PRAISE FOR
THE GARNER FILES

"James Garner stepped into two of TV's most calcified genres—the western and the detective series—and set a new standard that others have been chasing down since . . . having made up his mind to write [a memoir] . . . Garner follows his own heroic dictum: Plenty of self-deprecating humor, a general air of live-and-let-live, but when it comes down to it, no pulled punches. For Garner fans, *The Garner Files* is catnip . . . [Garner] is unfailingly candid about his own de-sires . . . it is a fine, frank and fun collection."

—*Los Angeles Times*

"Garner tells his life story with the same wry, self-effacing charm that characterized his classic TV characters: the laid-back cowboy Bret Maverick and the down-on-his-heels gumshoe Jim Rock-ford . . . Garner comes across as likable on the page as he does on screen."

—*Kirkus Reviews*

"Laid-back charm and a sense of humor fuel such memories, two qualities shared by the characters Garner often played in a career of 50-plus years . . . Full of funny stories and observations, *The Garner Files* offers the kind of clubhouse banter you might expect from a hardworking, successful guy who doesn't take himself too seriously—and doesn't want you to, either."

—The Associated Press

"[T]he narrative is genuine, candid, and more informative than usual for a Hollywood bio . . . Truly a cut above most actor bios, this is prime stuff for film and television collections."

—*Booklist*

"They don't make 'em like Jim anymore, that's for sure. And they don't write 'em like his new memoir much anymore, either . . . With equal parts old-school machismo and ageless charm—not to mention fisticuffs . . . *The Garner Files* is so blunt in its assessment of Hollywood old and new, it's often laugh-out-loud funny."

—*St. Petersburg Times*

"This is one of the better 'candid' celeb bios, with JG sharing stories about working with everyone from Brando to McQueen, Hepburn (Audrey) to Andrews. He writes passionately about his favorite pastimes—car racing and golf—and about his unabashedly liberal politics."

—*Barnstable Patriot* (Massachusetts)

"*The Garner Files* [is] real and compelling. A human being emerges from these pages, the guy I want to sit down with and talk about our shared era."

—*Los Angeles Daily News*

"In this long-awaited biography, Garner sets everyone straight on who he is, how he got there and the fact that he wants to be remembered 'with a smile' . . . Read *The Garner Files*. You may be surprised."

—*Lincoln Journal Star* (Nebraska)

"[V]ery candid . . . *The Garner Files* is for any fan of the actor who would like to know more about his life and work."

—*Midwest Book Review*

"Garner is a great storyteller."

—*Lancaster Sunday News* (Pennsylvania)

"I loved that I could hear James Garner's voice in the words I read on the page. I also loved that there were lots of surprises in this no-frills autobiography, which is reflective of his roles on big and small screens . . . He covers his life and his career . . . without pained explanations or any apologies; he also does it in a way that provides transparency to his life but preserves a wall of protection for his daughters—very classy . . . Some revelations in the memoir may surprise you, but I'm not about to divulge them here. Read the book!"

—*Courier-Journal* (Louisville, Ky.)

"James Garner's memoir is as easygoing and plain-spoken as his acting persona . . . [He] wouldn't have it any other way."

—USAToday.com

"[An] enjoyable memoir . . . there's plenty to love in this book. Garner . . . has a knack for telling a story and finding the perfect quote to tie it all together . . . charming . . . [It] resembles a conversation with an old friend who loves to tell colorful stories."

—PublishersWeekly.com

"*The Garner Files* is a classic tale of making it in Hollywood fueled . . . with Garner's good looks, fortune, charm, and sense of humor."

—*Christian Science Monitor* online

"The best advertisement for Garner's new memoir is that he relates the stories of his life in the same amiable and gentlemanly voice of his most famous roles . . . his honesty about himself and others is what makes this memoir a little different than the rest . . . An enjoyable look into the life of one of our most beloved actors."

—LibraryJournal.com

"For anyone who is in the business of acting, writing, producing, or creating music, this memoir has marvelous instructive thoughts about the entertainment world that are worth revisiting . . . In addition, readers are provided insight into [Garner's] favorite pastimes, which include golf, car racing and liberal politics. His affection for his wife and two daughters is also evident on the page, not to mention his personal integrity. He says who he is and proclaims that one value he holds for himself is that his word is his bond. This philosophy comes across throughout the book, creating a bond with the audience through his words."

—BookReporter.com

"If you buy one cranky celebrity memoir this fall, might we suggest James Garner's *The Garner Files*?"

—TheAtlanticWire.com

THE

GARNER FILES

JAMES GARNER

AND JON WINOKUR

INTRODUCTION BY JULIE ANDREWS

Simon & Schuster Paperbacks
New York   London   Toronto   Sydney   New Delhi

Simon & Schuster Paperbacks
1230 Avenue of the Americas
New York, NY 10020

First Simon & Schuster Paperbacks edition October 2012

SIMON & SCHUSTER PAPERBACKS and colophon are registered trademarks of Simon & Schuster, Inc.

For information about special discounts for bulk purchases, please contact Simon & Schuster Special Sales at 1-866-506-1949 or business@simonandschuster.com.

The Simon & Schuster Speakers Bureau can bring authors to your live event. For more information or to book an event, contact the Simon & Schuster Speakers Bureau at 1-866-248-3049 or visit our website at www.simonspeakers.com.

Designed by Joy O'Meara

Manufactured in the United States of America

10 9 8 7 6

The Library of Congress has cataloged the hardcover edition as follows:

Garner, James.
The Garner files / James Garner and Jon Winokur ; introduction by Julie Andrews.
  p.   cm.
Includes filmography and index.
1. Garner, James. 2. Motion picture actors and actresses—United States—Biography. I. Winokur, Jon. II. Title.
  PN2287.G385A3 2011
  791.4302'8092—dc23   2011044877
  [B]

ISBN 978-1-4516-4260-5
ISBN 978-1-4516-4261-2 (pbk)
ISBN 978-1-4516-4262-9 (ebook)

Contents

Introduction
by Julie Andrews

M y friend Jim Garner is a man's man, a ladies' man, a good ol' boy in the best sense of the word, a curmudgeon (he'll be the first to tell you) . . . and a sweetheart. I don't know a lady who isn't a little bit in love with him.

We met over fifty years ago on the film *The Americanization of Emily*. It was only the second movie I'd ever made, and I was nervous, gauche, and hopelessly inadequate in the heady culture of Hollywood in the '60s and the superb team of professionals with whom I was working. Mercifully, Jim made it easy for me. He was generous, gentle, and kind—and that was when I, too, fell a little bit in love with him. We both admired the brilliant screenplay by Paddy Chayefsky, and to this day, we agree that it was one of our favorite movies to make.

We've made two other films together since then—*Victor/Victoria* and the made-for-television movie *One Special Night*. You could say that the span of the three films is an index to the years of our friendship.

In *Emily,* we were young. It was intoxicating stuff—pure *fun.* *Victor/Victoria* happened some fifteen years later. We were more secure in ourselves, and there was security in working together. (Jim will never know how many times I copied his moves in order to learn how to act like a man . . .)

By the time we made *One Special Night* in the early '90s, we were in a more "pastoral" mode. That's a kind way of saying that we were a *lot* older. We shot the film in Montreal. It was the dead of winter, yet in spite of the *freezing* temperatures, the work felt so easy.

Every time we are on a set together, I marvel as I watch Jim weave his magic. Charisma simply oozes out of the guy. He owns his place on the screen, he *listens,* and he gives back. My husband, Blake, who directed Jim in two films—*Victor/Victoria* and *Sunset*—used to say that not only is he a good actor, he's a great *re*actor. As far as I'm concerned, few can match him in that regard. Watch his panic and fear in *Emily* as he heads for Omaha Beach. Watch him in *Victor/Victoria* when he discovers that the lady he's attracted to is actually a man. (Except that she's not!) Catch the pain he feels in *One Special Night* when he realizes there is nothing he can do for his dying wife.

Yet beneath the talent, charm, and a healthy dose of bravado, one senses that he's been hurt—more than once. So he's stubborn, a bit reclusive . . . defiant, too. Don't mess with Jim when he's fighting for a cause he believes in.

This glimpse into his early life, the cruelty and deprivation he suffered, his years in the service, his slow rise to fame, power, and fulfillment was a revelation for me. This memoir provides us all with a rare opportunity to get to know the captivating, enigmatic, complicated man that is the real Jim Garner.

Did I mention that he's a sweetheart?

June 2011

Dear Reader,

I've avoided writing a book until now because I'm really pretty average and I didn't think anyone would care about my life.

I'm still a little uncomfortable, but I finally agreed, because people I trust persuaded me you might be interested, and because I realized it would allow me to acknowledge those who've helped me along the way, from friends and family to the actors, directors, writers, and crew members I've worked with over the years.

I'll also talk about my childhood, try to clear up some misconceptions, and maybe even settle a score or two.

I don't like to brag on myself, and I won't start now, but I will ask people who know me to weigh in, for better or worse.

Above all, I want you to know I have no regrets. Here's this dumb kid from Oklahoma, raised during the Depression, comes to Hollywood, gets a career, becomes famous, makes some money, has a wonderful family . . . what would I change? Nothing. I wouldn't change a thing.

Yours truly,

THE GARNER FILES

CHAPTER ONE

Growing Up Fast

————

Jimmy is very close to his characters. That's the face he wants the world to see—the man who doesn't quite fit into any mold but is loved. The first thing I noticed about Jim was how funny he was. But Jim is a rather complicated man and is covering up lots of hurt. Growing up he was abused, lonely, and deprived.

—Lois Garner

Norman, Oklahoma, is located near the center of the state, in the middle of "Tornado Alley" where, April through June, dry polar air from Canada mixes with warm, moist air from the Gulf of Mexico to produce hundreds of tornadoes. If the southern Plains are a giant target for twisters, Norman is close to the bull's-eye, having taken as many hits, and even more near misses, than any other place on the continent. If that weren't enough, Norman is hot as hell in summer, cold as hell in winter, and windy as hell all year round. The landscape is flat and featureless . . . you might even say *bleak*.

But Norman was a good place to grow up. Everybody knew each

other, and you could walk the streets at night. It was a college town of about ten thousand, with three thousand University of Oklahoma students. Now, with thirty thousand students, the population is over one hundred thousand, and it's the third-largest city in the state, behind Oklahoma City and Tulsa. It's often mentioned as one of the best small cities in the United States, with its performing arts center, museums, theaters, parks, and annual festivals. But Norman in the 1930s was a sleepy little town.

My grandparents on both sides were among the first settlers of Norman. My father's father, Will Bumgarner, took part in the Oklahoma Land Rush and might have been one of the famous "Sooners."

On April 22, 1889, fifty thousand would-be landowners who'd come by train, covered wagon, on horseback, and on foot, gathered on the Arkansas, Kansas, and Texas borders. At high noon, at the sound of a cannon shot, they tore out to claim their 160-acre homesteads. By the end of the day, thousands had staked claims in Guthrie, Kingfisher, Oklahoma City, and on the sandy banks of the shallow Canadian River, where my grandfather had waited for the signal along with a few hundred others who would settle Norman.

Or maybe not. Grandpa Will might have slipped in beforehand: There were two kinds of settlers, "Boomers" and "Sooners." Boomers played by the rules and waited for the official signal to enter, but "Sooners" snuck in *sooner* than the law allowed to get the choice parcels. A few of them had to forfeit their land later on, but most got away with it.

Before statehood in 1907, Oklahoma was called Indian Territory, for good reason: the Indians were there first. Many tribes had roamed the Great Plains for thousands of years. It must have been beautiful country, with shoulder-high grass as far as the eye could see, pecan trees, and endless herds of buffalo.

The Creek, Choctaw ("Oklahoma" is Choctaw for "red people"), Blackfoot, Comanche, Arapaho, Kiowa, Cherokee, Cheyenne,

Pawnee, Shoshone, Crow, and Apache all depended on the buffalo for survival. They used every bit of the animal except the heart, which they buried ceremonially. When the settlers came, they slaughtered the buffalo, while the government put the tribes on reservations to "protect" them from homesteaders moving west. It shuffled them around for decades, uprooting them whenever the territory they occupied became desirable to whites, each time promising that the new land would be theirs forever. Norman is on ground that was "given" to the Creek Nation in 1832.

Bumgarner means "orchard tender," leading me to think that the Bumgarners, who came to America from East Prussia in the mid-1700s, were farmers. I have to guess, because I don't know much about them, and our German ancestry was never discussed. In my family, we never talked about feelings or about anything *personal,* like our roots. I learned only recently that my mother's family goes back to the Virginia colony in the early 1600s. I think that's remarkable, and I wish I knew more about her ancestors. All I know is that her parents, Charles Bailey Meek and Abbie Womack, were married in 1904 and that my mother, Mildred, was born a year later.

Charlie Meek, my mother's father, was Native American. My maternal great-grandparents disowned Abbie when she married him. I once asked my dad, "What was Grandpa Charlie like?" I'd never even seen a picture of him. All he said was, "He was a black, full-blood Cherokee. He was the blackest man I've ever seen." I don't know anything else about Grandpa Charlie because everybody pretended he didn't exist.

Growing up I knew I was one-quarter Cherokee, but I have to admit I was a little afraid of Indians. For one thing, I didn't *know* any. They were out of sight on reservations somewhere, or in the Little Axe community east of town. The schoolbooks didn't help. They gave the impression that Indians were "savages" who attacked without provocation. And our teachers didn't tell us that when Europeans came to North America, it was a disaster for the previous tenants.

I never knew my paternal grandfather, either. It wasn't until about twenty years ago that I learned anything about him. I'd flown from Dallas to Norman for a fund-raiser one rainy night with my friend Bill Saxon. After dinner, we went back to the airport to return to Dallas. My nephew Scott Bumgarner, our unofficial family historian, had dug up a newspaper article and left it for me with Bill's pilot. It was a report in the *Norman Transcript* from 1914. I picked it up while we were taxiing for takeoff and couldn't believe what I was reading.

It seems Grandpa Will Bumgarner was a bit of a rake. He and Grandma Lula (aka "Granny Bum") lived in Norman, but thirty-five miles to the north, in Yukon, Oklahoma, there was a widow woman he'd taken a liking to. Every so often, he'd go on a "whiz": he'd saddle up and ride for two days to see her. She must have been *some* woman.

The widow had a son who warned Grandpa to stay away from his mother. Grandpa didn't listen. One summer day he was sitting under a shade tree at a farm sale when the son approached and said, "I told you to leave my mama alone." He pulled out a nine-round repeating pistol and shot Grandpa five times. According to the newspaper account, Grandpa said, "Don't shoot me again, you've already killed me." But the kid put the other four bullets in him anyway.

Apparently, Will Bumgarner lived as violently as he died. Scott recently found some letters indicating that as a young man Will had a fight in a back alley and the other guy died, but Will was never convicted of a crime.

On the other hand, Scott points out that despite the fact that Will drank and fought and may have had affairs, Granny Bum apparently forgave his transgressions and in good moments even called him "sweet William." They had ten children, after all (three of whom died in infancy and another who died of burns at the age of six).

My mother, Mildred Scott Meek, and my father, Weldon Warren "Bill" Bumgarner, were married in 1921 and had three sons. Charles was born in 1924, Jack in '26, and I was born James Scott Bumgarner on April 7, 1928. "James" was for Jimmy Johnson, the owner of the local tobacco shop and a drinking buddy of my father's. Scott was my mother's middle name—after the doctor who had delivered her, and me. (It's also my daughter Gigi's, whose full name is Greta Scott Garner.)

In the depths of the Great Depression, my father ran a country store nine miles east of Norman in a speck on the map called Denver, population 5: Dad, Mom, my two brothers, and me. It was a combination hardware store/mail drop/service station on an old country road. Store in the front and two bedrooms and a kitchen in the back, and that was it. We didn't have indoor plumbing.

My mother died when I was four. I don't remember her, but I do recall riding in her funeral procession and passing by the country store. I couldn't understand why we didn't stop, because that's where we lived. It wasn't until I was fifteen that my cousin Betty told me my mother died of uremic poisoning after a botched abortion. She was twenty-six. To this day, I don't know the details, except that Grandma Meek and my mother were Christian Scientists. They never used a doctor, just prayer. I have no idea whether my father was involved in the decision to have the abortion or whether he blamed himself for her death. We never talked about it in the family.

Until I was five, I played every day by myself while my older brothers were at school. Well, I wasn't *all* by myself: I had "George," my imaginary friend. I was the sheriff of Denver, and he was my deputy. George was somebody to talk to. And I used him to get an extra piece of bread and peanut butter.

By the time I was six, I was working in the store selling peanut butter out of a five-gallon can. I'd scoop it, put it in a bucket, and smooth it out. I also pumped gas, and in those days, we pumped it by hand.

Everyone called my brother Charles "Bum." Jack was "Middle Bum," and I was "Little Bum," though I eventually grew to be physically bigger than both of them. They also called me "Babe" because I was the baby. One of my earliest memories is of the three of us riding bareback on an old horse with Bum in front, Jack in the middle, and me in the rear. Every once in a while they'd get mad and scoot me off the back. We rode that horse to a one-room schoolhouse. When we didn't have the horse, we had to walk. And, I swear, we often went barefoot. But not in the snow.

When I was seven, the store burned down and we moved to Norman. There were rumors my father set the fire. I don't know if he did, but it wouldn't shock me. In those days, people did all kinds of things to survive. It wasn't something we ever talked about in the family.

After the store burned down, my father basically left us to fend for ourselves. We were shuffled back and forth among relatives. I stayed with Grandma Louella Bumgarner at first, and then with "Grandma Meek," Abbie Womack Meek. We called her Maw. She was a feisty little ninety-pounder. Scotch-Irish. Brilliant. And so sweet. I could ask her for anything, and she'd give it to me, and if she didn't have it, she'd get it. I can still hear her calling me for supper: "Jimmy James Scott Bumgarner, get in here this very minute!" Without my own mother there to take care of me, I grew to love Maw very much.

During that period, I also lived with my Uncle John and Aunt Leona Bumgarner, while Bum and Jack were with other relatives. We brothers all lived in Norman, but we didn't get to see each other much.

Uncle John and Aunt Leona were *good* people, as close to parents as I could have gotten. I—along with everybody else in the family— called her Aunt Leone, but Leona was her real name. I loved Uncle John and Aunt Leone and they loved me. Their three children accepted me as one of the family.

Uncle John was a county commissioner, and he had a little dairy farm outside town. I loved to help him make butter and cream. And he was *smart*. In the wintertime, we used to sit in front of the fire with a dictionary to try to find a word he didn't know. I could never stump him. He knew the meaning of every word *and* the spelling *and* the derivation. He'd had some Latin because he'd studied to be a doctor, and worked as a Linotype operator and proofreader at the *Norman Transcript*.

Uncle John wasn't much to look at. His shirttail was always half-out and his hat was never blocked quite right, but I thought he was the most successful man in the world because he was content with what he had. And he had something many men never get: self-respect and the respect of everyone who knew him.

Our "home entertainment" consisted of a crystal set, a homemade radio you listened to with earphones. It wasn't powerful and you couldn't pick up many stations. You were happy to get dance music. If you were really lucky, you'd pull in *Fibber McGee and Molly* or *The Grand Ole Opry*.

We went to Saturday movie matinees. I liked all the heroes: Gary Cooper, John Wayne, Jimmy Cagney, and Henry Fonda, whom I saw in *The Grapes of Wrath* when I was twelve or thirteen. I was amazed that they actually made a movie about people like me, though I didn't like the term "Okie" for migrants who'd lost their farms during the Great Depression. The term's been widely used ever since Merle

Haggard's song "Okie from Muskogee" in 1969, but a lot of Oklahomans still don't like it, including me.

Fonda played Tom Joad, a young ex-convict whose family loses their farm in the Dust Bowl. With simple eloquence, he voices people's outrage at the greedy bastards who got the country into the Great Depression. I still remember his line, "I'm just tryin' to get along without shovin' anybody."

Spencer Tracy was my all-time favorite. Though I was only nine or ten years old, I remember him as Father Flanagan in *Boys Town* and as a Portuguese fisherman in *Captains Courageous*. I couldn't believe that one man could play such completely different characters so convincingly.

I loved Western stars such as Hopalong Cassidy, Buck Jones, and especially Bob Steele, because he was a little bitty guy. He had to reach up to punch someone. He was a terrific athlete. He could run up and jump on a horse from behind and land smack in the saddle. I got to know Bob and played golf with him years later in Los Angeles. He was a good player and a wonderful guy. Everyone called him "the Little Sheriff."

We attended the McFarlin Methodist Church on Sundays. It wasn't anything we enjoyed. Sometimes we'd set out for church dressed in our little black suits but take a detour to Massey's drugstore. My father wasn't much of a churchgoer, and Uncle John and Aunt Leone weren't exactly devout, either. They were fair-weather Methodists: if it was raining too hard, they didn't go. I count myself lucky they didn't jump all over me with Jesus, or with that hellfire and damnation crap. I had a lot of doubt. There were just too many miracles in the Bible for me. I still feel that way, and I haven't attended church since I was a teenager. I don't like people who try to ram their religious beliefs down my throat. Hey, if it works for you, fine, but it doesn't work for me, okay?

On the other hand, more than once I've tried to pray my way out of a tight spot, all the while thinking, *I wonder if this works.*

The Depression hit Oklahoma hard. Crop prices plunged and foreclosures and unemployment soared. There were bread lines, soup kitchens, and "Hoovervilles," temporary settlements where the homeless lived in crates and cardboard boxes. Drought turned the overworked soil to dust, and when the winds came, big hunks of Oklahoma, Kansas, Colorado, and Texas just blew away. They called it the Dust Bowl.

Small farmers got wiped out. The land was useless, and many saw their houses destroyed by storms. Most were sharecroppers who didn't own their farms, so the "Okies" packed up and pulled out, flooding the highways in their broken-down trucks and jalopies, just like in *The Grapes of Wrath*. Most drove west on Route 66 all the way to California. I remember seeing my father donate a few gallons of gas to countless travelers to help them get down the road.

Norman fared a little better than the rural areas. I guess because the University of Oklahoma and the state mental hospital employed a lot of people. And there were WPA projects in Norman as part of President Franklin D. Roosevelt's New Deal that put men to work constructing public buildings, many of which still stand.

We got by. We didn't have much, but nobody we knew had much either. We ate, slept, and played. What more could a kid want? I didn't have any great desire for *things,* and still don't.

My father eventually remarried. Her name was Wilma, but everyone called her "Red," because of her red hair. The family was reunited: Dad, Red, and my brothers and I all moved into a rented house together. But it wasn't a happy home.

Dad had hooked up with a man in Norman who owned two men's stores. "Shorty" was about six-foot-five. Like my dad, he was a widower with three boys. They had something else in common: they both liked to drink whiskey. They spent a lot of time together, and Shorty provided work for Dad building cabinets for the stores. Dad was also a part-time fireman. He did whatever he could to make a living. He worked hard whenever there was work to be had, but he drank too much.

Dad would come home drunk as a goat and make us sing for him or get a whipping. I hated to perform like that. I developed a phobia about getting up and talking in front of people. I wouldn't have passed speech class if my football coach hadn't been the teacher. To this day, I'm scared of public speaking. That's why acting was hard for me at first. I had to make a conscious effort to get over my fears, and I've had to work hard at that easygoing manner you see on the screen. I'm okay in front of a camera because I'm surrounded by familiar faces and I know I can do it again if I mess up. But I could never have been a stage actor.

It was a small house. From the room where my brother Jack and I slept we could hear everything my dad and stepmother did. They fought like two men. They got into some real knockdown, drag-outs, and she actually *could* knock my father down.

Red was a nasty bitch. She enjoyed beating the bejesus out of us. Sometimes she'd make us go out and cut willow switches so she could whip our butts with them. Other times she'd fly into a rage for no reason and hit us with whatever was handy, whether a stick or a board or a spatula. She loved to hit me with a spatula, and she had a favorite one for the purpose. I'll never forget that spatula.

I don't know why, but she picked on me especially. She gave me all the dirty chores, and when something needed to be blamed on someone, it was always me.

Red singled out Jack for a different kind of abuse. "I lost my virginity to her when I was just a little kid," he told me when we were teenagers. "I must have been in the third or fourth grade. I didn't really know what the hell was going on at the time. Later I realized what she'd done. I try not to think about it."

On top of the beatings, Red liked to put me in a dress and make everyone call me "Louise." Whenever I did anything wrong, I'd have to go put that dress on. My brothers would tease me and call me Louise and a fight would break out. And then I'd go hide. Now they'd put that woman in jail for what she did to us. But in those days nobody cared.

I'll tell you, it got to me. I became introverted, and it took a long time before I came out of my shell. I hated being ridiculed and never wanted to feel that way again. I think the experience shaped my acting style: I've always kept my tongue in my cheek and a twinkle in my eye because I want people to laugh *with* me, not *at* me. I don't want them to think I take this play-acting thing too seriously. I think it also gave me sympathy for the underdog. I can't stand to see big people picking on little people. If a director starts abusing someone in the crew, I'll butt in.

I finally took care of the problem with Red when I was fourteen. One day in the kitchen she raised her hand to me with that spatula and a voice inside me said, *"You're too old to take this anymore."*

I flattened her with one punch.

The next thing I knew I had her down and was choking her. Luckily, Dad and Jack came in just as she was turning purple and pulled me off her. Otherwise, I don't think I'd have let go until she quit breathing, because I thought she'd kill me if she got up.

Dad automatically took Red's side. He and Jack held me down while she took her revenge with the spatula. But a few hours later, Dad asked her what I'd done to deserve a whipping in the first place.

"Well, he did *something,*" she said.

Dad wanted to know what.

"I don't remember, but I know he did *something.*"

"You mean you were going to beat the hell out of the kid, but you don't know what he did to deserve it?"

They had it out right then and there. Red moved out of the house within a week, and Dad lit out for California soon thereafter, leaving us on our own again.

Years later, while I was doing *Maverick*, I was in a parade in Norman. Both my brothers were there. We'd heard that Red was in town and we were scared, because Jack and I had said things about her that were quoted in the local paper. I thought she might blast me with a shotgun or try to pick me off from a window. It sounds paranoid, but *we* knew she was capable of murder and we went to the police. They assigned plainclothes officers to Bum and Jack. As the parade came through town, Jack kept pace with me down one side of the street and Bum down the other to protect me. I was out there riding in a covered wagon, smiling and waving, all the while fearing I'd be shot at any second. Thank goodness, she didn't show up.

In my life, I've been on the wrong end of violence, and I've done violence myself. I'm not temperamental, but I do have a temper. Most of the time I direct it at myself. I think I'm harder on myself than I am with anybody else. Though I have a high boiling point and it takes a long time to get my goat, it can be got. I'll accept a lot before I snap, but when I do snap, I kind of go blind. I don't care what I do or what I say; I don't care about anything or anybody. Or the future. When I'm like that, it's best to stay out of my way. I've punched movie-set trailers out of frustration. I slugged a producer once. And I decked a guy on a golf course. In my opinion, they all deserved it. Except the trailers.

I refuse to glorify violence in my movie and television roles. The characters I've played, especially Bret Maverick and Jim Rockford, almost never use a gun, and they always try to use their wits instead of their fists. My favorite film character, Charlie Madison in *The Americanization of Emily,* is a downright coward and proud of it.

Though my brothers and I were separated a lot when we were young, we eventually got to know each other. Charles—"Bum"—was a natural leader and the worker in the bunch. He was always focused and would take charge while Jack and I would be screwing around. He was a surrogate father. I think he was the best of us.

Bum could do anything with his hands. When he was still a teenager he wanted an electric guitar, so he made one. He could build furniture, rebuild a car motor, do leatherwork, and make jewelry. He was also a crack shot: serving aboard a navy minesweeper during World War II, he exploded mines by shooting them with a rifle from the deck of the ship.

After the war, Bum got an industrial arts education degree from OU and went to work for the Norman school system teaching shop and mechanical drawing. If anything needed repairing at school, they'd come to him, and more often than not he'd fix it. He finally told the school board, "Either I'm going to be a teacher or a glorified janitor." They didn't want to lose him, so they promoted him to Assistant Superintendent, Director of Buildings and Grounds, and he thrived. He invented a special heating system and did architectural work on new school buildings. He eventually took charge of all the construction for Norman's public schools.

When Bum retired from the school system in 1982, he was immediately rehired as a consultant to manage new construction projects. He was looking forward to the part-time work and fishing the rest of the time. One weekend he drove up to a cabin on Lake Eufaula that he'd help build with his wife's sister and her husband, Lorita and Bill Lewis. There by himself, he died suddenly of a heart attack at the age of sixty.

I still can't believe he's gone.

When we were kids, Jack, two years older, would occasionally pull rank. Like the time I reached for the last piece of chicken-fried steak on the platter and he stabbed my hand with his fork. Then he lectured me: "Don't ever take food out of my mouth." It wasn't too long before I got to where I could whip his butt and there were no more lectures.

Jack was a hell of an athlete, and I always took a backseat to him. At Norman High, he was a point guard on a championship basketball team and quarterbacked an all-state football team. But his best sport was baseball: Jack was a pitcher in the Pittsburgh Pirates organization for eleven years. He was a better athlete than I was and a lot more outgoing. I was always in his footsteps.

When Jack came out to California in the early 1960s, he changed his name to Garner as I'd done a few years before. He was a singer with the house band at the Ambassador Hotel for a while, and then he asked me to get him in the movies. I said no.

"Why not?" he said. "You're a big-time star now."

"Well, you're my brother, and if I get you a job in the movies and you don't pan out worth a damn, it's not only bad for you, it's bad for me. If you want to get in the movies, you're going to have to do it yourself."

Jack got busy and worked in the business doing different television parts here and there. It was a good ten years before he ever worked with me. That didn't change how we felt about each other, because I think Jack understood what I was talking about.

It finally got to where occasionally Jack did work on my shows. But every time he did a *Rockford* episode, he had to go in and read. Sometimes he didn't get the part, sometimes he did. But Jack worked on many other shows, too. In fact, he worked so much that he finally got a Screen Actors Guild pension. Jack's day job was as a golf professional. He was a popular teaching pro in Los Angeles for thirty years. Jack died in September 2011 at the age of eighty-four. I miss him.

The set-to with Red and my father's departure for California when I was fourteen were my emancipation. The day my dad left Norman, he dropped me off at a dairy farm where he'd arranged for my room and board in return for doing chores. I slept on a cot in the cellar next to the washtub. I can still smell the damp laundry. And the cow shit, which I had to sweep up every morning. I lasted about three weeks.

That's when I began supporting myself. I got up at 3:30 every morning to sweep out the administration building at OU before going to my junior high classes. I understood right off that nothing would be given to me; still I daydreamed a rich relative somewhere would die and leave me a fortune.

Didn't happen.

My father wasn't bad. He just wasn't there. He couldn't handle the responsibility of raising three young boys. And he had several wives after my mother died, three or four; we're not sure to this day. Dad got married for the last time when he was in his mid-sixties, to a sweet woman named Grace. I called her "Mama Grace" and I loved her. She was the closest I ever came to having a real mother.

On my eighteenth birthday, I was in Odessa, Texas, out of work. The only thing I'd eaten in three days was the crackers I could steal off tables in restaurants. I called my father in California and said, "Dad, for my birthday, could you lend me fifty dollars?" And he said, "I'm sorry, son. I don't have it." Grace came on the line and said, "It'll be there in the morning." She wired the money, and I got back on my feet. I stood by her for the rest of her life.

Dad and I got closer after I became an actor, and toward the end of his and Grace's lives, I got to spend time with both of them. I eventually forgave my dad everything. He may have had a drinking problem and married the wrong women, but he wasn't evil. He died in 1996 at the age of eighty-five. We lost Mama Grace in 2002.

I'd started driving on country roads when I was ten and got my license the summer after I turned fourteen, when I was hired by a salesman for Curlee Clothes to drive him around the state of Texas. I was a combination chauffeur/traveling secretary/babysitter. I took care of the samples, kept the books, and tried to keep my boss away from whiskey. He had an ulcer and mixed his Scotch with milk. He wasn't supposed to smoke, either, so I doled out his cigars. He'd take a suite at the Baker in Dallas or the Rice in Houston where he'd sit around all day drinking with the buyers. I'd end up doing the selling. The guy offered to adopt me, but I wanted to be on my own.

I worked in food markets and clothing stores. I cut trees for the telephone company. I hauled Sheetrock. I was a dishwasher, a janitor, a dockworker, an oil field roughneck, and a carpet layer. I worked on a line cleaning chickens. (God help you if you accidentally nicked a gizzard.) I was a hod carrier on a construction site—that's the guy who brings bricks to the bricklayer in a box at the end of a pole.

I was also an insurance salesman, but not a very good one. I couldn't bring myself to do it. Here's some widowed mother of three who can't afford to put food on the table . . . I'd take one look at her and say, "No, ma'am, you don't really need insurance." Otherwise, I tried to give my all. I was usually the best worker they had, though I never really liked to work and never stayed on a job more than a few months. I don't think I was ever *fired,* but I'd quit as soon as I'd saved enough money to coast for a while.

In those days, I went whichever way the wind blew. I had no ambition and wasn't interested in getting an education. I just drifted here and there. I never had a job I liked enough to stick with until I took up acting, though it would be two or three years before I began to enjoy it.

When people ask me if I had a "bad" childhood, I'm never sure how to answer. I just did what was necessary. I had to make a living, because nobody was supporting me. While other kids my age had chores and allowances and curfews, I was holding down grown-up jobs because I had to feed myself and put clothes on my back and a roof over my head. It was simply a matter of survival. People have said it's right out of Dickens, but I didn't think I had it tough, because it was all I knew.

Looking back, I think I was better off having to do it earlier than later. Tell you what: You want to put pressure on somebody, live through the Depression. In Oklahoma. In the dust. After that, studio executives don't bother you at all.

Growing up in Norman I was lucky to have two great friends, Bill D. Saxon and Jim Paul Dickenson.

I've known "Billy Dee" almost my whole life. We're the same age. We went through grade school and junior high together, and we've stayed best friends these many years. Bill's late wife, Wylodean, was also a dear lifelong friend. She was in my class all through school. Over the years, she always welcomed me to the Saxon home, where I spent a lot of time. Most important, Wylodean made chicken-fried steak just the way I like it.

When I was growing up, Bill's family lived on the street behind us, and our back porches faced each other. I remember playing with him along a little creek that ran between the houses. When we were in our early teens, Bill and I worked together at a combination feed store and hatchery. We'd drive the truck to take feed and seed out to people, and we'd bring back chickens.

Bill's dad and another man owned a bank south of Norman in a little town called Paoli, Oklahoma. They had all their money loaned out on broomcorn and cotton. When the Depression hit, the bottom dropped out of the market for both crops. The bank went belly-up and Mr. Saxon came back to Norman, where relatives took him in and helped him get back on his feet.

Oklahoma was a place where people "hunkered up" with each other to survive. It was also a place where a man's word was his bond. Sure, we had hustlers, but they were so few and far between that you could spot them a mile away. Most people were honest, and they took care of each other. Not like LA. People here—at least those in the entertainment business—will look you right in the eye and lie to you. They lie even when there's no reason to. I've never understood that and never will. Out here, I'm a lead sinker in deep water.

Over the years, Bill Saxon and I played golf together all over the world. He owned a jet (he was in the oil business), and I had entrée to just about any course you'd want to play. We combined our resources, playing everywhere from Pebble Beach to St. Andrews to courses all over Europe and Asia.

Jim Paul Dickenson was also the same age. He was a smartass who thought he knew it all. The thing of it was, he *did*. He was a handsome kid; everybody said he looked like John Garfield. Jim Paul looked mature and he *was* mature. And suave. A real ladies' man.

When we were in tenth grade, Jim Paul dated a senior girl. The two of them were doing things Bill and I had only talked about. We'd be cruising in Jim Paul's mother's car and he would stop at his girlfriend's house and climb in her bedroom window. Bill and I would wait in the car, imagining what was going on. Later Jim Paul would fill us in on the details. Wow! We also thought it was cool the way he used the F-word in front of adults and got away with it. In short, we looked up to him.

Jim Paul's mother, Fern, was divorced. A lot of people in town looked down on her because she drank. I remember her driving down the street with a beer bottle in her hand. But Fern had a good heart. She owned a rooming house a block away from Campus Corner, a busy district across from the OU campus with shops, restaurants, beer joints, a pool hall, bookstore, and movie theater. "The Corner" was popular with both Norman youth and OU students—the fraternity and sorority houses were within easy walking distance. A number of OU basketball players lived in Fern's house and it was a great place to hang out because (a) it was near the Corner, and (b) Fern didn't care if you drank or smoked or stayed up late. There was usually an empty bed, so I often slept there, free of charge.

When World War II broke out, I, like most young men, was filled with patriotic fervor. I couldn't wait to get involved. And get away. I wasn't old enough to be in the regular service, but the minute I turned sixteen, Jim Paul and I quit school and joined the Merchant Marine. My dad had to sign papers for me because I was underage. As soon as we enlisted, Germany surrendered. They must've heard we were coming.

We went through boot camp in St. Petersburg, Florida, and then I took the train to New Orleans, where I shipped out on a seagoing tug bound for Cuba and South America. I was aboard ship for two months, and I was miserable every minute. I lost thirty-five pounds because I couldn't keep anything down. The ship's doctor said I had "mal de mer." Mal de mer? Hell, I was *seasick*. Fortunately, the Merchant Marine was like a civil service job: you could quit, and I did. But Jim Paul was a better sailor than I was. He stayed in for several years and went all over the world. I went to California.

When I arrived in Los Angeles, I moved in with Aunt Grace Bumgarner. She was what they used to call an "old maid," though we found out years later that she'd been married once. In my family, you thought you knew people, but you didn't.

Everybody said Aunt Grace was crazy about me, but I thought she was just crazy. She was a real busybody, always sticking her nose in other people's business. She knew exactly what was wrong with everyone, including the family back in Oklahoma. A domineering soul, she decided I should be an actor and would have talent scouts come and look at me at the A&P where I worked, but I refused to talk to them. I didn't want any part of it. She also tried to make me go back to high school, but I just wanted to goof off. After the set-to with Red, I'd gotten pretty cocky. Nobody was going to tell *me* what to do ever again. With my father absent and me supporting myself, I didn't have to answer to anyone.

Bill Saxon joined the Marine Corps late in 1945 and was stationed at El Toro, near San Diego. It was an easy hitchhike to Hollywood, where I was working at a filling station. On a weekend pass during the Christmas season of '46, Bill and a Marine buddy got a hotel room right at Hollywood and Vine. I joined them and we all went looking for girls. We didn't find any. It got late, and I stayed the night. There were only two beds so I slept on the floor. The two Marines stayed up all night moaning about how unhappy they were—it was their first Christmas away from home and we were all just teenagers—but I was quiet on the subject. When they pressed me, I finally flashed my good-ol'-boy smile and said, "You know, it doesn't make any difference to me where I sleep." Billy Dee told me he never forgot that. They were depressed and homesick, but there I was, lying on the floor, happy as can be.

I was never much of a student. I could get A's when I applied myself, but I rarely applied myself. I just wasn't interested in going to school. Not until the day when I saw two beauties on a streetcar. When I found out they went to Hollywood High, I enrolled right away. *Goodness gracious,* there were more good-looking girls at Hollywood High than in the whole state of Oklahoma.

While I was a student there, the Jantzen people were looking for guys to model their swimsuits, and the gym teacher gave them my name. I wasn't interested until I heard they were paying $25 an hour. That was more than the principal made! We went out to Palm Springs to shoot over a weekend, and I made good money, but I hated modeling. I felt like a piece of meat. The worst part was having to "look charming and smile," which is what they were always telling me to do.

I wanted to play football for Hollywood High, but there was a slight problem: I never went to classes and I got kicked out. I was still under eighteen and had to go to school somewhere, so I chose the Frank Williams Trade School, where I think I majored in first aid. I also played football for the Hollywood Boys Club as a punter and linebacker. A coach from Southern Cal saw me and said he wanted me to play for them if I ever graduated from high school.

About then I heard from Harley "Doc" Lefevre, the football coach at Norman High. He said he needed help fast or he was going to lose his job. So I went back to Norman and played for him. I won't say I was a *ringer* or that I got *paid,* but I was two years older than most of the seniors on the team and had open credit at a local clothing store. And I didn't have to get a job.

Doc wasn't exactly a role model. The only one of his players who had a car was Pud (rhymes with "good") Lindsay. Pud's family owned the Norman Steam Laundry. It was his folks' car, but he drove it to school every day. Doc didn't have a car, so he'd get Pud out of class to drive him around town. After running a few errands, Doc and Pud would go hang out in a coffee shop for the rest of the day. I'd get in on it, too.

Doc wasn't much of a disciplinarian, either. During a game against one of the high schools from Oklahoma City, some guys in the stands began ragging me. "Hey, pretty boy!" and stuff like that. They kept it up, and it got embarrassing. When I came in to punt, I kicked the ball and started jogging off the field, but I kept going right past the bench and into the stands after them. It turned into a brawl, and they had to get the police to break it up. The other guys got arrested and Doc winked at me as I trotted back to the bench.

was an introvert, but in a group of people, I was a show-off. I pretended never to take things seriously. I was probably trying to hide my insecurity. (What the hell, it worked for me. I'm glad nobody tried to fix it.)

One day a bunch of us were hanging out in front of Woolworth's in Norman and there were some gumball machines next to the door. I said to no one in particular, "I could steal one of those, easy."

"Well, bull*shit,*" they said.

That was all I needed. I sauntered over to a machine, swept it up with one hand, and kept on walking with it right down Main Street. None of the gang thought I could—or would—do it. They were so impressed at how smooth I was that one of the girls in the group nicknamed me "Slick."

The girl was Betty Jane Smith and she was my first love.

She was gorgeous, vibrant, full of life. I would have married her in a heartbeat. But there was a problem: Betty Jane was an older woman, by two years. While I was playing football and doing my best to flunk out of Norman High, she was attending OU and dating a college man.

Though I grew up fast in some ways, I was immature in others. I was a real wallflower. Women frightened the hell out of me. (Still do.) I didn't have a clue how to talk to them. Because I lacked the courage to tell her myself, a girlfriend told Betty Jane I was absolutely balmy about her. Unfortunately, the girlfriend told *me* Betty Jane wasn't interested. Not in a million years.

Broke. My. Heart.

I must have been out of my mind: Here *she* was, a beautiful former Football Queen and Pep Club president, and there *I* was, a ne'er-do-well with no prospects and no ambition, two years her junior.

Betty Jane eventually married the college man. He ended up a mogul in the record business, and they lived out in the Valley, a few miles from my house. As far as I know, they still do.

It took a long time to get over Betty Jane. I was sure I'd never fall in love again. A big cloud of gloom and doom settled over me, and I didn't want to do anything or talk to anyone. I just sat there brooding. I couldn't make a decision whether to take a bath or a shower, so I didn't do either. I just sat there. For days. At one point, I even contemplated suicide. But eventually I started to come out of it. Little by little, I began to feel like my old self again, until one day I realized that the cloud had finally lifted. I decided to go on living.

CHAPTER TWO

Korea to Broadway

I was the first Oklahoman drafted for the Korean War.

When I got the letter from Uncle Sam in late December 1950, I figured that if they needed *me*, they were in trouble: I'd already been in the National Guard. I tore up a knee during maneuvers, and they gave me a medical discharge. I had the knee operated on because I wanted to play football again.

When I reported for induction, I asked the doctor, "Hey, Doc, what about my knee?"

"What about it?"

"They operated on it, you know?"

"Well, they must have fixed it. Next!"

I went through basic training at Fort Sheridan, Illinois. One day they put up a list of a hundred guys who were being shipped out, and to my relief I wasn't on it. That's when I learned that nobody was supposed to go overseas unless they had boots. One of the guys on the list had feet the size of aircraft carriers and the army couldn't find boots to fit them, so they took *him* off the list and put *me* on it.

I was sent to Schofield Barracks in Honolulu and assigned to the

5th Regimental Combat Team of the 24th Division. It was a "bastard outfit," an independent unit with no permanent higher divisional headquarters. At one time or another, the 5th RCT had fought under the 1st Cavalry, the 45th Infantry Division, and even a Marine brigade, earning itself a distinguished combat record. In the parlance of the time, it was a "colored" regiment, because it had a large percentage of Hawaiians and Asian Americans. When the fighting heated up, the 5th was rushed to Korea. They needed fodder to stuff up the gap, and we were in the first group of replacements.

On my second day in Korea, as a rifleman in Able Company, I was bringing up the rear of a patrol when I was hit with mortar shrapnel. Most of it glanced off my helmet, but a few fragments caught me in the hand and face and one cut my watchband.

They sent me back to an aid station, but instead of going in, I started picking out the little bits of metal while looking in the mirror of a jeep. An officer came up and said, "Don't do that! Go inside and we'll get you a Purple Heart." So I went in, they bandaged my "wounds," and I went back to my unit.

A couple weeks later, on April 21, 1951, in what's now called the First Spring Offensive, 250,000 Chinese Communist troops swarmed across the 38th Parallel. The first thing they ran into was the 5th RCT.

Able Company was dug in on a ridgeline on the RCT's right flank, with elements of the Republic of Korea 6th Division protecting *our* right. On the night of April 24, the Red Chinese attacked us in force, bugles blaring. (They used bugles and whistles to signal infantry maneuvers, and it got so the sound of them was more unnerving than the roar of their artillery.)

As soon as machine-gun tracers and mortar rounds started coming in, the ROKs turned tail and ran, leaving our right flank wide open. We were overwhelmed by the sheer volume of incoming fire as wave after wave of infantry slammed our position. I took cover on the lee side of the hill and saw three enemy soldiers running along the ridgeline. Without thinking, I shouldered my rifle and started ripping away. I'm pretty sure I hit one of them because I saw the head snap and the helmet fly off.

The Red Chinese shot us to pieces. Before we knew it, we had only thirty men left out of one hundred thirty, and we were surrounded. Our company commander, Captain Horace W. West, assembled the survivors and told us we were going to execute a "retrograde" maneuver. Which is a nice way of saying we were checking out. Despite bleeding profusely from nine bullet wounds, Captain West led us off the ridge and we *retrograded* all night long, fighting as we went. None of us would have survived without his bravery and leadership, for which he ultimately received the Distinguished Service Cross.

At dawn the next morning we picked up some ROK stragglers just as our fighter planes began pounding the enemy positions. We were all sitting on a hilltop cheering them on, shouting, "Go get 'em, boys, blow the *shit* out of 'em!" when one of our own AT-6 spotter planes flew over. Because we'd lost our orange air panels that would have identified us as friendlies, the AT-6 radioed back about a concentration of "enemy" troops. The next thing we knew we were being strafed by US Navy Panther jets firing 20-millimeter white phosphorus rockets.

I was diving into a foxhole when I got hit. In the butt. (How could they miss?) The jets kept firing and there was white phosphorus streaming in all directions, so I figured I'd better get out of there. I jumped out of the foxhole and ran . . . right off the side of a cliff.

I rolled end-over-end about a hundred yards down the hill, dislocating my shoulder and tearing up my knees. Meanwhile, rockets were still raining down, with fragments ricocheting all over the place. I thought of the old line, "It ain't the one with your name on it you have to worry about, it's the one addressed, 'To whom it may concern.'"

A ROK soldier had rolled down the hill, too, and he was worse off than me: he had white phosphorus burns all down his back and I knew it was smarting, because that stuff *burns*. I could barely move because of my knees, but we slowly dragged ourselves back up the side of the hill. When we reached the summit, it was deserted.

There we were, alone on top of the hill. The ROK didn't speak English and I didn't speak Korean, but we could communicate with gestures. It didn't seem like a good idea to stick around, so we headed south, hoping to catch up with our retreating column.

As we made our way down the hill into another valley, I looked to my right and spotted a group of about one hundred fifty soldiers . . . *and they weren't ours*. It was what must have been a whole company of North Koreans. They saw us, too. My rifle had been blown to bits by a rocket, but the South Korean still had his, though it wouldn't have helped much if the North Koreans had decided to open up on us. I don't think I've ever been more scared in my life than I was at that moment. I didn't wet my britches or anything, but it wouldn't have taken much more.

We just kept walking, right past the North Koreans. To this day, I don't know how we got away with it. The only thing I could ever figure is that because the South Korean had a rifle and I didn't, the North Koreans must have thought he was one of them and I was his prisoner.

We walked for maybe six more hours, until we heard the sweet sound of American tanks. As we approached our own lines, I took the rifle from the South Korean so our guys wouldn't mistake him for an enemy soldier who had the drop on me. They sent me to an aid station right away. I don't know what they did with the South Korean. I've often wondered what happened to him.

The next day they airlifted me to a hospital in Japan. By the time I got there, my shoulder and the phosphorus wounds on my backside weren't too bad, but my knees had swollen up like balloons. I spent about two weeks in the hospital. Most of the guys there were a lot worse off than I was.

In his history of the 5th RCT, *Hills of Sacrifice,* Colonel Michael Slater writes that my unit fought one of the biggest and most pivotal battles of the Korean War. Of the 3,200 5th RCT troops deployed from Hawaii, more than a third were killed, wounded, or missing in action within six weeks of entering combat. Slater calls the battle "the most bitter close-combat struggle Americans have participated in since the Civil War." In terms of the big picture, our side had withstood a human wave offensive in which the Red Chinese lost 200,000 men and gained nothing. After that, it settled into a stalemate that finally led both sides to negotiate. The result half a century later is two Koreas tensely divided by the 38th Parallel.

You automatically get a Purple Heart if you're wounded or killed in action against an enemy of the United States. "Wounded" is broadly defined. The little shrapnel scratches I got were the same as my more serious knee injuries for the purpose. For that matter, a piece of shrapnel gets you the same medal for losing an arm. So I was awarded two Purple Hearts on my service record. But I never got a medal.

Years later, I wrote the army about it because I wanted to have something tangible to give Grandma Meek before she died. Didn't get an answer. I wrote again, and they finally dug through the old records and found my paperwork.

In 1983, in a ceremony that coincided with the two hundredth anniversary of the Purple Heart, a general pinned the medal on my chest, one Purple Heart decorated with an oak leaf cluster to indicate two awards. He said the army was remedying an error. It was sure better to get it thirty years late than posthumously. Sorry to say, it was too late for Grandma Meek, who had died in 1969.

I felt lucky to be recognized. Many other Korean War vets never have been. It was an unpopular war, coming less than five years after World War II. Nobody was ready for another war so soon. When we came home, there were no parades. The nation lost almost as many men in Korea as we did in Vietnam, but they didn't even call it a war—it was a "police action" or the "Korean conflict."

Korean War vets are ignored because Korea is a forgotten war. I hope that's changing. There's finally a Korean War Veterans memorial in Washington, and I've joined with Buzz Aldrin and others to help raise money to build a Korean War museum. (Many people don't know that before he was an astronaut or walked on the moon, Buzz flew sixty missions as a combat pilot in Korea.) Korean vets deserve the same recognition as vets of other wars.

Then again, Charlie Madison, my character in *The Americanization of Emily,* may have had it right: we'll end wars only when we stop glorifying those who take part in them. In any case, I want to be very clear about one thing: I was not a hero. If there were any heroes, they were the guys who never came back from Korea, or the ones who were wounded, captured, or risked their lives to save their buddies. I didn't save anybody but myself. I wasn't a hero; I just got in the way a lot.

After being discharged from the hospital, I was assigned to a base post office outfit stationed in a bombed-out shoe factory. That's when I started enjoying the war, because I became a "dog robber" like Charlie Madison and Bob Hendley, the character I played in *The Great Escape.* A dog robber is a soldier who knows how to work the system, a facilitator who can get just about anything done.

I decided to turn our area into a first-class recreation center. To do that I had to scrounge materials and supplies from other units on the base. They weren't always inclined to cooperate, so I had to give them an incentive: if they didn't come up with what I wanted, they didn't get their mail. Soldiers become unhappy when they don't get their mail, so they usually gave me what I asked for, including what we needed to build a bar and keep it stocked with whiskey. Graves Registration provided the ice.

I built a theater, laid out a baseball diamond, and ran in pipes so we could have hot showers. My crowning achievement was the swimming pool. We dug out the basement, painted the walls, cemented the floor, put in a ladder, and filled it with water.

But I couldn't do much about the food, which was standard army chow. We had fresh eggs, and you could get them cooked however you wanted, but we also had to endure the infamous creamed chipped beef on toast, what GIs unaffectionately called "shit on a shingle."

Still, army chow was bearable as long as I could keep the onions and garlic out of it. I cannot stand onions and I'm very sensitive to garlic. I can taste tiny amounts of it, like when they've cooked another dish with garlic before and don't wash the pan. If I get even a hint of it, I might throw up in my plate.

This violent aversion may have saved my life: like our South Korean allies, the Chinese and North Korean troops lived on a diet of fish heads, rice, and *garlic*. One night while on guard on the line, I caught a faint whiff of it coming from the direction of the enemy positions. I couldn't see anything, but I knew there was someone out there and they were coming closer. Once I sniffed them I could hear them, too. It turned out to be a patrol heading straight for our position. They were just the other side of a rise when I passed the word down the line. We were ready for them and stopped them in their tracks.

We got turkey for Thanksgiving and turkey for Christmas and turkey in between . . . and more turkey New Year's and . . . turkey, turkey, turkey! I got to where I didn't *like* turkey. One day I was bitchin' about it to the mess sergeant.

"Damn, don't we ever have anything except turkey?" I said.

"Come 'ere," he said.

He took me into the kitchen and showed me a refrigerated trailer full of turkeys. He pulled one out and handed it to me. It was cool— not frozen, not even cold—and it had a date on it: 1945.

They were feeding us World War II turkeys!

Needless to say, I never had another bite of turkey in the army, and I've tried to avoid it ever since. Unfortunately, I still have to eat it on occasion. But I don't have to *like* it.

After nine months, my hitch was up. They promised me another sergeant's stripe if I'd reenlist. I certainly enjoyed those months there. Though I was five thousand miles from the States, I felt at home. I knew who was who and what was what on the base. For the first time in my life, I had a sense of purpose and accomplishment. I even took the high school equivalency test and got my diploma.

But I didn't like the army *that* much.

I went home a happy man.

The only reason I'm an actor is that a lady pulled out of a parking space in front of a producer's office.

When I came home from Korea I visited my dad in California for a few months, but I still hoped to play football, so I went back to Norman and enrolled in the University of Oklahoma. Unfortunately, my knees were so messed up I couldn't play. I dropped out after one semester, even though I had a B average. I just wasn't interested in school.

I hung around the pool hall, racking balls and picking up a little change on the side hustling snooker and playing cards. One night I was in a card game with Jennings Nelson, a football player for the University of Oklahoma. I was always short of money, and I told him when we sat down: "I've only got so much money and when it goes, that's it." Sure enough, I ran out of money, and he called me a name. I had to do something, so I fought him. We went out to the back of the pool hall. He was a big guy, about six foot three. He wound up in the hospital.

Six months later, I was back in California, laying carpets for my father. I didn't *want* to lay carpets, but I didn't know what else to do.

I'd never found a job I liked and didn't have much of an education or any real skills.

One day I drove down to San Pedro to apply for an oil field job in Saudi Arabia, but it turned out they were hiring geologists, not roughnecks. On the way home, driving up La Cienega Boulevard feeling sorry for myself, I noticed a sign on a building: "Paul Gregory and Associates."

I'd met Paul in 1945, when I was seventeen and working at the Shell station on the corner of Hollywood Boulevard and La Brea. A fellow Oklahoman, Paul was a soda jerk at the Gotham drugstore across the street, but he really wanted to be an agent. He kept telling me, "You oughta be in pictures," and offered to "represent" me.

I laughed at him.

I ran into Paul a few years later, this time in Greenblatt's Delicatessen, when I was about to leave for Korea. By then he had an office across from Schwab's drugstore on Sunset Boulevard and he was driving a great big Cadillac convertible.

"See, I *told* you you should have been in pictures!" he said.

On my way back from Korea two years later, I saw Paul's name in *Newsweek* magazine. He was a big stage producer with three hits going, including *Don Juan in Hell* with Charles Laughton and Agnes Moorehead. So when I saw the "Paul Gregory and Associates" sign on La Cienega I thought, *Gee, maybe the soda jerk knows what he's talking about*. At that instant, a woman pulled out of a parking space in front of the building, and I pulled in. It was fate. Or at least serendipity: if the parking space hadn't suddenly been there, I would not have driven around the block looking for one. I'd have kept on going.

Paul saw me right away. He said he'd be willing to take me on as a client. (In those days, producers could be agents, too.) We talked for about an hour. Or rather, *he* talked. He told me I could have a "big career."

"Look at yourself, Jim," he said. "You could definitely be a success if you'd learn how to act."

I decided to give it a try. Though I wasn't much interested in acting, I was less interested in laying carpets. I wasn't looking for stardom. I just wanted a clean job for decent money. I was twenty-five years old and told myself I'd give it until I was thirty to see if I could make a living at it.

I also told myself I'd have to overcome my stage fright.

Paul sent me to Columbia to read for an acting coach named Benno Schneider. Afterward, Benno gave me some advice: "Whatever you've been doing until now, young man, I'd suggest you go back to it, because you'll never be an actor."

That was all I needed to hear. Rather than discourage me, it spurred me on. I don't like to be told I can't do something. I said, "I'll show *him*!" (About five years later, Benno and I were sitting on a couch in my business manager's office and he said, "I want you to know that I think you're wonderful. You have star quality." I said, "Really? That's interesting, coming from someone who told me I'd never be an actor." He claimed he never said it, but I told him, "Oh yes, you did! That's something you don't forget.")

My first part was in Paul Gregory's production of *The Caine Mutiny Court Martial,* a two-act drama by Herman Wouk based on his Pulitzer Prize–winning novel. (It was later made into a movie starring Humphrey Bogart, Van Johnson, and Fred MacMurray.) The play centers on the aftermath of a mutiny aboard a fictional US Navy minesweeper in the Pacific during World War II. Most of the action takes place in a military courtroom.

I played one of six judges on the bench. We were known on Broadway as "the silent six," because none of us had any lines. They paid us each a hundred bucks a week to just *sit* there for two hours every night.

But I didn't just sit there.

Being onstage without speaking for two hours every night taught me that the most important part of acting is *listening*. By listening, you keep yourself engaged. When you're not listening, you're daydreaming: "Where should I have dinner after the show? Maybe have a couple drinks first?" Your mind wanders and you lose track of what's happening on stage. That's the trouble with a lot of actors: they don't listen; they just wait for the chance to talk. Which means they're not involved in the scene. You can see the dead in their eyes as they wait to say their lines.

The production had three big movie actors: Henry Fonda, Lloyd Nolan, and John Hodiak. I learned a lot watching them work every night. Little by little, I saw what they were doing and why they were doing it. I learned about technique, and I learned how to concentrate, but most of all, I learned how to be a professional.

Henry Fonda had remarkable stage presence and tremendous self-confidence when he was in character. He knew how to capture an audience. The minute he walked on stage every eye in the house would go right to him and stay there. But he never thought he was any good. We'd have a great audience, they'd love the performance, and everyone would be happy but him. He was never satisfied, but never blamed anyone but himself.

I spent a lot of time with Henry over the years. We took vacations with our wives, and I got to know him well. He was a cultivated man, an intellectual, and a craftsman. He painted, had a vegetable garden, raised chickens, and kept bees. He even knitted!

And he was a gentleman.

I consider Henry a mentor, and not only as an actor. We never talked much about acting. We both just did it. We were the same in that respect. Henry had a code of honor: if he gave you his word, he meant it. I think a lot of it had to do with his Nebraska upbringing. That's true in Oklahoma, too, so it was common ground between us.

Henry was a good man. He was kind to people and treated everybody the same. His father had taken him to see a lynching when he was a boy and it had a lasting effect on him. To get the studio to make *The Ox-Bow Incident* in 1943, he had to do several stinkers in return. His Gil Carter, the lone voice of reason against a mob determined to hang three drifters, was more like Henry than any other character he played.

I admired him so much I even mimicked him. In *My Darling Clementine,* he did a little seated two-step in place by leaning back in a chair and pushing off a post, first with one foot and then another. I stole it for *Support Your Local Sheriff.* When Henry saw it, he said, "Why don't you imitate somebody good?"

We remained close friends until his death in 1982.

I was paid an extra twenty-five bucks a week to take care of Johnny Hodiak's wardrobe and keep his dressing room neat. I was basically his valet. I also understudied Hodi, who played Lieutenant Maryk, but I never went on. I respected him both as an actor and as a man. He knew his craft and, proud of his Ukrainian heritage, he had defied MGM boss Louis B. Mayer by refusing to change his name. It was a terrible shock and a great loss when, in October 1955, he died of a massive heart attack. He was only forty-one.

I used to go around with the three of them—Fonda, Hodiak, and Nolan—as a sort of bodyguard-gofer-mascot. On my first night in New York, they got me a date with a gorgeous model, a redhead named Barbara Walters (not the journalist), and they took us to the "21" Club. I *miss* those guys.

A month before rehearsals began, Paul Gregory assigned me to run lines with Lloyd Nolan. By that time, Lloyd was in his late forties, a master character actor who had done countless movies and plays. In the original script, Captain Queeg remained defiant until the end, but Lloyd had him slowly crumble under cross-examination. It added an extra dimension to the character and Lloyd stole the show. (Bogart played Queeg the same way in the film and got an Oscar nomination.)

But before Lloyd could put his mark on the character, he had to learn the dialogue. I would go to his house for two or three hours every day and cue him on Queeg's lines. At the table reading on the first day of rehearsals, Lloyd never had to look at his script. Everybody else was reading their lines, but Lloyd was letter-perfect, even on that long speech about the "stolen" strawberries.

Fonda was amazed, because Queeg was a difficult part.

"How the hell did you do that?" he wanted to know.

"I hired Bumgarner," Lloyd told him.

So Fonda asked me if I would cue him, too, and I gladly agreed. (The secret, by the way: It's like building blocks. You do one line at a time and stay on it until you've got it cold. Then you do the next line, and the next, and before you know it, you've got the whole thing.)

The play opened in Santa Barbara and toured the country for three months before its Broadway premiere at the Plymouth Theatre on January 20, 1954. It ran for more than four hundred performances. Fonda left the show before the end of the run, and Barry Sullivan replaced him. You could see the difference. No consistency. Sullivan had good nights and bad nights, but Fonda never let down. Lloyd Nolan was the same. They both gave a solid performance night after night.

William Inge said that after seeing me in *Caine Mutiny* rehearsals, he'd used me as the image of the character Beau in *Bus Stop* and he asked me to read for the part. The only thing I remember about the audition is that after I read two or three lines, they said, "That's nice, Mr. Bumgarner, but we can't hear you past the third row."

I was disappointed and relieved at the same time. I was so intimidated by everything, I just couldn't break out. You have to be much broader on the stage than on film, and I was just too introverted.

The New York office of 20th Century-Fox offered me a screen

test, but I declined. I figured there was a rivalry between the New York and Hollywood offices of every movie company, and I didn't want to get caught in the crossfire. I told them I'd only do a test in Hollywood. They thought I was crazy. After *Caine Mutiny* closed on Broadway, I went back to California and finally did the test for 20th, but nothing came of it because I was awful.

The first thing I ever did on film was a Winston cigarette commercial with a very young Ellen Burstyn; she was Ellen McRae then. A few years later, we did a play together, *John Loves Mary,* and I came back to Hollywood raving about her. I touted her to Marty Ransohoff and just about anybody else who would listen. Over the years, Ellen has proved me right. I'm proud of her.

After living off the Winston money for a year, I was about broke and wondering if I'd have to go back to carpet-laying when I was offered the part of Maryk in a touring company of *The Caine Mutiny Court Martial.* A previous road company had been a disaster because Paul Douglas, who played Queeg, gave an interview in Alabama. Douglas told the reporter he hated the South because it was "full of sorghum, sow bellies, and segregation." There were $30,000 worth of cancellations in about a week and they had to call off the tour.

They eventually put a new company together with Charles Laughton directing. Though I was still prone to stage fright, I jumped at the chance to work with the great English actor who'd created such unforgettable roles as Captain Bligh in *Mutiny on the Bounty* and Quasimodo in *The Hunchback of Notre Dame.*

One morning when we were still in rehearsals, Laughton said, "James, I'd like you to come up to the house and lunch with me."

I was *sure* he was going to can me, because I knew I wasn't very good.

After lunch he said, "James, do you know what your problem is?"

"No, sir, I don't."

"You're afraid to be bad, and therefore you don't do anything.

You stay in the middle of the road. You're not dull, but you aren't interesting, either."

It shook me to the core, but I knew he was right. I didn't care if the audience *liked* me, I just didn't want them to *dislike* me, and so I underplayed everything. I didn't want to do anything that might alienate them. As a result, I was mediocre.

Laughton said, "Don't worry about the audience. Just go out there and take the risk of being bad! I'll rein you in when necessary."

I suppose that applies to life, too: You have to take the risk. You may fail, but at least you've given it your best shot.

Laughton's advice helped me relax. Ever since then I just stick my neck out and let the director chop it off if he wants to. It also made me realize that if I wanted to be more than just another big ox standing there going "Duh," I'd have to distinguish myself somehow. I began to think I might be able to do it with humor.

I played Maryk in the road company for four months as we toured Oklahoma, Texas, Louisiana, and Arkansas. But I knew I wasn't cut out for the theater. It was great experience, but it finally dawned on me that if I were going to succeed as an actor, it would have to be on the screen. I recalled some advice I'd gotten from a friend in the *Caine Mutiny* cast, a fine actor named John Crawford.

John was staying at the stage manager's apartment while he was out of town. I asked if I could stay there, too, because I wanted to cut off the rent at the Belvedere Hotel. Late one night we were talking about what we wanted to do. John had already worked in films, and he said, "Jim, when you start making movies, learn what the camera can and cannot do, because that's your audience, that's your proscenium stage, the one you're playing to."

Then he gave me some "exercises."

"Jim, after lunch, don't sit around and bullshit with the crew," he said. "Go back to the set by yourself. They'll have the camera set up for the next shot. Pull up a chair and face the monster. Get about a foot away. Take a deep breath and look at that thing. There'll be a screw on the left and a screw on the right. Those are the 'eyes.' Look from one eye to the other as you say, 'I'm gonna kill you, you sonofabitch!' Do it again. And again. And again."

It made perfect sense. The camera isn't an object—it's a person. The most important person on the set.

"Now the camera is a woman," he said, "and you're trying to get her in bed. Look all over her face, but don't say anything, just think. Film is in the eyes. On a movie screen, your head is twenty feet high. If there's anything going on, the audience will see it. *Go make friends with the camera.*"

So I did.

I learned everything I could about what the camera does, including the technical stuff, and I got to the point where I *could* play love scenes to the monster.

I also lowered my voice and worked to get rid of my Oklahoma accent.

I was beginning to think of myself as an actor.

CHAPTER THREE

Maverick

By the end of 1955, I was back in Los Angeles, looking for work. I'd make the rounds of the studios during the day and drink beer at night with another struggling actor, Clint Eastwood. We'd talk about our plans for the future and what we wanted to do in the business.

In the mid-1950s, television was eating into movie ticket sales and the movie studios were losing money. Warner Bros. in particular was strapped for cash, so Harry and Albert Warner sold their shares to a banker named Serge Semenenko, who, against Jack Warner's wishes, steered the company into television production. Within a few years, Warner Bros. TV shows would be so profitable that Jack Warner bought back Semenenko's shares and wound up owning the whole studio himself.

Jack Warner tapped William T. Orr to head the TV division, not because of any great talent, but because Bill Orr was his son-in-law. A former actor, Orr was married to Warner's stepdaughter, Joy Page. ("The son-in-law also rises," some wag said.) It was comic at times: Orr and his two assistants would ride their little bicycles around the lot. Bill would be in front, then the first assistant, then the second. Nobody was allowed to pass anybody. It was like, "I'm the king!" If one of the assistants wanted to talk, he could pull up alongside Orr for a minute, but couldn't pass him. It was that kind of childish stuff.

Orr didn't want to pay for established talent for the new shows, so he had the producer-director Richard Bare scout around for unknowns who'd work cheap. One night I was in a bar with Robert Lowery, another out-of-work actor, when Dick Bare came in. Bob introduced me to Dick and we all had a drink. Dick mentioned he'd been looking for someone to star in *Cheyenne,* Warners' first Western series, but hadn't found the right guy. We talked a while longer and went our separate ways.

The next day it occurred to Dick Bare that the guy he'd met in the bar might be right for the *Cheyenne* lead, so he called Bob Lowery to track me down. Bob gave him my name but didn't know how to reach me, so all Dick could do was leave a message for me at the bar. I didn't go in there again until about a week later. I called Dick as soon as I got his message.

"If you can get to the studio right away, I may have a job for you."

"I'll be there in twenty minutes!"

Next thing I knew I was auditioning for Bare and Bill Orr. They'd already given the *Cheyenne* starring role to Clint Walker, but there was still one part left to cast. They were desperate because the company was going on location the next morning to begin filming the first episode. I'm sure that's why I got the part. It couldn't have been my acting.

I played a smart aleck Union Army officer I thought of as "the irate lieutenant." Just a couple of scenes. Over the next few months, I hung around Warners and did half a dozen small TV parts. One day somebody from the front office called and said they wanted to give me a screen test.

"What for? I've just done a bunch of jobs for you. If you can't tell by now, what good is a screen test?"

"Well, we like to test."

I didn't want to do it, but I finally said, "Okay, but you only get two weeks to make up your mind." They wanted a month, but I told them I might lose a job waiting, so they agreed to two weeks. I think they tested fourteen people in one day, including Dennis Hopper and Michael Landon. I told them, "Whatever you do about me, you ought to hire that Michael Landon. The kid's good."

Two weeks came and went and they asked for another week to make up their minds.

"Forget it," I said. "I didn't want to be under contract anyway."

Well, they picked me up that day. I was the only one of the fourteen they tested who got a contract.

I fell in love for the first and last time on August 1, 1956, at an Adlai Stevenson-for-President rally.

Stevenson lost.

I won.

That's where I met Lois Clarke.

It was love at first sight. The "thunderbolt." She was as beautiful as she was sweet. She reminded me of Audrey Hepburn, only full bodied, like Sophia Loren. And she was obviously a good Democrat. I was nuts about her from the moment we met.

Still am.

It was a barbecue and I ended up in the pool with the children. That's how I got to talk to Lois. It wasn't any strategy, it's just what happened. She was very nice. Within the first few minutes she told me she had a daughter from her first marriage, Kimberly, who had polio.

Lois and I saw each other every day—sometimes twice a day—until August 17, when we were married in the Beverly Hills courthouse.

My family was against the marriage. They pointed out that Lois and I had little in common. I was six feet three inches tall and Lois was petite; I was the outdoor, athletic type and she was the indoor type. I was practical and pragmatic, she was a dreamer. I was from a small town in Oklahoma, Lois had lived in LA all her life. The biggest objection was the difference in religion: I'm a Methodist, Lois is Jewish. But neither of us was ever what you'd call religious, so it wasn't an issue, at least not for Lois and me.

None of the naysayers had stopped to consider that Lois and I complemented each other. What they saw as weaknesses, we saw as strengths. Lois had what I lacked and vice versa.

Our honeymoon consisted of two days and one night at the La Jollan, an old hotel (a "dump," according to Lois) near San Diego. It was all we could afford on my contract player's salary. We didn't have the bridal suite, but a tiny room and bath overlooking the street. Lois now says she had to drag me to the beach during the day and to a play that night, and that I would have been happy just staying in the room, but that's not how I remember it. As I recall, if she wanted to go, I went . . . *cheerfully*.

Back home, we rented a small apartment on Dickens Street in Sherman Oaks. Its only advantages were proximity to the studio and affordable rent. Money was tight: Kim's condition had required expensive treatments, and the medical bills had piled up.

When I started acting, I didn't have a clue what I was doing. I was just stumbling around, hoping to get lucky. Getting married made me serious about my career and about my life. Suddenly I was the breadwinner for a family of three, soon to be four—our daughter Gigi was born a little over a year later. I had to buckle down and support these people. I welcomed the responsibility, but I also felt the weight of it. I think it focused me as an actor and motivated me to try to build a career rather than just drift along as I'd done before.

It wasn't easy. My signature on the Warner Bros. contract consigned me to the same studio system that Jimmy Cagney and Bette

Davis had rebelled against in the 1930s and '40s. For openers, the studio changed my name without my permission. I was born James Scott Bumgarner; the studio knocked off the "Bum." I accepted it because of Kim. Her name was Kimberly Clarke. She was known in school as "Kimberly Clarke," and "Kimberly Bumgarner," and "Kim Garner." That's confusing for a little girl, so I changed it legally—to make sure she knew who she was.

The contract was harsh. The studio owned you body and soul, and they had no qualms about putting you in a picture that was bad for your career. If you refused the part, they'd suspend you without pay and add the time to your contract. They could also make money "loaning" you out to other studios. Contract actors were indentured servants, like pro ballplayers before free agency.

I had a fifty-two-week deal, which meant they could use me for movies, television, public relations—they could make me sell pencils if they wanted to. They sent me all over the country for personal appearances and cast me in small character parts in several features, beginning with a William Holden vehicle, *Toward the Unknown,* directed by Mervyn LeRoy. When we started shooting, I was scared to death and had no idea what I was doing. I was so green I didn't even know what a producer was.

LeRoy was known for singling out one actor and picking on him for the whole shoot, and sure enough, he tried to make *me* his whipping boy on the set. He was especially nasty if he hadn't taken his pills that morning. Well, the first time he pushed me, I shoved right back, and he found somebody else to lord it over.

I got along fine with my fellow actors, including Lloyd Nolan, a pal since *Caine Mutiny Court Martial.* One day on the set, Bill Holden took me aside. "Jim," he said, "I saw the dailies, and you're gonna be a big star." What a generous thing to do. It gave me confidence when I really needed it.

Still a novice, I did small parts in two more features, *The Girl He Left Behind* with Tab Hunter, Natalie Wood, and David Janssen, and

Shoot-out at Medicine Bend, directed by Dick Bare. It was Randy Scott's last contract picture for Warners after a long run. The movie couldn't decide if it was a comedy or a drama, maybe because Bare had gotten his start directing the "Joe McDoakes" comedy shorts in the 1940s. Even the title is off; there's gunplay, but not one decent shoot-out in the whole picture.

Though my acting still wasn't very good, my next assignment was my first role of any consequence, and my first serious film.

Sayonara is the story of American servicemen in Japan who break the taboo against fraternizing with Japanese women. Based on James Michener's novel, it's a love story that also deals with racism.

Warner Bros. originally wanted Marlon Brando and Audrey Hepburn to play the leads, but they didn't have the budget for two big stars, so it came down to a choice between Brando and an unknown Japanese girl, or Audrey Hepburn and a newcomer in the Brando role. I figured I had a chance at the lead if they went with Audrey, but they decided on Marlon and a beautiful young actress named Miiko Taka.

Still a lowly contract player at Warner Bros., I was assigned to do screen tests with all the actors they were considering for the part of Marlon's buddy. The list included David Janssen, Robert Sterling, and Gary Merrill. When I heard they'd decided on a young actor named John Smith for the role, I asked to see the director, Joshua Logan, and the producer, Bill Goetz.

"Look," I said, "you've already got me, I'm a lot cheaper, and I think I'm better for the part."

And by golly, they hired me.

It's the only part I've ever gone after. (Okay, maybe I stole it.)

We shot *Sayonara* in Japan, in beautiful locations like the Imperial Palace in Kyoto, with its magnificent rock gardens and cherry trees. The movie showed tea ceremonies and traditional dances, and I think the portrayal of Japanese culture a decade after the end of World War II helped increase understanding between former enemies.

Marlon and I hit it off from the start. We gave each other the right of way, maybe because we had something in common: we were both rebels.

Marlon plays Major Lloyd Gruver, an Air Force ace and West Point graduate who risks a promising career when he takes up with a Japanese entertainer. I play Marlon's sidekick, Captain Mike Bailey, a Marine pilot.

The first scene we shot was in the back of a taxicab, and I couldn't help thinking about another taxi scene, Marlon's famous one with Rod Steiger in *On the Waterfront*. I knew I was no Rod Steiger.

I was so tense my palms were dripping wet, and Marlon noticed it. "What's the matter?" he asked.

"I'm so nervous I can't see straight. I've never done a first-class picture before."

Marlon immediately put me at ease. He took me aside and said, "If you have any problems, just let me know and we'll work 'em out."

That calmed me down. From then on, we worked well together.

Marlon had the reputation of being "difficult," but it wasn't with fellow actors, just producers and directors. For one thing, he liked to rewrite dialogue. For another, as Major Gruver he affected a Southern accent, which wasn't in the script.

Marlon was unhappy because he didn't feel Josh Logan was giving him any direction. He'd say to Josh, "Why don't you direct me?" and Josh would say, "Marlon, if you do anything I don't like I'll tell you." I think Marlon wanted a confrontation, but Josh was so agreeable, it was like pushing on a rope. That frustrated Marlon even more and he complained to me about it.

"Why are you doing this picture?" I asked.

"For the money."

"Okay, then, do it for the money, but don't give the director a heart attack!"

Josh didn't give me a lot of direction either, probably because Marlon became my personal coach. We'd go out to a rice paddy and "improve" the scenes. Then the two of us would rehearse and rehearse. I thought, *Josh is gonna kill me for this,* but when we showed him our stuff he usually liked it and wound up using it. But not because Josh was a pushover. When he made *Sayonara,* he was already a veteran stage and screen director, with film credits that included *Bus Stop* and *Picnic,* and he'd won the Pulitzer Prize for Drama as coauthor of the Broadway musical *South Pacific.* Josh had been around the block, and he was smart enough to stay out of Marlon's way.

Marlon Brando was the best movie actor we've ever had. I know that's not exactly going out on a limb, but I just want to be on record with all the other actors who feel the same way. He could make you forget he was the great Brando and you'd just see the character. Not many actors can do that. For what it's worth, I think he could have been even greater if he had chosen his material more carefully. But I never saw him do a bad job. Marlon was in a lot of bad movies, but he was always interesting.

Sayonara earned a bunch of Oscar nominations and wound up with several statuettes, including one each for supporting actors Red Buttons and Miyoshi Umeki. Though my role as Marlon's buddy wasn't outstanding, it was a big learning experience and a definite career boost. You're bound to get a little of it on you when you're in a film like that.

The studio bosses were absolute monarchs. Louis B. Mayer, Samuel Goldwyn, Harry "Genghis" Cohn, and Warner Bros. head of production Jack L. Warner—the Hollywood "moguls"—didn't like back talk from mere actors.

J.L., or "the colonel," as his subordinates called him—he'd wangled a commission in the Signal Corps during World War II— was the youngest of four brothers who'd immigrated to the United

States from Poland in around 1900. They were movie exhibitors, then distributors, and by World War I they'd opened a studio, Warner Bros., Inc., which introduced sound to the movies with *The Jazz Singer* in 1927 and made low-budget, socially conscious features in the 1930s and '40s.

Jack Warner treated everybody the same: lousy. He didn't spare his wife, his son, or his mistress. He hated writers ("schmucks with Underwoods," he called them), he hated actors, and he was cruel to his employees. According to Warner's own son, if Jack's brothers hadn't hired him, he'd have been out of work.

Someone once said in Warner's defense that he "bore no grudge against those he had wronged." But that wasn't true in my case, because Jack Warner hated me. Maybe it was because I said in a *Time* magazine interview that being under contract to Warner Bros. was like being a ham in a smokehouse: whenever they wanted some, they'd take it off the hook, slice off a few pieces, then hang it back on the hook. Word got back to me that the colonel didn't like that.

Warner was rude and crude—the most vulgar man I've ever met. He had terrible taste in most things and a filthy mouth. The first time Lois and I went to the Oscars, we sat at his table and listened to him tell one dirty joke after another. He actually thought they were funny. We got up and moved to another table. I told Bill Orr: "Don't you ever . . . don't you *ever* get me invited anywhere where he's going to be." Well, you don't say that about the boss.

Warner seemed to enjoy embarrassing himself and everybody in the room. When Madame Chiang Kai-Shek came to the United States on a fund-raising tour for China during World War II, she visited the Warner Bros. lot, where a dinner was given in her honor. After she delivered a gracious speech thanking her American allies for their continuing support and praising Warner Bros. for their contributions to the war effort, Jack Warner got up, waited for the applause to die down, looked at Madame Chiang, and said, "Holy cow, that reminds me, I forgot to pick up my laundry!"

I think Warner was scared of me. I mean *physically*. Whenever we were together, I'd catch him watching me out of the corner of his eye, as if he were afraid I'd pick him up and throw him out of a window, maybe because Errol Flynn had once threatened to do just that, and Warner thought I was the same kind of guy. I was careful not to dispel that notion, but I would never have laid a hand on him. A few years after I left Warner Bros., we were both at some premiere, and the minute he saw me he had his bodyguards circle around him as if he were in mortal danger.

Warner hated agents, especially Lew Wasserman and Jules Stein of MCA, who'd made a deal for client Charlton Heston to star in a Warner Bros. combat movie. While Heston was preparing for the role, Warner discovered that the contract gave the actor 10 percent of the movie's gross. He went ballistic and tore up the contract. Meanwhile, the studio ordered Heston to report for the start of production. When he refused on the advice of his agents, Warner Bros. declared him in breach of contract and lawsuits were filed.

Questioned by MCA's lawyer in a deposition, Warner ticked off his objections to the contract the agency had negotiated, and then blurted out: "Aw, those fucking actors deserve anything bad that happens to them anyway." The MCA attorney smiled and said, "Thank you, Mr. Warner, that's all we need from you." Heston got a big settlement.

At 5:30 on the same afternoon that Chuck Heston failed to report for the start of *Darby's Rangers,* I was called up to the Warner executive offices. They said they wanted to reward me for being such a great guy and offered to raise my salary to $350 a week and give me a two-year extension on my contract. I wasn't sure what they were up to, but I knew it was something, so I said no. Then they upped the offer to $500 a week. With Kim recovering from polio and Lois pregnant with Gigi, I took it. I didn't know that the $500 was really $285; the rest was withheld as an "advance against residuals" that I'd never see because actors didn't get residuals in those days.

On the following Monday morning, I learned I was to replace Heston as the lead in *Darby's Rangers*. It would be my first starring role in a feature, and they were getting me for $500 a week. They'd have had to pay anyone else many times that to star in the picture.

Early in 1957, as soon as I'd finished my work on *Sayonara* in Japan, Warner Bros. called me back to Hollywood to test for a new Western series. They'd looked at just about every actor in Hollywood to play a gambler wandering the frontier in the 1870s, but they picked me, probably because they saw the *Sayonara* dailies and figured, Hey— we've already got this guy under contract, we might as well save money. That's how they "discovered" me to play Bret Maverick. I wasn't happy about it. I wanted to make movies, not a TV Western. But I didn't have a choice.

Jack Warner had a firm policy against using original stories because he didn't want to pay a $500-per-episode "created by" royalty to a writer. He decreed that, whenever possible, scripts should be adapted from properties already owned by the studio. If the odd pilot was based on an original script, Warner would screen it once or twice in a movie theater in Bermuda or somewhere to establish technically that the series came from a Warner Bros. "film."

Maverick's pilot, "The War of the Silver Kings," was adapted from the book *The War of the Copper Kings,* which the studio had previously purchased. For another episode, they recycled an old Warner Bros. feature called *Rocky Mountain* starring Errol Flynn. They used stock footage from the movie, and our clothes had to match, so I wore Flynn's actual hat and vest. The rest of Maverick's costume was a conglomeration of stuff they had lying around in the wardrobe department: Monty Woolley's shirt from *The Man Who Came to Dinner,* Gary Cooper's coat from *Saratoga Trunk*. I even had to ride a certain horse. This was standard operating procedure at Warners in those days. People used to say that if there were ever more than two characters in a Warner Bros. TV show, it was stock footage.

In August 1957, on the strength of the pilot, ABC sold *Maverick* to the Kaiser Steel Company—in those days there was one sponsor for a whole show—for $6 million for fifty-two episodes, thirteen of them reruns. We had to deliver thirty-nine episodes the first season, giving us only a month to build up a backlog of shows before the series went on the air.

Henry J. Kaiser was an American industrialist who'd made his name and fortune building "Liberty" ships during World War II. He was a tough executive who figured out how to turn out a prefab cargo vessel in six days, which was a big boost to the Allied war effort. By the mid-1950s, his empire also included a steel and aluminum company based in Oakland, California. He wanted to go national, so he asked ABC for a suitable television show. ABC pitched *Maverick*.

Kaiser's friend, the TV host Art Linkletter, advised him not to buy it because, Linkletter said, there were already too many Westerns on the air. He predicted *Maverick* would "die like a dog" in the first season. Kaiser went ahead anyway, maybe because he saw a bit of himself in Bret Maverick. And I was told he liked the way I handled the character.

The *Maverick* pilot aired on September 22, 1957. After a few more episodes, the director Budd Boetticher and I started to play around with the scripts, injecting a little humor here and there. Soon Roy Huggins caught on. By the fourth episode, Roy was writing for it, and things got a lot more amusing.

One of the other *Maverick* writers, Marion Hargrove, liked to put little digs in the stage directions like, "Maverick looks as if he has lost his place in the script," or "Maverick looks at him with his beady little eyes." When someone told him you can't refer to the star as "beady-eyed," Marion said, "Leave it in. I know Garner, and believe me, he's beady-eyed."

By the tenth week, we were the top-rated show on television and were changing America's viewing habits. Before *Maverick,* when people went out to dinner on Sunday night, they made sure they were home by eight o'clock to watch Ed Sullivan or Steve Allen. *Maverick* came on at 7:30, so everybody had to get home a half hour earlier.

The show put the word "maverick" into the language. A "maverick" is "a refractory or recalcitrant individual who bolts from his party and initiates an independent course," according to *The Western Dictionary*. The word goes back to a Texas cattleman who didn't brand his calves. When they'd wander onto someone else's ranch, people started calling them "mavericks." In one of the shows, we defined a maverick as "a calf who's lost his mother, and his father has run off with another cow." I've always thought of it as a sort of freewheeling slick. In 1980, the name was used for a new NBA franchise—the Dallas Mavericks—and it's the name of a chain of convenience stores in the Southwest, though they spell it "Maverik."

Maverick's competition on Sunday night—Ed Sullivan, Steve Allen, and Jack Benny—were each making $25,000 a week, and we were burying them in the ratings. Sullivan had been on top for years and nobody had ever beaten him before, yet I was making $500 a week for doing not only *Maverick* but also appearing in feature films (*Up Periscope* and *Cash McCall* in addition to *Darby's Rangers*). I was also required to do publicity, including at least one interview a day at lunch, plus personal appearances on weekends. They also wanted me to go out at night and be seen around town, but I didn't have the money. I couldn't afford the clothes, and I couldn't afford the car. I had to borrow Natalie Wood's Cadillac to take Lois to the premiere of *West Side Story* because my car was an old clunker.

I figured that since *Maverick* was a hit, the studio would do the right thing and tear up the old contract. I figured wrong.

When *Maverick* was on hiatus, I hit the road at the rate of three cities a day. One weekend they sent me to Texas, and when we landed in San Antonio, there were five thousand people at the airport. They overran the gates and came right up to the plane. I did local TV, rode in a float with Miss San Diego, and was Grand Marshal at the Illinois State Fair, for which I received $100 pocket money while the studio got $25,000.

One time they put a bunch of VIPs on a Mississippi steamboat and pre-positioned me, costumed as Bret Maverick, on a small island in the middle of the river. When the boat came by the captain announced, "Ladies and gentlemen, we're going to pick up an extra passenger." They took me aboard and I mingled with the customers until we docked.

When I was asked to do *The Pat Boone Chevy Showroom* on ABC, I knew the usual fee was $7,500, but a Warner Bros. executive informed me I was expected to do it for nothing and I'd already been "committed" to appear.

"Then uncommit me," I said.

When they threatened to fire me, I said, "Up to you."

When they threatened to sue me, I said, "Go ahead."

We finally compromised: I got $2,500 for the Boone show, plus a new (1959) Corvette, tax-free, with a full tank of gas and the key in the ignition. (Wish I had that car today!) Plus, no more bookings without my permission, and I'd get half of all future appearance fees.

If you bring your personality to roles, people get to know you. When you play someone you don't understand, it doesn't work. I understood Maverick right away because a maverick is a rebel and I've always been a rebel. Maverick doesn't like to fight, but he'll use his fists if pushed to the wall. Me, too. (There's a line in *Murphy's Romance* that I think fits us both: "When I'm pushed, I shove.") Maverick is a drifter, and I was a drifter. He isn't anti-Indian, and neither am I, being one quarter Cherokee.

Maverick is quick-witted and quick on the draw, though he tries to avoid gunplay. But he's not a coward . . . exactly. He just believes in self-preservation. His attitude is, why risk your life over something trivial, like money? Or "honor"? But Maverick has his own moral code, and he does have a conscience. Yes, he cheats at cards, but he only cheats cheaters. He doesn't have to cheat anybody else because he's a great poker player. (That's one trait we *don't* share.) Maverick is often described as an antihero, but I don't think that's true. I'd call him a *reluctant* hero. He'll come to your aid if there's an injustice involved, and he'll always stand up to bullies. (Have I mentioned that I hate bullies?)

Mind you, I wasn't thinking about all this stuff when I was making *Maverick*. I just wanted that check at the end of the week.

It took us eight calendar days to make a *Maverick* episode: We'd start on Tuesday, shoot through Friday afternoon, break for the weekend, then come back and finish late Monday or early Tuesday. But since the episodes were being aired every seven days, we were losing a day a week, and it was only a matter of time before we would run out of shows. So after about the eighth week they got the idea of adding a brother who could alternate with Bret. They auditioned a bunch of actors, including Stuart Whitman, Rod Taylor, Richard Jaeckel, and Jack Kelly, the brother of the movie actress Nancy Kelly. One day they brought Jack over to the Warners back lot. We hit it off right away. They hired him to play Bart Maverick for $650 a week, $150 more than my salary . . . and he was *still* getting screwed. (My $500 a week increased to $600 the second year and to $1,250 the third, which, in those days, was . . . not a lot of money.)

Henry Kaiser wasn't just a sponsor; he was a 33 percent partner in *Maverick*'s profits, but as far as I know, he never interfered with the production. When the network accidentally forgot to tell Kaiser about the addition of another Maverick—he didn't find out until the first episode aired—he was livid. "I paid for red apples and they gave me green apples!" Kaiser said. ABC had to pay him $600,000 to smooth his feathers.

They created a second production company for Jack Kelly that worked simultaneously with ours. Jack and I did separate episodes, but all the scripts were written for *Maverick,* not for a specific brother, so they were interchangeable. Occasionally we'd cross over. He'd appear in my episode, I'd appear in his. Just a few scenes, though, usually to rescue each other from a tight spot.

Jack was a good guy and we got along fine. The only problem was, he drank too much. He wasn't *bad,* but whenever we'd go on an airplane, he'd get snockered and become *difficult.* And sometimes he'd arrive on set with a hangover and an attitude. But within a couple of hours, we were having fun again.

Jack's wife, the actress May Wynn, was another story. Born Donna Lee Hickey, she took her stage name from her character in the film version of *The Caine Mutiny.* She resented that Jack wasn't a bigger star, and I think she blamed *me* for it. She'd nag him about my having funnier scripts and getting more recognition. After a few drinks, she would needle Jack mercilessly. Then *he'd* have another drink, and they'd get into a big argument.

The audience somehow got the idea I was the senior Maverick brother, even though Jack was seven months older, maybe because I was there first, or because I was an inch or so taller than Jack. That may explain why Bart Maverick's episodes weren't as popular as Bret's. The audience was disappointed: All of a sudden, they weren't getting what drew them to the show in the first place. We tried to remedy that by having Bret introduce Bart's first few solo episodes.

These were the early days of television. We didn't have the time or money to do anything extravagant. The whole series was shot at Warner Bros. Studios. I don't think we went on location more than once or twice in three years. There were four units filming simultaneously on the lot in Burbank. We were literally back-to-back, one camera pointed at us, the other at *Sugarfoot* or *Cheyenne* or one of the other Westerns. The dolly grips were butt-to-butt and we had to take turns shooting.

Roy Huggins was the writer-producer and creator of *Maverick*. Roy was smart and he was successful, in a commercial sense. Look at the shows he created: *Maverick, 77 Sunset Strip, The Fugitive, The Rockford Files, Baretta*. Roy was a nice enough guy, I suppose, but he had strong opinions and would never listen to anybody. He borrowed just about every story he ever did and just changed it from one form to another. Somehow, I don't think he had the depth or the scope for the movies.

Roy did have a great line about me: "Jim Garner and I have a love/hate relationship: I love him and he hates me."

It wasn't true; Roy didn't love me at all.

But I may not be an impartial witness. I knew more than I should about Roy because my friend Luis Delgado was his brother-in-law. (Luis's sister, the actress Adele Mara, was Roy's wife.) More than that, I can't say.

Luis was Jack Kelly's stand-in on *Maverick* when I asked him to work for me. "I will on one condition," he said. "You take care of the acting and I'll handle everything else."

And did he ever. He looked after me like I was his baby. When we traveled, he made all the arrangements. He'd go to a city ahead of me and rent a car, check into the hotel, go to the production office and get our per diems, then pick me up at the airport. If I needed clothes, he got clothes. If I needed laundry or dry cleaning done, he saw to it. He'd drop me off and pick me up at the golf course (Luis didn't play); he'd get the script changes and put them in for me. He handled all the cash and made sure I always had spending money.

In short, Luis made sure I didn't have anything to worry about so I could focus all my energy on acting.

Luis ("LOO-ee") was a dynamic guy with a commanding

presence. My driver, Chester Grimes, could be across the room, Luis could just look at him, and Chester would straighten right up. (Chester, aka "Cheddar Cheese," has been with me for many years, and I can always depend on him to make me laugh. Sometimes so much I have to beg him to stop.)

I met Luis when I was eighteen and he was twenty, at the Dolores Drive-in at Wilshire and La Cienega where we both went to chase girls. The only difference was that Luis had a car.

Years later Luis owned a bar, the Laurelite, on Sunset Boulevard, next door to Greenblatt's Delicatessen and across the street from Schwab's drugstore. People in the movie business loved the place because he'd put them on the cuff. Luis never got wealthy, because he was too good-hearted.

Luis's nickname was "the Thin Man," and it fit: *delgado* means "thin" in Spanish, and Luis *was* skinny at six foot three, 185 pounds. He was too thin for the Army!

Luis always had good-looking cars—I remember a beautiful green Buick convertible he drove in the '50s. We both loved cars and at one time both had Mini Coopers. You'd see us going home from the studio, Luis in his purple one and me in my blue one. In 1972, Luis's wife bought him a custom van for his birthday. Luis was working as Steve McQueen's stand-in on *The Getaway*, directed by Sam Peckinpah. They were shooting in San Antonio, Texas, and I volunteered to drive the van there from Los Angeles to surprise Luis. He *was* surprised, and he loved the van, which had a lot of custom work by Tony Nancy.

While on the set of *The Getaway* I did a car stunt for Peckinpah. Drove an orange VW Beetle in a robbery scene. When I asked Sam to pay me, he said, "How much do you want?"

"Just give me what you think it's worth."

He reached in his pocket and pulled out a dollar.

I didn't tell him that I had so much fun, I'd have paid *him*.

Luis was excellent company and we had great times. Between

shots on the set, we played backgammon. On weekends, we'd go to auto races all over Southern California. When we weren't shooting, I'd go to his house in Sherman Oaks to play backgammon. Never played for money, and it's a good thing, because Luis was the luckiest damn roller you ever saw!

Luis and I understood and trusted each other. We never had a cross word between us in fifty years. I lost him to cancer in 1997.

I think Westerns are popular because they're pure escapism. They don't bother with the problem of how the hero earns his living. A cowboy rides into town, gets off his horse, and goes into a saloon. The barkeep pours him a shot and the cowboy sits down. He doesn't have to worry about anything. Nobody wants to know where he came from or what he does. When he ties up his horse, there's no parking meter on the hitching post. In *Maverick,* there's always good weather, and you know neither Bret nor Bart will have to worry about where their next meal is coming from. Or where they're going to sleep. They just get off their horses and lie down.

By the mid-1950s, there were a lot of "adult Westerns" on television, shows like *Wyatt Earp, Gunsmoke,* and *Have Gun Will Travel.* They had a more modern point of view than traditional TV shoot-'em-ups like *The Lone Ranger* and *The Cisco Kid,* which were so silly only a kid of ten could stand them. In adult Westerns, the hero didn't wear a mask and the writers tried to tell stories without using stencils. (Somebody said an adult Western is where the hero still kisses his horse at the end, only now he worries about it.) *Maverick* was the most adult of them all, including the other Warner Bros. Westerns, *Cheyenne* with Clint Walker, *Lawman* (John Russell), and *Sugarfoot* (Will Hutchins).

Maverick turned the genre upside down. It wasn't comedy and it wasn't satire, it was a Western with humor. Not slapstick, *situation* humor. Tongue-in-cheek. It let the air out of the stalwart TV

Western hero. Maverick was the first hero to wear black. He wasn't crazy about horses, so his mount was never a character in the show like Trigger and Silver were for Roy Rogers and the Lone Ranger.

Roy Huggins had his own ideas about the *Maverick* phenomenon. He distilled them into a list of instructions:

The Ten-Point Guide to Happiness While Writing or Directing a *Maverick*

1. Maverick is the original disorganization man.

2. Maverick's primary motivation is that ancient and most noble of motives: the profit motive.

3. Heavies in *Maverick* are always absolutely right, and they are always beloved to someone.

4. The cliché flourishes in the creative arts because the familiar gives a sense of comfort and security. Writers and directors of *Maverick* are requested to *live dangerously*.

5. Maverick's activities are seldom grandiose. To force him into magnificent speculations is to lose sight of his essential indolence.

6. The *Maverick* series is a regeneration story in which the regeneration has been indefinitely postponed.

7. Maverick's travels are never aimless; he always has an object in view: his pocket and yours. However, there are times when he is merely fleeing from heroic enterprise.

8. In the traditional Western story, the situation is always serious but never hopeless. In a *Maverick* story, the situation is always hopeless but never serious.

9. "Cowardly" would be too strong a word to apply to Maverick. "Cautious" is possibly more accurate, and certainly more kind. When the two brothers went off to the Civil War, their old Pappy said to them: "If either of

you comes back with a medal, I'll beat you to death."
They never shamed him.

10. The widely held belief that Maverick is a gambler is a
fallacy. In his hands, poker is not a game of chance. He
plays it earnestly, patiently, and with an abiding faith in
the laws of probability.

I've always enjoyed working. I feel at home on a set and I try to promote a relaxed atmosphere for everybody else. Jack felt the same, so we'd play little pranks to blow off steam. One day we rode our horses through all four sets shooting blanks and yelling and generally raising hell. Jack and I also played a game we called "BANG!" Whenever we saw each other, the first guy to draw his prop gun and yell "bang!" would get a point. One time he literally caught me with my pants down.

But it wasn't all fun and games. You were on stage shooting by 8:00 a.m. and you'd work until 7:00 or 8:00 in the evening. When you left the studio at night, they handed you the script for the next day. You went home and read it while you were having dinner . . . if you were lucky. Sometimes you wouldn't get the script until you were in the makeup chair the next morning at 6:45. I remember a director named Walter Doniger coming in one morning and saying, "Good script, isn't it?"

"I'll let you know when I read it."

"You haven't read the script?"

"No, I just got it, but don't worry, I'll read it before lunch."

We worked all morning without a problem—I could read eight or ten pages and pretty much know what it was about because the character was so strong. And I've always been a quick study when it comes to learning lines.

I had the privilege of working with a lot of good actors on

Maverick. In addition to the regulars, a succession of top-notch actors guested, including Mike Connors, Bing Russell (Kurt's dad), Fay Spain, Ruta Lee, Werner Klemperer (before he played Colonel Klink on *Hogan's Heroes*), Sig Ruman, Joanna Barnes, Hans Conreid, John Vivyan (before he starred on TV as *Mr. Lucky*), Jane Darwell, George O'Hanlon (the original Joe McDoakes in the movie shorts and later the voice of George Jetson), Claude Akins, Dan Blocker (Hoss Cartwright on *Bonanza*), Regis Toomey, Wayne Morris, Marcel Dalio (that wonderful French character actor), Edgar Buchanan, Abby Dalton, Robert Conrad (*The Wild, Wild West*), Louise Fletcher, James Lydon (we became good friends), Diane McBain, Connie Stevens, Adam West (*Batman*), William Schallert, Mona Freeman, Buddy Ebsen (Fess Parker's sidekick in *Davy Crockett* and later Jed Clampett in *The Beverly Hillbillies*), Richard Webb (*Captain Midnight*), Martin Landau . . . the list goes on. In one show, Clint Eastwood plays a smartass heavy who keeps calling me "Maver-ack," and a very young Robert Redford appears as a cowhand in another.

Fifty years later, two guest stars stand out in my mind: Kathleen Crowley was one of those actresses who worked a lot in the '50s. She did several *Maverick*s and always played charming grifters. Her character's relationship with Maverick was unusual: We didn't trust each other as far as we could throw a bull calf, but we liked each other. And Kathleen was gorgeous. She wasn't very tall, but she had classic beauty. Nobody considered her much of an actress, but I did.

Gerald Mohr was the one I had the most fun working with on *Maverick*. He appeared in several episodes, including one as Doc Holliday. Mohr was well educated. He was fluent in several languages, and he'd been a medical student when the radio bug bit him. He was good enough to be a member of Orson Welles's Mercury Theatre ensemble, and he did hundreds of shows during the 1930s and '40s, the golden age of radio. He made the transition to television and was one of the busiest actors in Hollywood for many years. He could tell a joke better than anybody, and he had a bunch of them.

Never repeated himself. And he was a pro. I learned a few things about acting from him.

A Shady Deal at Sunny Acres" is probably the definitive *Maverick*. It's certainly my favorite episode, because it's Bret at his coolest. One day Roy Huggins told me a script idea: One Maverick brother pulls off a complicated "sting" operation against a guy who had swindled the other brother out of some money while the brother who got swindled just sits on a porch all day and whittles. Every once in a while a citizen comes up to him and asks, "Why aren't you out trying to get your money back?" All he says is, "I'm working on it" and just keeps whittling. Roy gave me the choice of roles, and I took the one sitting on the porch. He was surprised, because it was the smaller of the two parts. But I needed to get off my feet!

Marion Hargrove wrote an episode that was a spoof of *Gunsmoke* called "Gun-Shy." Ben Gage played Marshal Mort Dooley, a send-up of the James Arness character Marshal Matt Dillon. In the opening, Ben stands at one end of a deserted street, his big butt filling the frame, and Bret Maverick stands at the other end. Ben draws and fires, but his first shot misses. So do five more. Bret shouts, "Shall we stand a little closer, Marshal?"

A wonderful character actor named Walker Edmiston played the Dennis Weaver part. In *Gunsmoke,* Dennis played Jim Arness's sidekick, Chester Goode, with a famous, stiff-legged limp. After the first day of shooting, I noticed that Walker wasn't limping. When I asked why not the director said, "That would be a little too much, Jim." I said, "No, if you're going to do it, *do* it!" So we added a little scene in which he comes into the marshal's office and he's limping all of a sudden. I say, "What's the matter, did you get hurt?" and he says, "A gol-durned horse stepped on my foot and it hurts like thunder!" and I say, "You should keep it, it gives you character." He limped for the rest of the show.

Almost from the beginning, there was an invisible character who was nearly as important as Bret or Bart: Pappy. His one-liners were a convenient way to end a scene on a humorous note, or to save face in a tough situation. They all began with, "As my old Pappy used to say . . . " Here are my favorites: "Man's the only animal you can skin more than once," "Marriage is the only game of chance where both people can lose," "If at first you don't succeed, try something else," "If you can't fight 'em and they won't let you join 'em, you best get out of the county," "Any man who needs to make out a will just isn't spending his money properly."

Warner Bros. made all the decisions for my career. The problem was, they didn't *care* about my career. *I* cared, though. If I was going to succeed, I wanted it to be *my* success. If I was going to fail, I wanted it to be *my* failure, not because someone else made the wrong choices for me. As old Pappy used to say, "Make a lot of mistakes but always be sure they're your own."

About a year and a half into *Maverick,* there was a Writers Guild strike, and Warner Bros. announced they were laying me off. They invoked the force majeure clause in my contract, which said if production was halted by circumstances beyond its control, like a strike, the studio wouldn't have to pay my salary. They claimed they didn't have scripts.

My reaction was, "Hey, I'm ready to work. You're paying me by the week and I'm here to do whatever you want."

"Nope, we're not going to pay you."

Well, bull*shit.*

I decided to sue them for breach of contract.

Almost everyone I knew advised me against it. I was actually threatened more than once that if I didn't drop the lawsuit, I'd "never work in this town again." (Life imitating art . . . or something.) I was told, "You'll be a dead man. You're a nobody just starting out—even if you win in court, your career will be over." I didn't want to be blackballed by the studios, but I was tired of being pushed around. I kept saying I could always go back to laying carpets for a living. I didn't really *want* to go back to laying carpets, but *they* didn't know that.

I was also a little concerned about being typecast as Bret Maverick. I didn't want to get too identified with the character and worried I wouldn't be able to make the transition from Bret to other roles.

I hired Gang, Tyre, Rudin & Brown, a prominent Los Angeles law firm, and they assigned a young attorney and former Rhodes scholar named Frank Wells. Frank turned out to be an outstanding entertainment lawyer and later ran Disney with Michael Eisner.

At first, I thought Jack Kelly was going to join me in the lawsuit, but then I heard the studio had upped his contract from forty to fifty-two weeks and promised him a feature film a year. To this day, I don't know if that's true, but if it is, I don't blame Jack. I just knew what I had to do for myself. After *Maverick,* Jack eventually left show business and got into real estate in Huntington Beach, California. He also served on the city council and was elected mayor, running on the slogan "Let Maverick Solve Your Problems." Jack died of a stroke in 1992 at the age of sixty-five.

Even though *Maverick* had ceased production because of the strike, there were still lots of requests for personal appearances, and I could have done movies while the writers were out. But the studio used the strike to teach me a lesson. So I went out and did eight weeks of *John Loves Mary* in summer stock and earned more than I had in a year at Warners. (For that matter, one year Luis Delgado made more money on *Maverick* as a stand-in than I did.)

By the time my case went to trial in Los Angeles Superior Court, Frank Wells had discovered that contrary to the studio's claim that it couldn't get scripts during the strike, it actually had fifteen writers working under the table churning out dozens of scripts as "W. Hermanos." Talk about prolific, that W. Hermanos really got around! "Hermanos," of course, is Spanish for "brothers."

When Frank cross-examined Jack Warner on the witness stand, it was a thing of beauty. Not flashy like in a courtroom drama, but cold and methodical. And devastating.

Warner claimed he didn't know about the "Hermanos brothers" scripts, but Frank used Warner's own testimony to prove otherwise. The Hollywood mogul seemed to get smaller and smaller as Frank caught him in one lie after another. By the time Frank was finished with him, Warner was a beaten man. He reminded me of Captain Queeg in *The Caine Mutiny Court Martial,* except that Queeg was worthy of sympathy.

The judge ruled in my favor, and after Warner Bros. lost its appeal, I was a free agent. As it turned out, I lost money on the original *Maverick:* I was paid $90,000 while I was under contract to Warners and it cost $100,000 in legal fees to escape. It was worth it.

Warner Bros. made 124 *Maverick* episodes, and I was in 52 of them. When I left, after the third season, they tried to get Sean Connery to replace me and they even flew him over from England, but he ultimately passed. Then they decided to bring in Roger Moore as Beau Maverick, Bret's English cousin. Roger had played a different character in a previous *Maverick* episode, "The Rivals," and he did a good job.

Roger was already under contract to Warners, and he insisted he'd do *Maverick* only if they'd release him at the end of the year. They balked at first, but he stood his ground and they finally agreed. After Roger worked the season, they did let him go, right into *The Saint,* which was a big hit for him. Good *on* ya, Roger!

Maverick lasted one more year with Jack Kelly and a kid named

Robert Colbert as Brent. They tried to sell him as a James Garner look-alike. They put him in my suit and underlit him, but as soon as he opened his mouth, you knew it wasn't me. Young Colbert wasn't happy. He complained about bad scripts and about having to wear my clothes. He pleaded with them not to make him a Bret Maverick clone. "Put me in a dress and call me Brenda, but please don't do this to me!" he said.

Over the succeeding years, we made several attempts to recapture the magic, but instead of reviving *Maverick,* we beat it to death.

I think the original *Maverick* series, which ran on ABC from September 1957 to April 1962, was a milestone. It was a fresh approach to episodic television, with an irreverence that anticipated a lot of what was to come in the '60s. In its own way, *Maverick* was "antiestablishment." It gave voice to viewers' dissatisfaction with the predictable, buttoned-down TV of the '50s, with its black-and-white morality. *Maverick* explored gray areas by questioning the authority of the conventional Western hero. After *Maverick,* it was hard to watch those steely-eyed cowboys without laughing.

If Warners had paid me a decent wage in the first place, I'd never have sued, and they'd have had me for life. I just needed to know I was appreciated. After we broke the contract, they offered me $5,000 a week to stay another year, and in those days, that *was* a lot of money. On top of that, Henry Kaiser offered me his one-third share of *Maverick's* profits. Old Henry J. had been good to me and I liked him, but at that point I just wanted out.

I'll never know how different my life would have been if I'd stayed in *Maverick,* but I probably wouldn't have had much of a movie career.

I've been told my lawsuit set a precedent that liberated actors from the kind of one-sided contract I'd been under, and that the court decision against Warner Bros. was one of the final blows against the studio system. The truth is, I wasn't thinking about anybody but myself. All I knew was I couldn't continue working under those conditions. That's why I was willing to risk my career to get out.

But that wasn't quite the end of the story. I can't prove it, but I'm sure Jack Warner tried to kill my movie career. On the same day in December 1960 that the judgment came down in my favor, I got a script from 20th Century-Fox called *The Comancheros*. Though I was anxious to work, I didn't much care for the movie and I turned it down. A few days later, when I heard that Gary Cooper had signed to do the other part, I said, "Whoa, send me that script back!" I looked at it again and decided to do it, just for the chance of working with a great star and a man I admired. As it turned out, Coop dropped out and Duke Wayne played the lead, but that would have been fine with me: I felt the same way about Wayne as I did about Cooper. The director and head of production both wanted me, and we thought it was all set. But I never heard from them again, and they wouldn't talk to my agent. Stu Whitman wound up with the part.

I'm convinced that Jack Warner called Spyros Skouras, the head of 20th, and told him not to use me.

Luckily, there were enough independent producers around that I didn't have to rely on a studio to get a job. It wasn't long before a big director cast me in an important film, and from then on, I could work anywhere.

CHAPTER FOUR

Big Screen

After I'd won my lawsuit against Warners, offers weren't exactly rolling in. Producers were understandably cautious. But my agent arranged a meeting with William Wyler and he hired me for *The Children's Hour* on the spot. I didn't even have to read for it.

Two schoolteachers, played by Audrey Hepburn and Shirley MacLaine, are accused of being lesbians by one of the students, a vicious little girl played by Karen Balkin. In those days, it was a touchy subject. We couldn't use the word "lesbian." Imagine. But the script wasn't about homosexuality anyway; it was about the harm rumors can cause.

William Wyler (*Wuthering Heights, Mrs. Miniver, The Best Years of Our Lives, Ben-Hur*) was one of our great directors. He had the reputation of being a perfectionist and a bit of a taskmaster, but I found him to be a pussycat. He didn't use force of any kind. He'd talk to you about the situation calmly and quietly.

But he didn't actually tell you anything. He had his own way of communicating, and it wasn't verbal. I don't think he knew how to express himself to actors. You'd do a take and all he'd say was, "Okay, let's do it again." He'd do five or six takes for every scene. In one scene, he did take after take to get Karen to cry. He finally got her so upset that the dam burst and she didn't stop crying for two days.

Shirley, Audrey, and I never knew what he was looking for so we kept searching, trying everything we could think of. We'd have these desperate little conversations: "What does he *want?*"

"I don't know, but let's keep going."

Looking back, I guess *he* didn't know what he wanted, either . . . until he saw it. Or, rather, heard it: Wyler didn't watch what we were doing; he turned his back and listened. He was hard of hearing, so he'd hook up his hearing aid to the sound system and keep shooting until he *heard* what he wanted.

And he'd keep changing things. He was actually working from three scripts: In addition to ours, he had the original Lillian Hellman play, which is based on a true story and was done on Broadway in 1934. He also had the first movie version, *These Three,* with Merle Oberon, Miriam Hopkins, and Joel McCrea, which he'd also directed. It left out the lesbian stuff because of the Hays Code. He'd take a line from here and a line from there and keep moving them around. Then he'd change a line and have you do it again.

Wyler was a brilliant, talented man, and I considered it a privilege to work with him. I simply put myself in his hands. It made me proud whenever I did something that pleased him. He was a great director, and I think it was his judgment and dedication to what he felt was right that made him great.

It was wonderful working with Audrey and Shirley. They were very different, of course. Audrey was quiet and demure, a very proper lady, though she had a great sense of humor. I fell in love with her. (I could never figure out how she could have married that guy Mel Ferrer. She was way too good for him.)

I love Shirley, too. Terrific actress, wicked sense of humor, like one of the guys. One day Shirley and I were kidding around just before a take and Willy Wyler came over and told me, "Don't do that! Think about the scene." Shirley could laugh and tell jokes one minute and flip a switch and be in character the next, but Wyler didn't think I had that ability, and at the time he was right.

The Children's Hour is a poignant film. In one scene, I cry in front of a mirror. Coming right after years of doing light humor on *Maverick,* it was a departure. The first time I had to cry on camera was hard, and I didn't like it. I've never gone back and looked at it because I know it would make me wince. But the role propelled me from TV Westerns into major motion pictures.

The *Great Escape* is based on a true story, the mass breakout of Allied fliers from a German prison camp, Stalag Luft III, during World War II. Almost everything in the movie is accurate, though some incidents are condensed and a few characters are composites. It was such a good story that director John Sturges didn't have to take liberties. Well, not many. Two of its most exciting sequences never happened.

The screenplay is credited to W. R. Burnett (*Little Caesar, The Asphalt Jungle*) and James Clavell (*Shogun*), who had himself been a prisoner of the Japanese during World War II. There was trouble with the script, so by the time we were done shooting, there'd been four more writers and about a dozen drafts, and we still wound up improvising scenes.

The film is based on a nonfiction book of the same name by Paul Brickhill, who'd been a POW in the real Stalag Luft III after his Spitfire was shot down over Tunisia. As a prisoner, Brickhill had been involved in the tunneling but ultimately couldn't join the escape because he was claustrophobic.

Sturges bought the rights to Brickhill's book in 1951, but it took ten years to get the picture made. The studios were afraid of it because there were no female characters, and because they thought it would be too expensive to shoot. Then there's the unhappy ending, which prompted Sam Goldwyn to complain, "What the hell kind of escape is this? Nobody gets away!" But in 1962, after the success of *The Magnificent Seven,* Sturges was suddenly bankable, and the Mirisch brothers and United Artists put up $4 million to make the picture.

Allied airmen captured during World War II were sent to prison camps run by the Luftwaffe, the elite flying corps and the least Nazified branch of the German military. For the most part, these camps honored the Geneva Convention and treated prisoners decently. In 1943, the Luftwaffe built Stalag Luft III in Sagan, about one hundred miles south of Berlin, to house prisoners who'd already made escape attempts. In putting the hard cases in one maximum-security camp, the Germans unwittingly created a cadre of super escape artists, men who refused to sit out the rest of the war as POWs. They were determined to create a diversion that would draw German troops away from combat against the Allies, and they knew it would be a propaganda coup if they could break out of what the Luftwaffe boasted was an "escape-proof" camp.

Roger Bartlett, Big X, played by Richard Attenborough, is based on Roger Bushell, a South African pilot who led the actual escape attempt. He wasn't the ranking officer in the camp, but he was a clever and resourceful leader who knew how to harness the diverse skills of his fellow prisoners. Bushell considered it his duty to "harass, confound, and confuse the enemy." He'd already tried several escapes when he devised a daring plan to break out 250 prisoners, the greatest escape ever attempted.

As shown in the film, the POWs simultaneously dug three tunnels, code-named "Tom," "Dick," and "Harry." Each tunnel began with a thirty-foot, vertical shaft to make it deep enough so the Germans couldn't hear the digging with underground microphones. The prisoners built a ventilation system and a trolley to move the dirt out of the tunnel. The soil was sandy and the tunnels were prone to cave-ins, so wooden slats from prisoners' bunks were used to shore up the walls. There were in fact escape attempts by hiding in a truck loaded with tree cuttings, and by trying to blend in with a detail of Russian prisoners. The inmates actually did sing Christmas carols to drown out the sounds of tunneling, and there really was a Fourth of July celebration with moonshine. (None of us could play fife and drums, so we faked it.)

A Canadian mining engineer named Wally Floody, the real "Tunnel King," was a technical adviser on the film. A downed Spitfire pilot, he was captured by the Germans and sent to Stalag Luft III, where he was in charge of tunnel construction. Wally made sure the details of the tunnels in the film were accurate down to the color of the dirt.

Even the prison slang in the movie is correct: *Goons* were the Germans; when interrogated, the POWs told their captors "goon" stood for "German officer or noncom." The sentry platforms were *goon boxes,* harassing the guards was *goon baiting,* the lookouts were *stooges,* and the guards assigned to escape-detection were *ferrets.* The prisoners who carried dirt in bags inside their trousers and released it in the yard, right under the *goons'* noses, were *penguins.*

Sturges had wanted to shoot the picture at Idyllwild, in the mountains near Los Angeles. It would have been too expensive to bring hundreds of extras in from Los Angeles every day, so he planned to hire college students from nearby Palm Springs. But the Screen Extras Guild wouldn't give him a waiver. In need of a new location fast, assistant director Bob Relyea went to Germany and reported back to Sturges that, lo and behold, it looked just like Germany. Even better, the German government was offering all kinds of incentives, so Sturges bit the bullet and flew the whole company across the Atlantic.

We shot the interiors at Bavaria Studios in Geiselgasteig, just outside Munich, and on location in an exact replica of Stalag Luft III built for us on the edge of a pine forest. Because it was an ensemble cast, there were stretches where an actor wouldn't have a call for days on end, and the cast used the downtime to travel all over Europe. That was fine with Sturges, who liked to issue tourist information to the cast and crew on his movies. He asked only that they check in by phone every night. I decided to stay close and explore Munich, except when Lois flew over toward the middle of it and we spent a few days together in Paris.

For the most part the German people were friendly and hospitable, though there was one columnist who didn't want us there reminding everybody we'd won the war. He ripped the studio for bringing in a bunch of "television actors." I guess he meant me and Steve McQueen.

Though I felt comfortable in Munich and tried to behave myself, I still managed to get in trouble. Believe me, I never intended to take part in the Munich riots. I was just in the wrong place at the wrong time.

In that summer of 1962, the student quarter along Leopoldstrasse was a vibrant section of Munich and a top tourist attraction, with sidewalk cafés, restaurants, clubs, and a large public park. The endless stream of people of all shapes and sizes strolling up and down the boulevard reminded me of the Via Veneto in Rome.

One evening a student with a guitar plopped down in the middle of the sidewalk and began playing. Pedestrians had to thread their way around him, and somebody complained. Loudly. The argument attracted other pedestrians, and there was pushing and shoving. Pretty soon, hundreds of people had gathered around, most of them students. The police waded in to break it up, swinging their nightsticks, and that's when it got out of hand.

More students showed up, outnumbering the police, who in turn called for reinforcements. A line of mounted police advanced. As their riders swung rubber truncheons, the horses stepped on and kicked the students, who fled in all directions, many of them bloodied. It was a police riot, with cops beating and arresting defenseless kids.

The next night was worse. Police arrived in even greater force and there were ambulances standing by. The students were now armed with rocks, and there were more casualties. By the third or fourth night, the story was international news. Spectators came to watch the battle from the sidelines, and tourists got caught in the crossfire, including me.

It was a Friday night. I had just parked my car on a side street when two policemen approached. I thought they'd recognized me and were going to ask for an autograph. Instead, they demanded my passport. It was in the breast pocket of my jacket, along with my wallet, and when I pulled it out, one of the cops snatched the passport and the wallet, which he promptly emptied of its contents, about a thousand bucks' worth of German marks, and threw the wallet on the ground. When I protested, he laughed in my face. When I asked for my passport back, he told me I could pick it up at police headquarters after they investigated my "case." I asked him for his badge number, but he just laughed again.

That's when I lost my temper. A reporter had witnessed the whole thing, and I gave him a spontaneous interview that I would later regret. I told him that the Munich police were out of control, that the situation was worse than what I'd seen in Tokyo while we were shooting *Sayonara*. I said the Japanese police were tough on student demonstrators, but the Munich cops were much worse. And then I added, "What I've witnessed here reminds me what it must have been like under the Nazis in the thirties."

That little nugget touched a nerve.

The Germans were still sensitive in 1962. They didn't want to be reminded of the Third Reich, so when I compared the Munich police to Nazis, all hell broke loose. The German public was up in arms and the government demanded an apology.

Despite pressure from the studio, I refused to apologize. I'd hated seeing the kids bullied by the police and I meant what I said. But a few days later, after they'd threatened to deport me, which would have prevented us from finishing the picture, I caved in. I realized it would hurt too many other people. So I issued an apology. But I didn't mean it.

My character, an American in the RAF named Bob Hendley, was a composite. His part in the actual escape was done by several individuals. It wasn't a stretch to play Hendley the Scrounger; that's what I'd done in Korea. Hendley was a hustler who could bribe, barter, or con his way around anything. He'd do whatever necessary to get what he needed, whether an identity card or an expensive camera, and he wasn't afraid to take a risk when he had to.

Sturges had German actors playing all the Germans, which was unusual for a Hollywood film. It worked: Hannes Messemer was convincing as Kommandant von Luger, as was Robert Graf as Werner the Ferret.

The prisoners were well supplied with cigarettes, coffee, chocolate, and canned goods from Red Cross packages. The Germans didn't have such luxuries, so it was easy to bribe the ferrets, and Hendley plays Werner like a violin. I think some of the scenes between them were among the best in the film, and Graf was a delight to work with, as were all the German actors. I didn't feel any animosity from them, even though they were making a film about their side losing the war.

For the most part, it was a happy set and everyone in the diverse cast got along. Donald Pleasence and I became good friends, just like our characters in the film. He plays Flight Lieutenant Colin Blythe, the camp forger who goes blind from working by candlelight. Big X tells him he can't join the escape, but I promise to take care of him: "Colin's not a blind man as long as he's with me, and he's *going* with me!"

By the time he made *Great Escape,* Donald was an accomplished stage and film actor. An officer in the RAF during the war but too old to fly, he was a "boffin"—a desk jockey. One day in 1944, he went on a mission in a Lancaster bomber just to see what it was like. The Lancaster was shot down over France and Donald spent the rest of the war in a fliers' camp like the one in the picture.

In a sequence that didn't happen in real life, Donald and I steal a German two-seat trainer with an old-fashioned crank starter to make our escape. In the script, I sit at the controls while Donald cranks the engine, then I have to get out and help him into the plane because he can't see. The crew could never get the engine to turn over in rehearsals, so Sturges told Donald to go through the motions of cranking it and then he'd do the rest of the scene in cuts. I said, "What if it starts?"

"Don't worry, it won't."

"Okay," I said, "but if it does we're in trouble, because I'm not a pilot."

Just to humor me, Bob Relyea, our production manager and a weekend pilot, gave me a quick lesson on how to use the brakes and throttle. The cameras rolled, Donald turned the crank, and sure enough, the damn thing kicked over on the first try. With the cameras still rolling, I throttled back and tested the brakes. When I realized the plane wasn't moving, I got out and helped Donald into the cockpit, then got back in myself. I revved the throttle, eased off the brake . . . and the damn thing began to taxi! You should have seen the look on the faces of the crew. But they kept rolling and got the scene. Nobody was more surprised than I was.

In the script, Donald and I run out of gas and crash before we can make it to Switzerland. They couldn't get a stunt pilot to crash it, so it fell to Relyea. Bob took most of the fuel out of the plane, flew it across a field, and pancaked it, tearing both wings off in the process. Sturges wound up with some great footage and Bob wound up in a back brace.

John Sturges was a man's man and a good director. He'd started as an editor for David O. Selznick and worked his way up to directing. He really knew how to cut a picture together. His specialty was action-adventure and he had a good track record—he'd done *Gunfight at the O.K. Corral, Bad Day at Black Rock,* and *The Magnificent Seven* before *The Great Escape.* He knew how to take a bunch of characters coming from different directions and draw them together in one purpose. In *Magnificent Seven,* it was protecting a village from bandits. In *Great Escape,* it was busting out of a German prison camp.

John would assemble a great cast and let them do their thing. He got the most out of actors by bolstering their confidence with a pat on the back at the right time. He was easygoing but could be tough when he needed to be. He was always fair.

In the middle of the shoot, McQueen walked out of the picture. He'd seen about an hour's worth of dailies and didn't like how he looked. Wanted to reshoot the whole thing. Of course, they couldn't reshoot that much footage—it would have taken too long and cost too much money. Steve's agents flew in from the States and had a showdown with Sturges.

The next day Sturges called me in and said, "Jim, McQueen's out and you're the star of the picture. We'll change a few things here and there. It'll work."

I didn't see how it could possibly work, and neither did Jimmy Coburn, so the two of us sat down with Steve at my rented house in Munich and asked him what the problem was.

"I don't like the part. I'm not the hero. And the stuff they have me doing is corny."

"Well, Steve, the reason you're not *the* hero is because it's an ensemble cast. There are a lot of heroes."

Steve could be a stubborn little cuss, but Jimmy and I finally convinced him to stay on the picture. To pacify him, Sturges added some motorcycle stunts and changed his character, Hilts, the Cooler King, to a guy who goes out to reconnoiter the surrounding countryside, then unselfishly allows himself to be recaptured so he can share the information with the others.

There were no Americans in the actual escape; they'd all been transferred to other camps before the tunnel was finished. And there never was a motorcycle chase, but I think it's the most exciting and memorable part of the movie. When people think of *The Great Escape,* they think of Steve on that motorcycle.

The bike was actually a 1961 Triumph 650 painted green and dressed with Nazi insignia, including swastikas. Steve did most of the driving, including the part of a German soldier chasing him, but not the now famous leap over the barbed wire barricade at the Swiss border. The insurance company wouldn't allow it, and Sturges didn't want to risk injury to Steve, so the racer and stunt driver Bud Ekins made the jump—off a wooden ramp just out of frame. Bud estimated that he flew sixty-five feet at a good twelve feet off the ground.

Steve went nuts over there. He was always getting into scrapes. When he wasn't working, he'd race that motorcycle with the swastikas on it all over Munich just to annoy the Germans. And people would yell. He also totaled a Mercedes Gullwing. Stuck it right into the pine trees. The police finally set up a roadblock and nailed him. They put him in jail for a few hours and took his driver's license away.

Hilts was a great character and Steve did a good job. He had a persona he brought to every role, and people loved it, which is fine, but you could always see him acting. That's the kiss of death as far as I'm concerned.

Someone once asked me if Steve was "trouble." Steve was trouble if you invited him for breakfast. He didn't like *anything*. Like Brando, he could be a pain in the ass on the set. Unlike Brando, he wasn't an actor. He was a movie star, a poser who cultivated the image of a macho man. Steve wasn't a *bad* guy; I think he was just insecure. His wife Neile told me that he'd coveted the turtleneck sweater I wore in the picture. If I'd known that, I'd have given him the damn thing. Neile said that Steve had always been envious of tall, dark men, and that he was jealous because she and I had known each other during the Broadway years, when she was in *Kismet* and I was in *Caine Mutiny*. Though Neile and I were only casual acquaintances, Steve was convinced, she said, that we'd had an affair.

Yet Steve and I were good friends for a long time, probably because we had a couple of things in common besides acting. We both liked cars, and we raced together in the Baja 1000. We were also next-door neighbors.

Steve and Neile had a unique house in the hills above Los Angeles. It was built like a castle, out of stone, with turrets and secret passageways. Lois and I were there one day and noticed the property next door. It was a good-size piece of ground and we could see the potential. I told Steve, "I think I'll try to buy that," and he was all for it. We wound up building our dream house there.

As neighbors, Steve and I hung out a lot. We'd tinker in the garage and ride our motorcycles on a nearby fire trail. After *The Great Escape,* we both brought Mini Coopers back from Europe and we'd race them up and down our street. There were big speed bumps, so we'd shoot down either side, just a few inches from parked cars.

One thing Steve and I didn't have in common was our politics, because Steve was a Republican. The only saving grace was that he somehow made Nixon's enemies list, an honor I would have given anything to have achieved.

Steve liked to lob his empty beer cans into my backyard. Claimed he couldn't resist because it was always so neat, with the flowers trimmed and no newspapers lying around. He thought I didn't know it was him. That was Steve. Deep down, he was just a wild kid. I think he thought of me as an older brother, and I guess I thought of him as a younger brother. A delinquent younger brother.

Charlie Bronson was a pain in the ass, too. He used and abused people, and I didn't like it. Charlie Buchinsky. He'd been a coal miner in Pennsylvania and a B-29 tail gunner in the Pacific. He was a bitter, belligerent SOB. I don't know why he had a chip on his shoulder. He wasn't a barrel of laughs on the set, I can tell you. His character, a claustrophobic Polish prisoner nicknamed Danny the Tunnel King, is loosely based on Wally Floody.

About a year after we made *Great Escape,* I had a little set-to with Charlie during a poker game at my house. He made a bet and then withdrew it after it was too late. I said, "Sorry, you can't do that." I wasn't even in the hand; Charlie was against a street kid who was working extra in Hollywood. I made Charlie pay him, probably no more than fifty bucks, because that money meant a lot to the kid. Charlie got upset and we got head-to-head, but it didn't come to blows.

After that, Charlie went around swearing he'd never work with me again. Throughout my life, there have been a few guys who didn't like me because I was outspoken. Hell, I never thought I was outspoken, I just told the truth.

A few years later, I was in an Italian restaurant in Beverly Hills waiting for Lois. I'm back in a booth having a beer and I look up and there's Charlie and he says, "How *are* ya, Jim?" and I say, "I'm fine, Charlie, how are you?" Next thing I know the four of us are having dinner together—Lois and me and Charlie and his wife, Jill Ireland.

It was all so very pleasant. But I think Charlie held a grudge. I know *I* did.

Sturges called one day while he was editing the film and invited me to lunch. "Jim," he said, "the two best scenes in the picture are with you and Donald, but they're on the cutting room floor. I had to stay with the goddamn motorcycle."

They *were* touching scenes. In one of them, Donald and I are looking out the window in a blackout. All you could see was explosions, with us silhouetted in the distance light. I thanked Sturges for being considerate enough to break the news to me in person, before I saw the movie and got upset. I told him that I understood, and I did. The motorcycle action is exciting and gives the film a more upbeat ending.

The actual great escape took place in March 1944. Seventy-six prisoners got out before the tunnel was discovered. Only three made it to freedom. Yet the escape accomplished its goal: the Germans had to divert thousands of troops to round up the escapees. Hitler was so enraged he ordered fifty of the recaptured prisoners shot. The film's dedication, "For the fifty," refers to those men. In one of the closing scenes, Kommandant von Luger informs Group Captain Ramsey, played by James Donald, that the men were "shot while trying to escape."

"How many were wounded?" Ramsey asks.

"None," von Luger replies.

After the war, British Intelligence tracked down the murderers and brought them to justice. Most were convicted and either imprisoned or hanged.

Though the German government had been cooperative, the picture went over budget. Sturges cut scenes and used crew members in bit parts to economize, but the studio still wanted to pull us back and finish the picture at Arrowhead. To avoid that, a few of us deferred salary for the overage. We never expected to see any money—you rarely do in that situation. But the movie turned out to be a summer blockbuster, and we all got paid.

I knew *Great Escape* was going to be good, I just didn't know how good. It had a little bit of everything: humor, pathos, and a wonderful sense of camaraderie among the fliers. Its pacing and suspense are a tribute to Sturges and to film editor Ferris Webster, who was nominated for an Oscar. The movie was both entertaining and educational: it introduced the younger generation to World War II and got people to look up the real story. It's one of the few pictures I'm in that I'll watch when it's on television, even though it's almost three hours long.

But the greatest accolade came prior to the picture's release: Just before *The Great Escape* opened in movie theaters, Sturges took a print to London and screened it for a group of survivors, and they loved it. Sturges said he felt vindicated by their approval, and that he was glad he'd been true to what he called the "nobility and the honor" of the brave men of Stalag Luft III.

Early in 1963, the producer Martin Ransohoff signed William Wyler to direct and William Holden to star as Lieutenant Commander Charles Madison in an MGM feature about a cowardly US Naval officer. After a few weeks, Wyler backed out of the picture. I'm not sure why. I'd heard that MGM wouldn't pay him what he wanted, but the real reason may have been that the script was just too radical for the man who had directed two great World War II pictures, *Mrs. Miniver* and *The Best Years of Our Lives*.

I was already cast as Lieutenant Commander Paul "Bus" Cummings when Marty Ransohoff asked whether I would play Charlie Madison if Holden dropped out. "Oh, you bet!" I said. I knew it was a hell of an actor's part. It was a different kind of role than I'd been doing, with a brilliant script by Paddy Chayefsky from William Bradford Huie's novel. A lot of drama and a lot of humor. The only possible drawback: it required me to deliver long, dense speeches.

Bill Holden was having trouble with the IRS, something about doing his banking in Hong Kong, and there'd been some publicity about it. A columnist accused him of being unpatriotic. On top of that, Holden kept making one demand after another, and Marty Ransohoff got fed up. He provoked an argument with Holden's agent, Charles Feldman, and offered him $200,000 to get out of the picture. Feldman grabbed it. I don't think he wanted his client doing an antiwar picture at a time when he was being skewered in the press as un-American.

A long line of directors had turned the picture down before Marty reluctantly offered it to Arthur Hiller. Marty didn't think Arthur was ready for it because he was still young and hadn't tackled anything so meaty. As it turned out, Marty needn't have worried.

By then color had become the standard, but Arthur wanted to shoot the picture in black and white because he thought it would be more realistic. MGM balked—they were afraid people would think it was an old movie. But Arthur fought for it and the studio finally gave in.

I'd worked with Arthur on *The Wheeler Dealers* and we got along fine. He has a gentle demeanor but knows what he wants, and for me that's the first quality of a good director. I'm not looking for a pat on the back; I just want to know if I'm on the right path. Arthur gave me a valuable bit of direction early on. He told me I was trying too hard to protect the writing, that I was delivering each line as if it were the most important in the movie. He explained that you can't do that because it turns everything into a monotone. You have to have ups and downs. "Just play the character," he said, "and don't try to peak on every line."

He was right.

I'd worked with James Coburn in *The Great Escape*. He was a good guy and a terrific actor. When I recommended that Jimmy take over the Bus Cummings part, Marty Ransohoff and his assistant, John Calley, agreed. It turned out to be a great choice.

Arthur Hiller once said that Paddy Chayefsky was the only genius he'd ever worked with. Same here. He saw the insanity of life and described it with wit and compassion. I've never had finer words to say on a movie screen.

His given name was Sidney. He got "Paddy" in the army, when an officer woke him at four o'clock one Sunday morning for KP. Sidney asked to be excused so he could go to mass.

"Mass?" the officer said, "I thought you were Jewish!"

"Yeah, but my mother's Irish," Sidney lied.

"Okay, Paddy, go back to sleep," the officer said, and the name stuck.

Paddy was an intense man, short and stocky and bristling with energy. He had an irreverent sense of humor and an explosive temper. And he was the most articulate person I've ever known. His dialogue is like fireworks, it *crackles*. Paddy once said that he collected words "the way other people collect postage stamps." He was fascinated by the English language and he delighted in the sound of it. I don't think this exchange could have been written by anyone else:

EMILY: That's a piquant thing to say, wouldn't you agree?
CHARLIE: Yes, I think I'd call that piquant.

Some people complain that Paddy's scripts are too "talky." To me that's like saying Van Gogh's paintings have too much color. To this day Paddy's the only screenwriter to have won three solo Oscars, for *Marty, The Hospital,* and *Network*. He died of cancer in 1981 at the age of fifty-eight. Imagine what he could have done with another twenty years.

One of my proudest moments happened at a preview of the picture in Beverly Hills. Paddy said, "Let's take a walk." As we strolled around the block, he told me he was pleased with my performance. It thrilled me to hear that from a writer, especially one I respected so much. It felt like I'd won an Oscar.

Set in London in the weeks before D-Day, *The Americanization of Emily* is the story of Charlie Madison, who, as the opening credits explain, is a "dog robber," the personal attendant of a general or admiral whose job it is to keep his man "well-clothed, well-fed, and well-loved during the battle." Charlie is an admitted coward who likes his job because it keeps him out of combat. When he meets Emily Barham, a driver in the local motor pool who has lost her father, brother, and husband in the war, she despises him at first.

The meaning of the title is revealed in an exchange between Emily and Charlie early in the picture: "I don't want oranges, or eggs, or soap flakes, either. Don't show me how profitable it would be to fall in love with you, Charlie. Don't Americanize me!" Emily isn't just talking about little wartime luxuries, but also about Charlie's cynicism and cowardice. Despite her grief, she's still patriotic. It takes Charlie's supposed death to finally Americanize her, to make her abandon her conventional view of war.

When we began shooting, Julie Andrews had just completed her first film, *Mary Poppins,* but it hadn't been released. She was nervous at first, and so was I. We'd met seven years earlier when we were both on Broadway. I was playing a judge in *The Caine Mutiny Court Martial* and Julie was starring in the hit musical *The Boy Friend.* Later

I saw her as Eliza Doolittle opposite Rex Harrison in *My Fair Lady* and, like the rest of the world, I was bowled over by her talent.

Julie was just wonderful as Emily. She stepped out of the Broadway mold to play a complex character convincingly: an outwardly priggish but inwardly passionate war widow. Though Julie wasn't nominated for the role, it showed her range as a performer, which may have helped her win the Oscar for *Mary Poppins* when Academy voters realized that she could play a serious character without having to sing.

Julie and I have made three films together (*Victor/Victoria* in 1982 and *One Special Night* in 1999 are the other two). She's always been a joy to work with. She's a team player who cares about her colleagues and coworkers: in 1996, Julie turned down a Tony nomination for the Broadway version of *Victor/Victoria* because no one else in the production had been nominated, including the director, her husband Blake Edwards. Julie explained that she preferred to stand with the "egregiously overlooked." That's Julie.

There was a lot of pressure about the script. The Motion Picture Association of America's production code office was afraid of it. They thought it put US servicemen in a bad light and they worried about a box-office backlash that would sink *The Americanization of Emily* and maybe even taint other films. They thought the movie was just too extreme for the American public.

Well, we weren't a bunch of wide-eyed pacifists; we knew what we were talking about. I'd certainly experienced the stresses of combat. (I am, by constitution, a coward, so you could say it was type-casting.) Paddy had been wounded by a land mine while on a patrol as an infantryman in Belgium during World War II. He stepped out of line to relieve himself, went into the woods, dropped his pants, and sat down on a mine. The wounds were serious, but Paddy used to roar when he told the story. Arthur Hiller had been a navigator in the Royal Canadian Air Force and Jimmy Coburn a radio operator in the US Army. Melvyn Douglas, who played Admiral Jessup, had served in *both* world wars. We'd all witnessed the kind of snafus, interservice rivalries, and insanity portrayed in the film that cost people their lives.

In those days, censorship was unpredictable. We couldn't use the F-word—that's why a British officer berates two enlisted men by calling them "featherheaded." We thought there might be a problem with the censors because of Jimmy Coburn's character. Every time you see him, he's got another girl in bed, including Judy Carne, who has a ten-second nude scene. But nobody complained about it, except maybe Burt Reynolds, who was married to Judy at the time.

We had zero cooperation from the US Navy, which usually pulls out all the stops for war movies. So long as the movies are gung-ho. The navy brass knew we were making an antiwar movie and they didn't want anything to do with it. (When Marty Ransohoff made *Ice Station Zebra* a few years later, the navy remembered *The Americanization of Emily* and refused to cooperate. They gave in only after he convinced them that *Ice Station Zebra* was pro-navy.)

Without support from the navy, we had to improvise. We used the same damn landing craft over and over. Arthur shot it every which way. We couldn't get right-hand drive British army trucks, so Arthur had to have them mocked up and he "cheated" the shots where they appeared.

After ten days' filming in London, we came back to LA. The MGM lot in Culver City was already booked, so we shot the rest of the picture at the Selznick Studio in Century City. We also used the Santa Monica Airport, where we created our own rain—a *lot* of rain—and we went up to a beach near Oxnard aptly called Hollywood-by-the-Sea for the invasion sequence.

Admiral Jessup is determined that "the first dead man on Omaha Beach must be a sailor" because he feels the army is getting all the glory and too big a share of congressional appropriations. He wants a record of the event, so he orders Charlie to accompany the first wave with a camera crew. It's nothing but a public relations stunt to help Jessup persuade Congress to create a "tomb of the unknown sailor." Charlie begs to be excused, then refuses to go. But Jessup is adamant, threatening to have Charlie "brigged" if he disobeys the order, and Charlie soon finds himself in a landing craft heading into Omaha Beach. When the door opens, Charlie refuses to move, but Bus is right behind him with a .45 and he shoots Charlie in the leg, just to kind of encourage him.

The beach scene runs only a couple of minutes on the screen, but it took a week to shoot and cost a quarter of a million dollars, a big chunk of the movie's budget. With all the explosions, it had to be choreographed just right or we could have been seriously injured or killed. There's a moment of unintentional realism in the scene. If you look closely when I stumble onto a land mine and get blown into the air, you'll see me do a little bounce when I hit the ground. That's because I cracked two ribs on the point of the metal canteen on my web belt. (The movie gods were getting even for what I'd done to Doris Day on the set of *Move Over, Darling*. In one scene, she was standing on a bed and I reached up, grabbed her by the waist, and carried her off. In the process, I broke two of her ribs. I didn't know it until one of the assistant directors told me the next day, because Doris never complained.)

On Friday, November 22, 1963, while we were shooting the party scene, someone came in and said that President Kennedy had been shot in Dallas. We all gathered around a radio. Everyone was stunned. Some were crying. We quit work and didn't come back for several days. It was Arthur Hiller's birthday that day, but we never celebrated it.

Paddy Chayefsky broke a lot of rules, including the old Hollywood taboo against trying to make "message" pictures. (Sam Goldwyn warned screenwriters: "If you want to send a message, call Western Union.") Paddy's movies and plays are *full* of messages. I think his message here is that sentimentality is as much a cause of war as greed or racism or religious hatred. A lot of antiwar movies are preachy, but not this one. As Charlie says, "I'm not sentimental about war. I see nothing noble in widows." But the picture isn't really antiwar. It allows that sometimes war is necessary, like when you have to defend yourself from an invader. But don't make war seem so wonderful that kids want to make "the ultimate sacrifice" when they grow up. If we ever want to end war, we have to stop building shrines to dead soldiers—they just perpetuate the carnage. The most patriotic thing we can do is be yellow for our country. As Charlie Madison says:

> War isn't hell at all. It's man at his best; the highest morality he's capable of. It's not war that's insane, you see. It's the morality of it. It's not greed or ambition that makes war: it's goodness. Wars are always fought for the best of reasons: for liberation or manifest destiny. Always against tyranny and always in the interest of humanity. So far this war, we've managed to butcher some ten million humans in the interest of humanity. Next war it seems we'll have to destroy all of man in order to preserve his damn dignity. It's not war that's unnatural to us, it's virtue. As long as valor remains a virtue, we shall have soldiers. So, I preach cowardice. Through cowardice, we shall all be saved.

In a long scene with Emily and her mother, played by Joyce Grenfell, Charlie gets up on a soapbox to make his point about cowards saving the world. We're having tea in the backyard—sorry, the "garden"—and I just talk and talk. Joyce would ask me a question and I'd do two pages and then Julie would say, "Isn't that wonderful," and I'd do two or three more. I think the whole speech was eleven or twelve pages. It says, in part:

> *I don't trust people who make bitter reflections about war, Mrs. Barham. It's always the generals with the bloodiest records who are the first to shout what a Hell it is. And it's always the widows who lead the Memorial Day parades . . . we shall never end wars, Mrs. Barham, by blaming it on ministers and generals or warmongering imperialists or all the other banal bogies. It's the rest of us who build statues to those generals and name boulevards after those ministers; the rest of us who make heroes of our dead and shrines of our battlefields. We wear our widows' weeds like nuns and perpetuate war by exalting its sacrifices. My brother died at Anzio—an everyday soldier's death, no special heroism involved. They buried what pieces they found of him. But my mother insists he died a brave death and pretends to be very proud.*

I worked on it a lot at home, and we rehearsed it so much it was probably the best speech I ever gave in terms of understanding what I was saying. But at the end of day, I wasn't happy with my work in the scene. I asked Arthur if we could do it over. He reshot the close-ups, but I don't think it helped much. I failed to do the job I wanted to do.

I have to say that if I'm not a downright hypocrite, I am, at the very least, inconsistent. Though I've never thought war is noble, and though I always understood the absurdity and brutality of it, I still wanted the Purple Hearts I'd earned in Korea and went out of my way to get the medals. So I contributed to the problem by buying into the whole glorification of war thing. Maybe I'm splitting hairs, but in truth I don't want Korean War vets glorified, I just want them recognized for their service along with vets of other wars. It's a fine line.

The *Americanization of Emily* got good notices from the "important" critics. Bosley Crowther of *The New York Times* wrote that it "says more for basic pacifism than a fistful of intellectual tracts" and he also found it "highly entertaining." But the picture was a commercial failure. After Julie won her Oscar for *Mary Poppins,* the studio tried to capitalize by reissuing it with the shortened title *Emily,* but that didn't make it a woman's picture and didn't help at the box office. Ted Turner colorized it, then saw the light and apologized. A legal dispute kept it unavailable until 2005, when a court decision rescued it from obscurity. You can see it now, uncut and uncolorized.

The Americanization of Emily is my favorite of all the films I've done. Julie has said it's one of her favorites—as did Jimmy Coburn and Marty Ransohoff. Paddy once said that it was one of his two favorites, along with *The Hospital*. I think it was ahead of its time. When it was released in 1964, the country was still in turmoil after the Kennedy assassination, and the public hadn't yet turned against the Vietnam War. Most Americans who saw the picture were outraged by it. It was, after all, the first major Hollywood picture with a hero who was proud to be a coward. But its message dovetailed with the growing conviction that Vietnam wasn't worth dying for. Audiences have come around to it, and it's now a cult favorite and a minor classic.

Unfortunately, it hasn't put war out of style.

CHAPTER FIVE

Politics

———

I'm a "bleeding-heart liberal," one of those card-carrying Democrats that Rush Limbaugh thinks is a communist. I'm proud of it. And proud to have been part of the March on Washington for Jobs and Freedom on August 28, 1963, when 250,000 Americans of every age, race, and religion came to the nation's capital to support passage of a landmark civil rights bill.

I was there for one reason: I didn't think it was right that a hundred years after President Lincoln signed the Emancipation Proclamation, African Americans still didn't have basic rights of citizenship. In the South they couldn't vote or sit together with whites on a bus, they couldn't eat at the same restaurants or use the same water fountains or restrooms. Black children couldn't go to school with white children or use public swimming pools or libraries. Things weren't much better in the North, where blacks were relegated to inferior schools and low-paying jobs.

President John F. Kennedy proposed a bill to remedy the situation, but there was strong opposition in Congress and the bill wasn't given much chance. A. Philip Randolph, head of the Brotherhood of Sleeping

Car Porters, came up with the idea of a mass demonstration, a "living petition" to pressure Congress to do the right thing. He enlisted master organizer Bayard Rustin, who'd been fighting racism since the 1930s. A coalition of unions, churches, and civil rights groups joined in support.

In hindsight, the march was a turning point in the civil rights struggle. It was the largest demonstration for equality in American history, where Dr. Martin Luther King Jr. delivered his now legendary "I Have a Dream" speech. But in the weeks before the march, there were serious doubts.

The summer of 1963 had been a violent one. African Americans who dared to protest in public had been jailed, beaten, and even killed. Alabama governor George Wallace declared: "Segregation now, segregation tomorrow, segregation forever!" In Birmingham, Bull Connor turned fire hoses and attack dogs on peaceful demonstrators and put two thousand children in jail.

In that atmosphere, we didn't know if hate groups like the Ku Klux Klan or the American Nazi Party would attack the marchers. A few black leaders, including Malcolm X, were advocating violent revolution, so no one could guarantee that the marchers themselves would be peaceable. And while organizers hoped for one hundred thousand marchers, there was no telling how many would show up.

About a week before the march, with the press warning that a large mob would be uncontrollable and with critics claiming the march was a communist plot to overthrow the government, President Kennedy tried to stop it. He thought the sight of thousands of blacks parading in the streets of Washington would anger whites and hurt the civil rights bill rather than help it. But when the leaders refused to cancel the march, Kennedy endorsed it.

March organizers insisted on a peaceful protest in line with the nonviolent picketing, sit-ins, and boycotts that had been going on in the South. Bayard Rustin tried to ensure an orderly crowd through careful planning: he secured plenty of pay phones, water fountains, and portable toilets along the route, had thousands of box lunches on hand, and somehow convinced local police to patrol the crowd in plainclothes so as not to intimidate marchers.

On a warm, sunny Wednesday, hundreds of "freedom buses," "freedom trains," and chartered airline flights converged on the city carrying marchers from all over the country. I flew in the day before on the "celebrity plane" that Harry Belafonte had arranged. For security, we weren't told when and where to board until the last minute. The night before the march, FBI agents called the "celebrities" one by one and warned us to stay away, saying they couldn't guarantee our safety.

The Hollywood contingent included Charlton Heston, Sidney Poitier, Burt Lancaster, Paul Newman, Joanne Woodward, Ossie Davis, Ruby Dee, Blake Edwards, Rita Moreno, Lena Horne, Diahann Carroll, Sam Peckinpah, Sammy Davis Jr., Anthony Franciosa, Tony Curtis, and Marlon Brando.

Before we left Los Angeles, Chuck Heston, the Screen Actors Guild president and self-appointed leader of our group, presided over a planning meeting where Marlon held up a cattle prod that had been used against demonstrators in Gadsden, Alabama. Marlon wanted us all to chain ourselves to the Lincoln Memorial. Chuck didn't like that. He said we should play by the rules and threatened to bail out of the march if we did any "militant" stuff. Marlon shut up and we did it Chuck's way.

I was not a fan of Heston's, either as an actor—he was stiff as a board—or as a defender of civil rights. It turned out my instincts were right. About a year after the March on Washington, during the 1964 presidential race between Lyndon Johnson and Barry Goldwater, Heston had an epiphany. Stuck in traffic in his limousine on the way to the studio one morning, he looked up at a campaign billboard with a photograph of Barry Goldwater and the slogan, "In Your Heart, You

Know He's Right." Chuck stared at that billboard and said to himself, "Sonofabitch—in my heart, I *do* know he's right!" That was it. That was how Chuck Heston went from liberal to conservative, from the SAG president who marched for civil rights to the NRA president who said they'd have to pry his gun from his "cold, dead hands."

We got a lot of flak for joining the march, and there was pressure from the Hollywood establishment. When a studio head told Paul Newman that our presence would alienate Southern theater and TV station owners, Paul said, "I'm not going to ignore a great injustice merely because it might be bad for business."

That about says it all. Civil rights is a matter of conscience. I had to express myself on the issue because I'm a citizen as well as an actor. It's not only my right to speak out—it's my responsibility. If my celebrity draws extra attention to my cause, all the better.

Marchers assembled at the Washington Monument and walked the mile or so up the Mall to the Lincoln Memorial, where entertainers performed and leaders gave speeches from a temporary podium in front of Lincoln's statue.

The great Jackie Robinson, the first black baseball player in the major leagues, was there with his young son. The writer James Baldwin and the entertainer Josephine Baker flew in from Paris. The comedian Dick Gregory was there. Marian Anderson sang "The Star-Spangled Banner" and "He's Got the Whole World in His Hands." Bobby Darin, Peter, Paul and Mary, Joan Baez, Bob Dylan, Odetta, and Mahalia Jackson all sang.

Roy Wilkins announced the death of NAACP founder W. E. B. Du Bois in Ghana the day before. Walter Reuther of the AFL-CIO, John Lewis of SNCC, and Whitney Young of the National Urban League all gave short speeches. James Farmer of the Congress of Racial Equality sent a letter from his jail cell in Louisiana, where he'd been arrested during a demonstration.

Dr. King was the last speaker. I was seated in the third row when, standing before the columns of the Lincoln Memorial, he gave his "I Have a Dream" speech. I've never experienced such powerful oratory before or since, and I knew I was witnessing history.

We heard later that the "I Have a Dream" section was not part of Dr. King's prepared text. He had improvised it, inspired by the occasion and by Mahalia Jackson, who, seated behind him, leaned down and whispered, "Tell them about the dream, Martin." She'd heard him talk about "the dream" in an earlier speech.

The March on Washington was, as Dr. King called it, "the greatest demonstration for freedom in the history of our nation," and a resounding victory for the cause of civil rights in America, leading to passage of the Civil Rights Act of 1964. But it wasn't the end of the struggle: Two weeks later a bomb planted by Ku Klux Klan members exploded in the basement of a black church in Birmingham, killing four young girls. Three months later, President Kennedy was assassinated in Dallas. Five years later, on April 4, 1968, Dr. King was struck down in Memphis.

Everybody I knew in Oklahoma was a Democrat, but the first time I voted, in 1952, it was for Eisenhower. I felt we needed a strong military man in there because the world was in turmoil. I learned my lesson. Never voted Republican again. I don't understand the conservative way of thinking. The next time I voted, it was for Stevenson. I think he's still the most intelligent presidential candidate we've ever had. I think Obama runs a close second.

In 1962, they asked me to run for Congress on the Republican ticket. It didn't stop them when I told them I was a Democrat. They didn't know anything about me, and they didn't care about my politics. They just thought I could win.

The Democrats wanted me to run for governor of California in 1990. A group from the party came over to the house. The discussion soon got around to the issue of abortion and they asked my opinion.

"I don't have an opinion," I said, "because that's up to the woman. It has nothing to do with me."

"Well, you can't say that. They'll kill you."

"What do you mean, I can't say that? It's how I feel, and I'm not going to say anything else."

They sat there for a few more minutes trying to get me to change my mind, then they got up and left.

It was reported during the 2008 presidential campaign that I took out an injunction against John McCain to stop him from calling himself a maverick. I was quoted as saying:

"Maverick, my chapped old-man ass! Ask anyone and they'll tell you, I was the original Maverick! I was a maverick back when you were just another asshole in danger of failing out of Annapolis! I played the title role of Maverick on ABC between 1957 and 1960. That means I've been Maverick to two hundred million Americans for fifty-one years! Take it from me, young man, the camera may love you, but you sure as shit ain't no maverick."

I want to squash this rumor once and for all: It was a hoax. I never said it. Let me make it crystal clear: I never said any of those things.

But I wish I had.

I'm tired of hearing that actors shouldn't take positions on public issues. We're citizens, and I think it's our obligation to take a stand. But there's a big difference between speaking out and holding office, which involves abilities actors don't have. Unfortunately, a lot of people in office don't have those abilities, either.

Too many actors have run for office. There's one difference between me and them: I *know* I'm not qualified. In my opinion, Arnold Schwarzenegger wasn't qualified to be governor of California. Ronald Reagan wasn't qualified to be governor, let alone president. I was a vice president of the Screen Actors Guild when he was its president. My duties consisted of attending meetings and voting. The only thing I remember is that Ronnie never had an original thought and that we had to tell him what to say. That's no way to run a union, let alone a state or a country.

My decision not to run for governor was also influenced by Lois's reaction to the idea. Her exact words were: "I'd rather die." But Lois is very passionate about issues. She writes letters. Sometimes, when she's *really* passionate, she says, "Jimmy, I want you to sign this one, too." I have a standard answer for that: "Yes, dear."

The cause closest to my heart is the environment. Lois and I supported the efforts to prevent oil drilling along the Southern California coast, to stop logging in Northern California forests, and to create a nature conservancy in the Santa Monica Mountains. Is there anything more crucial or more urgent than saving the planet?

CHAPTER SIX

Racing

———————

Late in 1965, I heard that John Frankenheimer was about to direct a big-budget, CinemaScope feature about Formula One racing. I'd done a series of small films and felt I needed an "epic," so I had my agent get the script. I didn't know that Steve McQueen had already been signed for the part.

As it happened, Steve couldn't get along with the producer, Ed Lewis, so he backed out of the picture, flew to Taiwan to make *The Sand Pebbles* instead, and I got the part, even though Frankenheimer had wanted an unknown to play Pete Aron. I think he was looking for someone he could control. He had worked a lot with Burt Lancaster, and Burt always had an opinion, so Frankenheimer didn't want anyone with an opinion. But both Ed Lewis and the studio wanted me, and they overruled Frankenheimer.

Just to be nice, I called Steve to tell him. When I said, "Steve, I'm gonna do *Grand Prix,*" there was about a twenty-five-dollar silence. He finally wished me luck, and I didn't think any more about it. But Steve wouldn't talk to me for a long time afterward. He eventually made his own racing picture, originally called *The Champions,* directed by John

Sturges. It came out in 1971, retitled *Le Mans*. Years later, Steve's wife, Neile, said he resented me for taking the part, even though he'd already turned it down.

The movie follows four drivers through a season of racing for the world championship in the Grand Prix series. Antonio Sabato plays a promising rookie, Yves Montand a former champion at the end of his career, and Brian Bedford a Scotsman recovering from a crash. My character, Pete Aron, is an American trying to make a comeback after being thrown off his racing team for recklessly causing injury to a fellow driver. Eva Marie Saint, Jessica Walter, and Françoise Hardy play the love interests, but the story is pure soap opera.

Making *Grand Prix* was the most fun I've ever had on a movie. Hell, it was the most fun I've ever had, period! Six months with the best cars and the best drivers on the best circuits in the world . . . for a guy who'd always loved cars and racing, it was a fantasy come true.

We filmed at actual races at Monte Carlo, Clermont-Ferrand in France, Spa Francorchamps in Belgium, Brands Hatch in England, Zandvoort in the Netherlands, and Monza in Italy. The crowds in the movie are real. We shot before, during, and after the races and blended our footage with film of the real competition.

Formula One is the elite class of single-seater auto racing. Along with Indy Car racing, it's at the pinnacle of motor sports. The "formula" is the set of rules prescribing weight, length, width, and engine capacity (three liters or 3,000 cc.). No two race circuits are the same; they have unique lengths, configurations, and local conditions.

The filming got off to a rocky start. The drivers were skeptical at first, and no wonder: we crowded into the pits with our cameras and lights, ate into their practice time, and were a hazard on the track. Most of all, I think they doubted whether we cared enough to get it right.

Ferrari refused to allow its cars or even its name to be used in the movie at a time when Ferrari was synonymous with Grand Prix racing. There was no way to make the film without their cooperation, so Frankenheimer cut together an hour's worth of footage, took it to the factory in Maranello, and screened it for Enzo Ferrari, the former racing driver who manufactured the fastest sports cars in the world and founded the Ferrari Grand Prix team. He immediately gave his blessing. After that, the drivers came around, too. I guess they needed to know we were on their side and wanted to give a true picture of their sport.

If I hadn't been an actor, I'd like to have been a race driver. I've always admired them because what they do takes so much courage and skill. I was especially in awe of the Grand Prix drivers. It was an honor to be on the same track, and those guys went out of their way to help me. They pointed out the correct line through corners, briefed me on what to do in a spinout, and generally showed me the ropes. Between shots, we did some impromptu racing. We'd do a choreographed shot with five or six cars passing and jockeying, and when we cut we'd all turn around and race back. Fuuun!

Frankenheimer put as many Formula One drivers in the movie as possible. Phil Hill, then the only American to have won a world championship, and Graham Hill—I called him "Mr. Smooth"—both played drivers and had a few lines in the picture. Richie Ginther, Jochen Rindt, Jack Brabham, and Bruce McLaren had walk-ons. The legendary, five-time world champion Juan Manuel Fangio came out of retirement to do a cameo and almost caused a riot when he appeared at Monza.

I started driving when I was ten years old, as soon as I was big enough to reach the pedals. I began playing "Ditch 'Em" around Norman not long after my fourteenth birthday, when I got my driver's license. We'd line up half a dozen cars, and the first guy would take off and try to lose the rest. Or I'd be cruising around town in my dad's Ford sedan or my Uncle John's Chevy and I'd see Jim Paul Dickenson in his mother's Ford V-8 or Pud Lindsay in the family Packard (with the gear shift *right on the steering column*) and off we'd go. No comments—you'd start driving on the other guy's bumper and the race was on.

It was during the war and gas was rationed, so we had to steal it. We'd go up to somebody's car at night with a siphon hose and a five-gallon can. Then we'd chase each other all over the county. It was great fun, with a lot of whoopin' and hollerin', but it wasn't as dangerous as it sounds. Nobody ever got hurt—never even rolled a car, because we were all good drivers. Or so we thought.

Before I went to Europe, I worked for two months in Southern California with Bob Bondurant. Bob was a successful sports car and F1 driver who now has the largest driving school in the world, but I was his first student. I went at it like I'd never driven a car before in my life, because driving a race car is completely different from driving a passenger car on the highway.

Bondurant and I went up to the track at Willow Springs. At first, I sat in the passenger seat and watched him drive. Then we switched places and he coached me. We started slowly and gradually built up speed on each lap until I reached my limit. You have to know your limit, go to the edge of it, and stay there. But I was never afraid of it. We worked four or five days a week and every day I'd drive home on the freeway thinking it was more dangerous than the race track.

I went over to Europe early, and while the other actors attended Jim Russell's racing school in England, I worked with some of the real F1 drivers who were in the movie. You'd be surprised how fast you can learn when you have teachers like Phil Hill and Richie Ginther. We worked in a two-seater at first, and then I'd drive a single-seater. I learned the tracks in sections, a few hundred yards at a time, and eventually memorized the whole circuit down to each bump and oil spot. I learned there's a perfect way to drive a course, and you strive to come as close to that ideal as possible. With *that car*. The car dictates what you can do. Taking an 80-mile-an-hour corner at 80 miles an hour is very satisfying. Not 79, which is too slow, or 81, which will spin you out.

You don't so much sit in a Formula One car as wear it. The cockpit was so cramped I couldn't fit, even though I'd lost twenty pounds for the part. They had to raise the roll bar and take the seat out. I sat smack on the frame, on a little piece of leather wrapped around a towel. I'd get quite a jolt when the car bottomed out at 130 mph.

Frankenheimer was a good director. He'd begun in live television in the 1950s directing episodes of *Playhouse 90* and *Climax!* and went on to direct feature films including *The Manchurian Candidate, The Birdman of Alcatraz,* and *Seven Days in May.* But he was a bully. If he wanted something, he *made* you do it. No arguments, no compromises, no suggestions, just do it! We got along okay, except for one little set-to when he was picking on somebody in the crew and I had to speak up. After that, everything was fine between us.

I don't think Frankenheimer knew how to smile, but at least you knew what he wanted. He was trying to make a big movie under tough conditions, and I still don't know how he managed the logistics of moving two hundred people, thirty race cars, and tons of equipment all over Europe for six months. At every stop, he had to shoot on the fly, regardless of weather or available light, with little or no chance to stage anything or shoot a scene more than once. As a result, it was an expensive movie to shoot: early in the production, we were already over budget and there were rumors the studio was about to pull the plug. On our first day in Monte Carlo I was in the hotel elevator with Frankenheimer and he said, "Well, we've got 'em now!"

"Got who?" I said.

"The studio. I have a five-million-dollar budget and I can't bring in the picture for less than eight million dollars, but MGM is *committed,* so they've *got* to let us finish it."

Frankenheimer wanted to put viewers in the car and give them a sensation of speed. But he didn't cheat anything: no rear projection, no process shots, no speeded-up footage. The technology he needed to get the realism had to be invented. Special effects man Milt Rice rigged a motorized, swiveling cockpit for close-ups of spinouts, and devised a tubular catapult charged with compressed nitrogen that was in effect a cannon for Formula One cars. In a split second, it could launch a mock-up car—with or without a dummy in it—from a standstill to 120 mph.

Because Frankenheimer was obsessed with details, the movie is almost a documentary in terms of the racing. Someone called it a "porno film for gearheads," with tight close-ups of instrument needles, spinning wheels, drive shafts, suspensions, gear changes, heel-toe pedal work. The sound is deafening, with the thundering roar of engines and cars surging off the line. Sound effects editor Gordon Daniel prerecorded a whole library of motor sounds with Phil Hill driving on a straightaway in California. Phil simulated hundreds of gear changes specific to the corners on all the circuits. Gordon then matched them in postproduction to what the drivers were doing on the screen, so aficionados heard the exact sounds they expected at every corner of every track.

Former World Champion Phil Hill drove the camera car, a Ford GT-40, a Le Mans–type racer capable of hitting 200 mph. Some of the camera techniques invented for *Grand Prix* are still in use today, including helicopter shots, some of which were taken from only ten feet above the action. There were complaints about it flying too low, so they backed off for a while . . . then went back to flying low again. How low? The cameraman, John Stephens, would hang out of that chopper with his feet dangling, and at the end of the day, his pant legs would be green from brushing the trees.

Lionel Lindon was the cinematographer, but Saul Bass directed the second unit and designed the multiscreen montages. The technique first appeared in the 1960s and soon became a cliché, but at the time, it was revolutionary, and all the more striking in Cinerama, a process that doubled or tripled the size of the screen and curved it around the audience. With a high-quality sound system and the advanced cinematography, some viewers actually got motion sickness.

NASA developed special microwave cameras to be mounted on the cars. Johnny Stephens put cameras over wheels, on hoods, in drivers' laps. Those big, heavy, 70mm cameras—housed in special glass shields to protect the lenses from kicked-up pebbles and rain—were difficult to work with. Mounted on the chassis, they upset the aerodynamics so much that the cars had to be counterweighted. Stevens rigged special remote controls for them and experimented with antivibration mounts. He finally decided to let the camera shake because it looked sexier. Today's cameras are so tiny they can fit several in the cockpit without bothering the driver, and television viewers are used to seeing what the driver sees from the cockpit. But in those days, Frankenheimer struggled for months trying to shoot from the driver's point of view until Bell Labs created a camera that could be strapped to a driver's helmet.

The white "BRM" I drove was actually a Formula Three car, a disguised Lotus-Ford with a one-liter, four-cylinder engine. It was rigged with fake exhausts and carburetor stacks to make it look exactly like a three-liter V-8. It could hit 130 mph, while the real Formula One cars could do 160. Frankenheimer was so thorough, when he realized my car didn't have enough torque to spin its wheels on the starting grid, he coated the tires with oil to make it smoke like the real thing.

I did all my own driving in *Grand Prix*. The other actors weren't so gung ho. Yves Montand scared himself to death when he spun out in front of the Hôtel de Paris and almost put the car in the police station. Antonio Sabato seemed to think he was Fangio, until he spun it in the pits, and from then on he looked terrified of the car. Brian Bedford didn't know how to drive at all before he got the part—he'd had a driver's license for only a few months when we began shooting. Before long he said, "Look, I can't do this. Either double me or replace me." Frankenheimer got a stand-in who did all his driving. Brian later said, "Asking an actor to drive Formula One is like asking Phil Hill to play Hamlet."

During practice for the Belgian Grand Prix at Spa Francorchamps in June, Lloyd's of London found out I was running 120 miles an hour in the rain. The district manager from Lloyd's came down to the pits and said, "We can't have that, Mr. Garner." We managed to calm him down. Birds were another hazard at Spa. They kept bouncing off the windshield. I half expected one to bounce off my face.

There was a sudden downpour at the start of the actual race, and the drivers ran into a curtain of rain. Half of them crashed on the first lap, including Jackie Stewart, whose BRM hit a stone wall and went upside down in a ditch. There he was, trapped in the cockpit with a broken collarbone and high-octane racing fuel leaking all over him, terrified that the car's hot exhaust pipes would turn him into a human torch at any second. There were no marshals or emergency personnel handy, so it was fellow drivers Graham Hill and Bob Bondurant who rescued Jackie—after they pried the steering wheel off with a wrench borrowed from a spectator. By the time they pulled Jackie from the car, he was soaked with gasoline. He had to wait twenty minutes for an ambulance, his skin blistered by the additives in the fuel.

The experience turned Jackie into a crusader for driver safety, which made him unpopular with the Formula One establishment, including some of the drivers. Jackie maintained that he was being paid to drive, not to risk his life week after week.

Jackie was talented as he was tenacious. Between 1965 and 1973, he won twenty-seven races and three World Drivers' Championships. In his spare time, he formed a drivers' union that demanded changes and eventually got them. Because of his efforts, barriers were erected, medical support was improved, and some venues were closed, including Spa.

It was a simpler time when we made *Grand Prix*. Formula One racing was a lot more seat-of-the-pants. The teams were run by individuals, not giant corporations. The drivers were a swashbuckling band of brothers, and they had personalities: you could actually recognize them in their open helmets as the cars streaked by. Now the drivers look like faceless robots when they're in the car and walking billboards when they're not.

Though today's Formula One cars go much faster than their 1966 counterparts—220 mph now versus 160 then—modern cars are a lot safer. In those days, safety measures were crude at best. The Ferraris, BRMs, Maseratis, and Lotuses didn't have seat belts, because in a crash the cars would either disintegrate or catch fire or both, so drivers had a better chance if they were thrown free. Driving a Formula One car then was more physically demanding than it is now. They were hard to steer and the insides of your fingers would blister and bleed from constantly changing gears. Today drivers shift with a flick of a paddle on the steering wheel.

The old cars were slender and beautiful, but they were death traps: between 1960 and 1969, on average, two Grand Prix drivers were killed every year. In 1996, I went back to Monza with Formula One World Champion Jacques Villeneuve. He took out a restored 1963 Brabham that was older than he was. Though Jacques was used to driving a much faster car, he said the Brabham scared the hell out of him. I had the chance to drive a couple of laps myself, and as I brought the car back to the pits, I caught myself giggling.

I still have the open-face helmet I wore in the picture. At the time, I thought it was really something, but compared to what they have now, it was awful. Made of fiberglass, the only thing it protected you from was the wind. Today's full-face helmets are much stronger and give a lot more protection. The Lexan visor protects the driver's face from pebbles and bits of debris thrown up from the track that can travel at 300 mph, and it has multiple layers of clear film that can be peeled off as they get dirty. There's a tube connected to a supply of drinking water—the temperature in the cockpit can reach 120 degrees Fahrenheit, so drivers have to fight dehydration, which can lead to muscle cramps and loss of concentration. Today's helmets also allow two-way radio communication with the pits. In the old days crews had to write on message boards on the side of the pit wall and the driver tried to read it while speeding by.

At one point, the shopkeepers along the race route in Monte Carlo revolted because we'd blocked off the streets and their customers couldn't get to them. We'd already paid them, but I guess it wasn't enough, because one day they came down and disrupted filming. I was on a boat in the harbor, soaking wet from the previous shot and eager to get on with it. When I realized that a shakedown was in progress, I went ashore and pretended to blow my stack. Well, half-pretended. We were soon filming again.

Toward the end of the shoot, I did a fire stunt with butane bottles that I ignited with a switch in the cockpit on the final turn. When I crossed the finish line going about 120, I slammed on the brakes and threw another switch to put out the flames. But something went wrong and the car erupted in a giant fireball. I scrambled out of the cockpit as the crew blasted me in the face with fire extinguisher and smothered me in an asbestos blanket. I wasn't hurt, but it shook me up. The producer wasn't happy that I'd done the stunt and neither was Lloyd's of London. They canceled my policy, and for the rest of the picture I drove without insurance.

One of the top-grossing films of 1966, *Grand Prix* won Oscars for editing, sound, and sound effects. The movie captured the beauty and spectacle of Formula One racing in its golden age, before it became commercialized and high-tech. It looked real, sounded real, and felt real. At the end of three hours, you felt you'd been *in* the races, not *at* the races. I think it's still the greatest auto racing picture ever made.

Grand Prix was a high point in my film career, and I owe the whole experience to Steve McQueen for dropping out of the picture in the first place. Steve's son Chad finally dragged him to see it. I ran into them on our street as they were coming home. Steve stopped and said his first words to me in two years:

"Well, we went to your movie."

"Yeah? What'd you think?"

"Pretty good picture. Pretty good."

Coming from Steve, it was high praise.

When you get behind the wheel of a race car, it's just you and the car. It takes complete concentration. You can't fake it. I wasn't a thrill seeker, and I didn't have a *need for speed,* but I liked the challenge of controlling your machine and outmaneuvering your opponents.

Making *Grand Prix* gave me the racing bug. After soaking up the atmosphere on the Formula One circuit and driving fast cars on race tracks all over Europe, I *had* to be involved in the sport.

So I formed American International Racers.

The first thing we did was buy three brand-new L-88 Corvettes. Big mistake. They were so unreliable, we raced them only once, at

Daytona in 1968. We sold them and moved up to Formula A with three Lola T-70s.

In Formula A, which is just a cut below Formula One, the cars can reach speeds of 180 mph. Formula A cars aren't easy to handle. They're too light overall, and the weight is in the back, so the rear end swings all over the place. But the Lolas were sweet. *Great* race cars. What I wouldn't give to have one now. I drove one on the street for quite a while, but the lights were too low. Totally against the law.

We entered long-distance endurance events—LeMans, Daytona, Sebring. We raced two cars and kept a third as a backup. At our first Daytona, our Lolas finished second and seventh.

In those days auto racing was friendly competition. You thought nothing of helping a competitor fix his car during a race. I remember doing that for Roger Penske at Sebring. To me that's what racing is all about.

It was fun and exciting owning AIR while it lasted, but I disbanded the team at the end of 1969 after discovering that racing is a big commitment of time and money. I didn't have enough of either to continue.

We chronicled AIR's 1969 season in *The Racing Scene,* a ninety-minute documentary directed by former ABC Sports director Andy Sidaris and written by William Edgar. The film follows us as we race at Daytona, Sebring, and on the Formula A circuit at Lime Rock and St. Jovite. The title sequence shows Scooter Patrick and me driving in the Baja 1000.

I couldn't drive in Formula A because I was busy working. Even if I'd had the time, the insurance companies wouldn't have covered me. But for some reason they did allow me to drive in the Baja 1000. I'm not sure why they made that exception. Maybe they thought it was a rally because there were checkpoints. Whatever the reason, I'm glad I fell through that crack.

———

First run in 1967, the Baja 1000 is the granddaddy of off-road races and the longest nonstop, point-to-point race in the world, running over a thousand kilometers through the beautiful desolation of Mexico's Baja Peninsula from Ensenada, 100 miles south of San Diego, to La Paz, near the peninsula's southern tip.

The Baja had already been a popular playground for dune buggy and dirt bike enthusiasts, so it was a natural for a big off-road race. The course starts on the Pacific Ocean side of Baja California in Ensenada and zigzags from east to west.

It's an eerie, majestic, untamed landscape where the terrain changes suddenly and drastically, going from seaside to desert, mountains to cactus forest, salt marsh to lava field. There's every road hazard you can imagine: auto parts, fenders, and tires litter the course; there are steep grades, sharp switchbacks, rocks, washouts, sand pits, sagebrush, scorpions, poisonous snakes, and blinding, smothering silt beds. The most feared hazard of all, silt is like talcum powder. It can be several feet deep with sharp ruts at the bottom. The silt cloud gets so thick, you just point the car, put your foot down, and hope.

If all that weren't enough, the course is open to local traffic during the race! Livestock wanders onto the course. Spectators build hidden ramps to send vehicles airborne to enhance their viewing pleasure. Nobody sells tickets; people just walk onto the course and stand there, a few feet from the action. There can be tree trunks across the road and other fun-loving sabotage, like when spectators switch course markers to lead drivers astray. One year there was even a speed trap: a pair of enterprising local cops pulled competitors over *during the race* to sell them tickets to the policeman's ball.

Baja 1000 drivers are celebrities in Mexico, where they're admired for their proficiency and daring. The greats from all forms of auto racing have driven there: Indy Car racers Johnny Unser, Jimmy Vasser, Roberto Guerrero, Danny Sullivan, and Mario Andretti ("You don't fall asleep at the Baja," Mario said); desert racers Rod Hall, Larry Roeseler, and Ron Bishop; and NASCAR champions Jimmie Johnson and Robby Gordon. Robby was one of the best I ever saw down there. He was so good, I swear he hardly ever touched the ground. And there were sports car drivers like Paul Newman who, in 2004 at the age of seventy-nine, was the oldest person ever to compete in the Baja 1000. Paul was *good*. Very precise. In the 1970s and '80s, "P. J. Newman" won a bunch of SCCA (Sports Car Club of America) national titles. In '78, he won his class at LeMans and finished second overall.

The first official Baja 1000, in 1967, had sixty-five entries. Now the vehicles are all high-tech, with factory support teams and corporate sponsors. But back in the old days, it was friendly and relaxed. There were hardly any rules and very little prize money. Everyone was there for the fun of taking part in a crazy carnival.

I drove the Baja five or six times, beginning in 1968. That year there were 250 entries, half of which didn't finish. (In 2010, there were more than 1,200 entries.) I finished the race every year, whether in a truck or car, which is a testament to the people who built the vehicles, not the driver.

In '68, Larry Bergquist and Gary Preston finished first overall on a motorcycle. Larry Minor and Jack Bayer finished first in their class in the Number 3 Bronco, but not before hitting a cow on the way in. I drove the Number 59 Bronco with Scooter Patrick and we came in fourth in our class.

Scooter and I split the driving, but you couldn't get any rest while your partner was behind the wheel because it was such a rough ride. You had to vise-grip the handles on the side of the car just to stay in it.

Another year I started from Ensenada while my codriver (and future *Rockford* assistant director) Cliff Coleman flew to El Larco, five hundred miles farther south. Cliff, a good night driver, took over there and finished the race.

My mother, Mildred Scott Meek
Bumgarner, circa 1929.
(Personal collection)

My father, Weldon Warren "Bill"
Bumgarner, circa 1935.
(Courtesy of Terry Bumgarner)

With my mother and older brothers
Jack (left) and Charles, circa 1930.
(Courtesy of Terry Bumgarner)

James Scott Bumgarner, age four. *(Personal collection)*

At the Denver, Oklahoma, country store with the hand-operated gasoline pump, circa 1933. Left to right: brother Jack, me, my father, and brother Charles. *(Personal collection)*

My first-grade class at Washington school, circa 1935. I'm in the back row, fourth from the left. *(Personal collection)*

Left to right: Charles, Jack, and me, circa 1935. *(Personal collection)*

My Lucky Strike "endorsement," seventh grade at Norman Junior High. *(Personal collection)*

At the Pickwick pool in Burbank, California, circa 1944. *(Personal collection)*

My first "head shot," circa
1945. *(Courtesy of Bill Saxon)*

Left to right: Jack, me, and Charles, in 1949. *(Courtesy of Terry Bumgarner)*

Hollywood, 1949.

(Personal collection)

With my father in Los Angeles, on my way to Korea in 1951. *(Personal collection)*

Private Bumgarner, 1951.
(Courtesy of Terry Bumgarner)

Ralph Edwards springs the trap:
"James Garner, this is your life . . ."
(Personal collection)

On the set of *This Is Your Life,* June 1958. Left to right, standing: Ralph Edwards, Jack Garner, Uncle John Bumgarner, Aunt Leona Bumgarner, Charles Bumgarner. Seated: Grandma Abby Meek, Grandma Louella Bumgarner. *(Courtesy of Terry Bumgarner)*

Gary Cooper gives Kim his autograph in the Warner Bros. commissary.
(Courtesy of Kimberly Garner)

Fisticuffs at the Crosby Pro-Am, 1981.
(Courtesy of Bill Saxon)

With Gigi, in her favorite photograph. *(Courtesy of Gigi Garner)*

With Gigi, Henry Fonda, Lois, Shirlee Fonda, and Kim on Henry's seventy-fifth birthday. *(Personal collection)*

With Tom Selleck, 1978. *(Personal collection)*

Luis Delgado at the 1978 *Rockford Files* Christmas party.
(Courtesy of Robert Howe)

Left to right: Jack Garner, Bill Saxon, and Jim Paul Dickenson at the Bel-Air Country Club, circa 1991.
(Courtesy of Bill Saxon)

A word about Cliff: He's crazy as hell, but he's a good man to have around. In addition to his talents on a sound stage, Cliff is a terrific cook. Whenever we were stuck in a little Mexican village, he'd go to the local grocery and pick up canned meats and whip up a stew or some eggs and hash. He's also a mechanic and a carpenter. I used to tell everybody, "Don't go anywhere without Cliff."

Anybody can enter the Baja 1000 with almost any kind of vehicle, and there are now more than forty classes: small- or large-bore motorcycles, dune buggies, stock VW bugs, trucks, custom desert vehicles, ATVs. Each class goes off separately, the faster ones first. The heavyweights are the trophy trucks, the largest and fastest vehicles in the race, some with 800-horsepower, V-8 engines. These monsters can reach speeds of 140 miles per hour and cost $1 million to set up for the race.

For a couple of years we ran Ford Broncos prepared by Bill Stroppe. They were good, rugged vehicles, but they weren't pretty. People were always coming up and asking, "Are you really gonna *race* in that thing?"

The 1963 Indy 500 winner Parnelli Jones was on the Bronco team. Parnelli, who won the Baja 1000 twice, said the race was "like being in a twenty-four-hour plane crash." He'd go out in pre-runs and mark bad spots in the road with pink toilet paper and silver tape so we could see them at night.

Parnelli and I became good friends. In 1970, his Bronco broke down, so we picked him up and gave him a ride hanging on our roll bar. After we got in, I thought I saw the imprint of his face on it. Another time he broke a steering rod, so I took two open-end wrenches, put one on this nut and one on the other, wired it together, secured it with 200-mph tape, and it held.

I changed a tire during the race one year and forgot to strap down the tools when I put them back in the trunk. Every time I hit a bump, they rattled around, making a tremendous racket. After the race, I looked in. The tools had scoured all the paint off the inside of the trunk. It looked like someone had gone in and polished it.

Vic Hickey, a senior engineer at General Motors, designed the Oldsmobile Banshee in 1972. I drove it in the Baja 1000 a couple of times and managed to come in second in my class one year. I was interested in the development of the car, so I would drop in on weekends while it was being built. I'd remembered that Formula One cars had the engine positioned toward the rear instead of in front, to prevent the weight from making the car nose down when it went airborne after hitting a bump. So we put the Banshee's engine next to the driver. With all that weight in the right-center and my weight on the left-center to balance it out, the Banshee flew straight and landed flat, a big advantage in both handling and safety.

The Banshee was unique for its time. It looked like an Olds Cutlass, but shorter and wider. It had a 500-horsepower aluminum block engine to give it a little more power. The Banshee placed high in a few races and won the Riverside Grand Prix, even though I hit the sand and had to jump the car into a mud pond near the start/finish. I was so disgusted with myself, I jumped out of the car and smashed my helmet on the ground. (The crowd loved that.) I also rolled it a few times in a practice run, but it was strong enough to protect me.

Steve McQueen and Bud Ekins, who'd done the motorcycle jump for Steve in *The Great Escape,* drove the Vic Hickey–designed Baja Boot, a four-wheel-drive vehicle custom-made by GM. Steve was a good driver, but nobody else was as good as he was, according to him. He was competitive with me, but it wasn't mutual. I'd go through a checkpoint and they'd say, "McQueen just came through and wanted to know where you were." I didn't give a damn where *he* was.

On the way to the Baja one year, McQueen, Cliff Coleman, and I flew from LA to Nogales, Mexico. As soon as we got off the plane, the local police arrested us, herded us into a room, and made us take off all our clothes. That's right: *strip-searched in a Mexican jail!* There we were, lined up with our backs against the wall, side-by-side, buck naked. It was a humbling experience in more ways than one: not only was it demeaning to stand there bare-ass next to your peers (more or less), it was also deflating that the policemen, most of whom were snickering at us, didn't seem to know or care that Steve and I were movie stars. They kept us locked up for a few hours and then let us go without explanation or apology.

Driving the Baja 1000 is a world apart from Formula One, where finesse, precision, and, above all, speed are essential. I didn't have a clue about off-road racing at first, but I learned the desert's secrets pretty fast. I was born in the country and drove on country roads where if you hit one bump, you remember it. That background came in handy.

Running the Baja is mentally exhausting. You're paranoid. You're never sure what's over the next rise. You look at every tree, bush, and shadow in the road that can tell you, "There's a hole here." And it's hard on the body, especially the back. Even though we'd worked on the suspensions to soften the bumps, at the end of a run I could barely stand up. Felt like I'd been gone over with a rubber hose.

But the fun outweighed the pain.

In the Baja, you drive just as fast as you can and hope your car doesn't break. We'd get up to 90 miles an hour in the Bronco on those desert trails. If you got stuck behind a slower car, you ran up, gave him a little bump in the back, and kept bumping him until he moved over. At night, you flashed your lights to signal a slower car in front of you to get out of the way. If you drove the Baja alone, you were in the car fifteen to twenty hours in 100-degree heat during the day and subfreezing temperatures at night. Darkness complicated everything, of course.

The vehicles need a lot of logistical support, so there are dozens of mechanics, welders, fabricators, and fuelers on hand with stockpiles of food, gasoline, and spare parts. In the old days, you had to stop at eight different checkpoints along the way and actually have a paper ticket punched at each one. You'd stop, get gas and oil, take a drink, grab a hot dog, and off you went again. The crews would leapfrog ahead and wait for the racers at the checkpoints, which were spaced at about every hundred miles, usually in a little town. After the driver went through, the support people would pack up and jump to the next checkpoint. A few drivers took shortcuts between checkpoints. Now they track all the vehicles with GPS and the course changes from year to year, with secret checkpoints to discourage cheating.

The Baja 1000 is generally recognized as the most grueling off-road race in the world, and I'm told it's become a test bed for passenger cars and off-road vehicles. Lessons learned in the Baja help manufacturers improve drivetrains and suspensions.

Once ABC's *Wide World of Sports* began covering it, the Baja 1000 was on the way to becoming the major international event it is today. Winning it is right up there with the great accomplishments in motor sports, and there's a lot of money and glory on the line. But all I know, it was a lot of *fun*.

Speaking of fun, I drove the pace car at the Indianapolis 500 three times, in 1975, 1977, and 1985. It's a great honor: Some of the others who've done it are Eddie Rickenbacker, Carroll Shelby, Chuck Yeager, and General Colin Powell. Driving the pace car puts you on the same track with three dozen of the most advanced race cars in the world.

Formula One and Indy are the two fastest forms of motor racing. The cars are similar, but because Indy cars run on oval circuits, they're built heavier, to hug the tracks, while Formula One cars are quicker and more agile in the turns.

Unlike F1, the Indianapolis 500 uses a rolling start. The pace car ensures that nobody gets an advantage. On the three pace laps, the cars form into eleven rows of three. They gradually build speed while warming up their engines and tires until they get the green flag signaling a clean start, and the pace car leaves the track.

During the race, whenever there's a yellow caution light, the pace car comes out and the race cars have to bunch up behind it without changing position. The pace car leads the field at a safe speed—100 mph or so, until the green light comes back on. Casual viewers may not know that it's a different pace car driver, a professional who does it every year rather than the driver who does only the first three laps.

Some people get bent out of shape when they drive the ceremonial pace car, so race organizers want somebody who's used to being in crowds and knows something about driving. Officials got even more nervous in 1971, when an auto dealer from Indianapolis lost control of the pace car and wiped out a photographers' stand in the pits, injuring twenty people.

The pace car is always a street-legal American car. In '75 it was a Buick Century, in '77 an Oldsmobile Delta 88, and in '85 an Olds Cutlass Calais. Car companies jockey for the privilege of having one of their models selected as the year's pace car for the prestige, and for the revenue from sales of pace car replicas with special performance packages and "Indy 500" decals.

I love the traditions and camaraderie of "the Brickyard." With 400,000 people cheering and singing "Back Home in Indiana," it's a unique experience. Even when I wasn't driving the pace car, I tried to go back every year to renew acquaintances and soak up the atmosphere. And whenever I was in Indianapolis, I made the pilgrimage to the Iron Skillet for fried chicken and to the Kountry Kitchen for the best chicken-fried steak, mashed potatoes, and gravy in the world.

I've made some great friends at the Indianapolis 500: Lloyd Ruby, Roger Ward, Mario Andretti. I first met Jim Murray at Indy. We'd sit up under the tree at the first turn. We played a lot of golf together at Riviera over the following years. I met Jim Cook and his son John there when he was a boy. John and I would later partner up at the Crosby Pro-Am. One year Bill Saxon joined me at the 500 and brought his friend Tom Davis. I wasn't driving the pace car that year, but Saxon and Davis got in a convertible with me and we did a lap. I wanted them to feel the warmth and energy from the stands washing over them as I had. Every time I raised my hand to wave, the crowd roared. Billy Dee said he felt like a Roman gladiator.

CHAPTER SEVEN

The Rockford Files

R*ockford* began as a character in *Toma,* a series that Roy Huggins and Stephen J. Cannell were doing at Universal. When Steve turned in the script, they realized they had something bigger, so they pitched it as a Movie of the Week with an eye toward making it into a series.

Frank Price, the head of television at Universal and, by the way, Roy Huggins's son-in-law, liked the concept and practically guaranteed the show would get on the air if they'd make one little change: turn Rockford into a *short* private detective. Evidently, the executives at Universal had seen Robert Blake in *Electra Glide in Blue* and were hot to do something with him. Price said, "Make the PI five-foot-six and you've got a hit." Well, Roy Huggins didn't like that idea, and he sent *me* the *Rockford* script instead.

At that moment, I was negotiating with MGM to do a television series based on my character in *Support Your Local Sheriff.* When I got the *Rockford* script, I read it, loved it, and agreed to do it the same day, and Universal dropped the short detective idea. I asked for one change of my own: the character was originally named "Tom" Rockford. I said, "I'm not a *Tom.*" They changed it to Jim.

Frank Price pitched the show to NBC, and *they* wanted to change the character, but in a different way: they didn't want Rockford to be a "coward." I told them, "Look, I said I'd do the show based on the script, and if you change a single word, I'll walk."

The pilot was a ninety-minute Movie of the Week with a very young Lindsay Wagner, who hires Rockford to find her father's killer. When it aired on March 27, 1974, it got good ratings and NBC picked it up for the fall.

The series debuted on September 13, 1974, on NBC at nine p.m. on Friday night. *Rockford* ran for six seasons—a total of 122 episodes—until July 25, 1980. It went straight into syndication and hasn't been off the air since.

My company, Cherokee Productions, produced *The Rockford Files*. I wanted Steve Cannell to be our supervising producer. Besides being a talented and prolific writer, Steve understood the character because he had created it.

The first time I met Steve, he said, "When I was a kid, my father let me stay up to watch *Maverick* if I was a good boy."

"There are a lot of things you could have said to me that would have been better than that," I said.

At that point, Steve had no interest in producing—he just wanted to write. But I insisted, and the studio finally talked him into doing it for one year. That first year went so well that Steve said he'd continue for as long as I wanted him, and we lasted for almost six years, the entire run of the series, and never had a single disagreement.

Early in the first season, there was a script that just wasn't working. I called Steve to tell him, but he didn't know what I was talking about. He came down to the lot and found that we had pages that Roy Huggins had sent through without consulting Steve or anybody else, and they just didn't fit in the script. Steve told us to go back to the original and it worked like a charm.

That convinced me that Roy should not be involved in our day-to-day operations. When I put out the word that he'd have nothing to do with the scripts, he went ballistic. But I had a company to run. After that, I never had to send a script back. Just for conceiving the character, by the way, Roy made himself over a million bucks. I often thought that if we'd had that money, we could have put it to work on the screen where it belonged.

When my former agent, Meta Rosenberg, became our executive producer, her assistant, MaryAnn Rea, came to work for me, and we've had a close working relationship ever since. I tell people, "If you want to reach me, call MaryAnn, because she always knows where I am, what I'm doing, and what I'm *thinking*." It's a credit to her that we can work so well together while so far apart geographically: for the past ten years, she's lived in Northern California, yet she runs everything like clockwork. MaryAnn is my right arm. Make that right *and* left. I've been lucky to have her in my professional life all these years.

Meta was a first-rate organizer who knew a good script when she saw one, and it all starts with the writing. Without good writing, you're not going anywhere. Fortunately, we had the best writers in television. Steve Cannell oversaw the scripts and wrote about fifty episodes himself. Nobody could write as fast or as well as Steve. He could sit down and bang out a script a week for an hour show on that electric typewriter of his. I've never heard of anybody else who could do that.

Steve had a tremendous career after *Rockford,* with shows like *Baretta, Wiseguy, The A-Team, The Greatest American Hero,* and *The Commish.* He was responsible for something like forty TV series, and for three decades Steve always had at least one show on network television. He personally wrote hundreds of episodes of various series, primarily crime dramas, and in his spare time, he turned out a couple of dozen best-selling crime novels. All despite a severe disability:

Steve was diagnosed with dyslexia as an adult. He became an advocate for people with learning disabilities. Steve was about the finest human being I've ever known. It was a devastating loss when he died in 2010 after battling melanoma.

We also had Juanita Bartlett, who'd been Meta's secretary when we were doing *Nichols*. Juanita wrote some of the best *Rockford*s, including "The Great Blue Lake Land and Development Company," inspired by a *60 Minutes* story about land fraud, and "So Help Me God," about the abuses of the grand jury system. I'm proud of that show, because it was instrumental in bringing about changes in the law. Juanita eventually became a successful writer-producer in her own right.

Meta hired David Chase for the third season as a writer-producer and he stayed on the show until the end. David, of course, went on to win a slew of Emmys for creating, writing, and producing *The Sopranos,* one of the great American drama series of all time. I'm proud of him.

Charles Floyd Johnson, our producer, was an attorney who'd worked at the US Copyright Office before going into television. He was also executive producer on the *Rockford* movies and has produced a bunch of other hit series including *Magnum, P.I.; Quantum Leap; Simon and Simon;* and *JAG*.

In addition to his other duties, Chas was the guy in charge of the notorious phone messages. Each episode began with Rockford's answering machine: "Hi, this is Jim Rockford. At the tone, please leave your name and I'll get back to you." You'd hear the tone and then the message, which was usually bad news:

"Jim, this is Norma at the market. It bounced. Do you want us to tear it up, send it back, or put it with the others?"

"Gene's 24-Hour Emergency Plumbing. Your water heater's blown? We'll have somebody out there Tuesday . . . Thursday at the latest. "

"Hi. Just wanted to put your mind at rest . . . found your address book in the theater last week. It's in the mail. By the way, Carol's okay—but Linda?"

"It's Lori at the trailer park. A space opened up. Do you want me to save it, or are the cops gonna let you stay where you are?"

"This is the Message Phone company. I see you're using our unit . . . now how 'bout paying for it?"

"Jim, it's Shirley at the cleaners. You know that brown jacket—the one that looks so great on you—your favorite? We lost it."

It got to the point in the third or fourth season where the writers were running out of messages. It was the biggest problem they had writing the show! They got desperate there toward the end and were asking secretaries, Teamsters, everyone.

We rotated directors so they could prepare during the week or ten days before the episode began filming. We had people like Lou Antonio, Jackie Cooper, William Wiard, Ivan Dixon—the best in the business.

In our second season, CBS scheduled the popular *Hawaii Five-0* against us in the nine p.m. Friday night slot, and the studio got nervous. They decided Rockford should be a straight detective to compete with macho man Jack Lord, and they wanted us to take the humor out.

Take the humor out?

As soon as I heard that, I called Frank Price and asked him to come out to the location.

"When are you breaking for lunch?" he said.

"We've broken for lunch," I said.

"Well, okay, I'll be out in a couple of hours."

"Fine, but we're not going back to work until we talk."

Frank was there in twenty minutes.

We were shooting at Riviera Country Club and we met in my motor home. I explained to Frank that I'd been in the business a long time and that humor is what I do best.

"That's what people hire me for," I said. "If they don't want it, I'd just as soon do something else. I'm not going to change at the whim of somebody with no experience and no judgment, so either fire me or don't mess with it. If you don't like the series, cancel it."

I don't think Frank expected me to talk to him like that and it obviously shook him up. I might have raised my voice a little. I may have even broken one or two small pieces of furniture. Whatever I did or said, it got them off our backs once and for all. After that Frank and I got along just fine, though from then on he insisted on having at least one other person in the room whenever we met.

In the 1970s, Universal was a factory for prime-time television series: *Columbo, Quincy, The Six Million Dollar Man, The Bionic Woman*—all the shows had a similar style, or lack of it. Bland. Cookie-cutter. The studio cared more about getting them out than getting them good. I didn't want *Rockford* to be tainted by that attitude, so I hired my own production crew and bought my own location equipment. I wanted to get off of Universal's back lot. and I wanted the camera to follow Rockford wherever he went, so we shot more than half the scenes on location.

Universal's trucks were always breaking down, so I bought two semis and outfitted each to carry three or four different departments, which eliminated eight drivers and trucks. All those drivers cost money! The union wasn't happy about it, and when they complained, I said, "Well, gentlemen, why should I spend money on something I don't need?" After further discussion, they ended up making me an honorary Teamster.

I did everything I could to minimize production costs because I thought it would increase my share of the profits. In fact, the crew had a running joke: "Let's get to work—it's *Garner's* money we're wasting." They were a solid group who all knew their craft and worked well together. That's what makes a successful series. One guy can't do it alone. You've got to have all those people working together. If we ever had a bad apple, he was out like that. Otherwise, I let people do their jobs and I didn't look over their shoulders. I always tried to promote a family atmosphere on the set. That's what made me comfortable, and I think everybody else liked it, too.

Hour shows usually took seven or eight days to shoot; we shot an episode in six. In five and a half years, we were never over budget and only a handful of days over schedule. No other television show came close to that record. When Universal noticed it, they sent efficiency experts down to find out how we did it.

Even our theme music was a departure from the standard TV fare of the time. Steve Cannell brought in Mike Post and Pete Carpenter to write it: bluesy harmonica and a bluegrass instrument called a Dobro guitar, backed by a big band. The *Rockford* theme made the Top Ten on the *Billboard* charts, and Post and Carpenter won a Grammy for it. They also wrote the score, deliberately avoiding what they called "Mickey-Mousing," the common practice of punctuating action and telegraphing emotion with music.

If you look at Maverick and Rockford, they're pretty much the same guy. One is a gambler and the other a detective, but their attitudes are identical.

Rockford isn't your typical detective. He's a quirky character who turns all the private eye clichés inside out: he works out of a broken-down trailer at the beach instead of in a seedy downtown office; he's got a telephone answering machine rather than a leggy secretary; and while most private eyes are loners without families, Rockford has his dad, Rocky.

Instead of being a tough guy who thrives on danger, Rockford is *cautious*. He believes bravery gets you nothing but hurt, and he'd rather quit than fight. (When he absolutely can't avoid violence, he fights dirty.) Rockford doesn't like to hit people because it hurts the hand. He owns a gun, but he keeps it in a cookie jar and rarely carries it because, he says, "If I carry a gun, I may have to shoot somebody." (Though Rockford did fire his gun on a few occasions, he never killed anybody.)

Rockford softened the hard-boiled-detective image made popular by Humphrey Bogart, Dick Powell, and Robert Mitchum. Every real private detective I've ever talked to said Rockford was much closer to the truth than a lot of the tough ones on the screen.

Rockford has a bad back and worse luck. He has a problem with authority, so he tends to mouth off at the worst possible time, like when he's being beaten up by a thug: "Does your mother know what you do for a living?"

Rockford's tricky, but he isn't *bad*. He's an ordinary guy. He's a bit thick around the waist because of a weakness for tacos and Oreo cookies. He helps people who've been wrongly accused, just as he'd been. He spent five years in San Quentin for something he didn't do. He was convicted of armed robbery, but it was a bum rap and he got a full pardon.

"I have expenses," he's always saying. He runs credit checks on prospective clients, even if they're beautiful women, but he isn't greedy. "I won't kill for money," he says, "and I won't marry for it. Other than that, I'm open to just about anything." But Rockford only pretends to like money. In truth, he isn't in it for the money because there isn't much money in it, and deep down he knows that: two hundred bucks a day plus expenses wasn't a lot, not even in the 1970s. Most of his clients stiffed him anyway. That's okay, because Rockford has no ambition beyond being able to pay his bills, go fishing with his dad, and drink a few beers while watching football on TV.

Rockford is always suspicious of people's motives, but he isn't a cynic. When the chips are down, he's up there on his white charger fighting like hell for what's right. On the one hand, he's seen it all, but on the other, he's naive. He usually gets screwed in the end, but he's never bitter. He's a realist, but he has a good heart. In short, Jim Rockford is an honorable man.

Speaking of honor, or rather the lack of it, there was a producer at Universal named Glen Larson who stole a bunch of *Rockford* stories. He had the gall to lift the plots and just put different characters in them! When we caught him, we complained to the Writers Guild and they fined him. The fine obviously didn't teach him, because he copied the *Rockford* theme music for one of his shows.

One day on the back lot he came up, put his arm around me, and said, "I hope there are no hard feelings, Jim."

"Take your arm off me," I said.

He didn't listen. I told him again to take his arm off me, but he still didn't listen. I was so goddamn mad at him for stealing our stuff, I hauled off and belted him. Knocked him clear across a curb and into a motor home and he came out the other side. It's a good thing I only hit him with my left hand, because if I'd hit him with my right, I'd have killed him.

It was crazy: the studio had wanted us to change *our* show to look like *Hawaii Five-0,* but now they had this guy changing *his* show to look like ours. We weren't dealing with creative geniuses up there in the Black Tower.

We had a wonderful cast. Noah Beery Jr., or "Pidge," as everyone called him, played Jim Rockford's father. Pidge was a fine actor and a gentle man. He was a complete professional who always showed up on time, knew his lines, and never complained. But then, he had acting in his blood: his father was a silent film star and his uncle, Wallace Beery, won an Oscar for *The Champ* in 1931.

Pidge's character, Rocky, is a retired trucker who isn't happy that his son is a private detective. He's always saying things like, "Sonny, how can I tell my friends my son's a private eye?" or "Sonny, you never gave trucking a chance." Rocky loved to fish, and he passed that love on to his son. The moments when they're fishing together are among my favorites, and I think Rockford's relationship with his father is the emotional backbone of the show. Sometimes they get on each other's nerves, but the affection is there through it all.

Stuart Margolin, as Angel Martin, is a perfect foil for Rockford. Though Rockford is smarter than just about everybody else, everybody takes advantage of him, even his friends. Especially Angel, who was Rockford's cell mate at San Quentin.

Angel is a weasel. He double-crosses Rockford again and again. He's always getting in trouble, and Rockford always has to bail him out. (Few people know that Angel's first name is Evelyn. No wonder he's got issues.) I confess that I've never understood why Rockford likes Angel so much, because he's rotten to the core. But there's something lovable about him. I don't know what it is, but it's all Stuart's doing.

NBC didn't want Stuart in the show, but I was crazy about him and we cast him in the pilot as a snitch. NBC said they didn't like his performance, but we put him in a second episode anyway, then a third. NBC still didn't want him and they told us point-blank not to use him again. Then he got an Emmy nomination.

"Do you think we can get him for next year?" they said.

"I don't know. He's pretty busy. I'll have to talk to him."

Of course, I told Stuart all about it, and he was able to make a pretty good deal. He wound up with two Emmys for his work on *Rockford*. Stu is also a talented director, and a fine singer! We've remained great friends down the years.

Joe Santos played Detective Dennis Becker. He's a good cop and they have a good relationship, even though they use each other. Rockford gives Dennis a tip here and there, and in return Dennis keeps his superiors from pulling Rockford's PI license. The top brass can't stand Rockford because he makes them look bad by solving cases.

I just love Joe. He's the kind of guy who lights up a set just by showing up. He's so good and so professional, and he's got so damn much enthusiasm that it's always fun working with him. He's a hell of an actor and one tough little dude. But mostly, what Joe is, is a pussycat.

Gretchen Corbett played Rockford's lawyer and sometime love interest Beth Davenport. She was as smart and tough as she was beautiful.

Tom Selleck appeared in two episodes as an intrepid detective named Lance White. Lance is rich, he has all the advantages, and all the luck: clues appear for him as if by magic. Tom was so funny and so good in the role, I was positive he'd be a big star and I told him so. "Tom," I said, "you're a good actor and, looking the way you do, just keep doing what you're doing and it'll come sooner or later." Sure enough, the next thing I knew, he was starring in *Magnum, P.I.*

Rita Moreno appeared in three *Rockford* episodes as a needy ex-hooker called Rita Capkovic and won an Emmy for it. I've known Rita a long time: we worked together in *Marlowe,* and she'd made a screen test with me at 20th Century-Fox years before. Rita is incredibly talented, one of the few performers to have won all the major show business awards: Oscar, Emmy, Grammy, Tony, and Golden Globe.

We were also fortunate to have had Dennis Dugan as Richie Brockelman and Isaac Hayes as Gandolph Fitch in the cast, and week after week we had terrific guest stars like James Woods, Lauren Bacall, Jill Clayburgh, Ned Beatty, Rob Reiner, and Mariette Hartley.

Rockford's Firebird was also a character in the show. I've been asked why he didn't have a TransAm instead. Well, he would've *liked* one—it's much sexier—but I didn't think he could afford it. The Firebird was more of a blue-collar car, a stripped-down version of the TransAm, with a sticker price of about $3,000 for the 1970 model. And I thought it handled better than the TransAm.

We got a new car every season, actually three—two backups in case of breakdowns or damage—until the last two seasons, when we stayed with the '78 model. The official color was Sierra Gold and the interior was Camel Tan. Standard equipment on the Firebird Esprit was a 400-cubic-inch, 6.6 liter V-8 engine, with dual exhausts and an automatic transmission. Which was fine for our purposes. The only modification we made was to stouten up the suspension to handle all the stunts.

I've heard different stories about the significance of the license plate number, 853 OKG. I think the OKG stands for "Oklahoma Garner," but I don't know about the 853.

Car chases and car action were a big part of the series, and I did most of the driving myself. That was my *fun*. I'd driven race cars a little in *Grand Prix* and gotten the bug. One maneuver became a kind of signature of the show. People thought I invented it and began calling it a "Rockford," but it was really just a reverse 180, also known as a "moonshiner's turn" or "J-turn." When you're going straight in reverse at about 35 miles an hour, you come off the gas pedal, go hard left, and pull on the emergency brake. That locks the wheels and throws the front end around. Then you release everything, hit the gas, and off you go in the opposite direction.

People have no idea how physically punishing it is to do an action series. You're producing twenty-two one-hour movies every year. You're on the set fifteen hours a day with no time to do anything else but get a few hours sleep before you have to start all over again. Wore me down to a nub!

You show me a leading man who's done a drama series for more than two or three years and I'll show you somebody who's beat to a pulp. Our legs are gone, our backs are gone, and generally our brains are gone, too. (I just barely managed to hang on to mine.)

David Janssen and I grew up in the business together. I saw what the demands of doing a television series did to him. He had three or four knee operations, and while he was making *The Fugitive,* he'd call and say, "I don't know if I'm going to make it." David drank too much—not because he was an alcoholic, but because of the pressures of being on the screen for an hour every week. He died in 1980 at the age of forty-eight. The work killed him.

For the last ten years of *Gunsmoke,* Jim Arness just phoned it in. Everyone else carried the show. He'd come in one day a week and they'd give him his script and tell him what to do. He had terrible arthritis and couldn't work any more than that. If he had a normal job, he'd have been on disability. David Soul had to go into the hospital after two years on *Starsky & Hutch.* It's just pure overwork. Nobody talked about it, because they didn't want to tarnish their tough-guy image.

I limped through every episode of *The Rockford Files.* I had a double, my good friend Roydon "Roy" Clark, but only for long shots. The stunt guys used knee pads but I couldn't—they'd show. I needed muscle relaxants and painkillers to get me through a day's filming. I took Robaxin, Percodan, and codeine on a regular basis.

I got beat up a minimum of twice per show. I don't know why, but viewers loved to see me get whipped. Maybe they knew I'd get even later on. In staged fights, the big danger is slipping and hitting something. I hit a dolly once and broke a piece off my spine. Otherwise, I've been lucky doing fight scenes: I've never been accidentally hit with a punch.

But I have been hit on purpose: there was an actor in *Maverick,* a burly guy named Leo Gordon, who played Big Mike McComb. Leo was a genuine tough guy who had served time in San Quentin for armed robbery. Everybody in the crew was afraid of Leo because he was a scary guy. In one fight scene, he nailed me right in the gut. I looked at him like, "Huh? What was *that*?" He just grinned and kept doing it. Well, the fight turned around and I got to beat on *him* a little, and I buried my fist right down to the spine. He looked at me like, "HUH, what was *THAT*?" We got along fine from then on. We understood each other. (Hey, if you give it, you've gotta be able to take it, right?) Leo did three or four *Rockford*s, and he was also in the *Maverick* movie, and we never had a problem.

In the six years I did *Rockford,* I had seven knee operations. Every hiatus, I had one or both of them operated on, but I didn't have enough time to recover, so I'd be back working on them and they'd give out again. When I was in the hospital for one of the operations, Burt Lancaster was in the next room having a prosthetic knee put in. He raved about it. Said it worked fine and there was no pain. That's what it was like in those days; we were constantly comparing notes on doctors and procedures. I remember Joe Namath calling to tell me he'd found a great new orthopedic guy.

I finally had both knees replaced. They didn't give me any trouble after that, but they were stiff. If only I could've had my feet and my back replaced.

In the first year, after I'd done five or six *Rockford*s, I asked Steve Cannell, "Could you please write for somebody else? I'm in every shot!"

Steve said, "Jim, just give us eight shows where you're prominent and then we'll back off."

Every year after that I said the same thing: "Guys, can you please write something for somebody else?"

Never happened.

My contract with Universal was for six years, but Universal had only a five-year contract with NBC. After the fifth year I was in such bad shape I asked Fred Silverman, NBC's head of programming, not to pick up *Rockford* for a sixth season. But he didn't want to let *Rockford* go. I didn't blame him; he had a winner and they needed to fill the hour. I'd have done the same thing in his shoes.

One day on the set in October 1979, I suddenly doubled over with stomach pains and I was bleeding rectally. The studio doctor diagnosed ulcers. I went down to the Scripps Clinic in La Jolla and they told me I had to stop working. I took their advice, because I was literally sick and tired. I was a plow horse who'd pulled the plow too long.

By the time I was anywhere near able to go back to work, we'd missed our air dates and NBC had canceled *The Rockford Files* with ten episodes of the sixth season still unfinished. They claimed I was malingering.

On January 16, 1980, at about six p.m., I was driving my 1979 TransAm north on Coldwater Canyon Drive, a steep, winding road that connects Beverly Hills with the San Fernando Valley. The rush-hour traffic was down to a crawl when I noticed an El Camino in my rearview mirror passing cars on the right shoulder. I sped up a little and moved over to let the guy back into line behind me, but instead he tried to pass me on the right and he hit my right rear fender. I put my turn signal on and began to pull over to check the damage, but the El Camino tried to pass me on the left. I thought he was trying to get away without exchanging insurance information, so I swerved to the middle of the lane, stopped in front of him, and turned off the ignition. Just as I was about to open the door I heard, "YOU MOTHERFUCKER!"

That's when I got clobbered. This character was punching me through the open window! I couldn't get out from behind the wheel because he'd grabbed hold of the gold chain around my neck and kept flailing away, and I didn't have room to throw a punch. All I could do was reach up and grab him by the throat. At that point a woman—his sister, it turned out—opened the passenger door, reached in, grabbed my keys, and said, "Let's go, Aubrey, I've got his keys." I guess she thought they'd throw my keys away and take off, leaving me bleeding at the wheel.

Didn't happen, because I wouldn't let go of that sucker. While he was still hitting me, I pulled him so close to the car that his chin was pinned against the roof. But he kept punching! And he was doing some damage. At that point, I was holding him with both hands and he had me with his left and was punching with his right. I finally managed to lean back and kick him in the chest hard enough to push him away.

I opened the door and swung my feet onto the pavement. As soon as I stood up, I caught one flush in the mouth. I threw a punch and missed, and then I grabbed him. I held on, we stumbled clear across the highway, tripped over a curb, and I landed on top of him.

The next thing I know I'm lying facedown and he's kicking me in the head. I couldn't believe he got up so fast. He kicked me up one side of my body and down the other. It suddenly dawned on me that he was trying to kill me and that he might succeed, so I yelled, "Someone get this son of a bitch off me!"

There were lots of bystanders, but nobody wanted any part of this guy, and I don't blame them because he was out of control. But I don't think I would have stood by and watched someone take a beating like that.

When nobody came to my aid, I figured I'd better play dead, so the next time he kicked me in the head I sort of shuddered and went limp. That's when he hauled off and kicked me like you never *saw*! He was wearing pointy Italian shoes and he nailed me right behind the ear. He tried to kick me in the cojones but got my tailbone instead and fractured it. Then he kicked me *again,* and I heard the sister yell, "C'mon, Aubrey, let's get out of here."

They started to leave, but I figured anybody who could hit and kick me so many times without killing me wasn't *that* tough. If he'd had any punch at all, he'd have knocked me out halfway through the first round. So I got up and went after him.

I couldn't see very well, but I made it to the passenger side of his car. I reached in to grab his sister's hair, thinking I'd hold on to it even if he started to drive away. But one of the bystanders—Lew Wasserman's chauffeur, as it happened—grabbed me from behind and Aubrey and his sister took off.

I spent three days in the hospital. In addition to the cracked tailbone, I had a concussion and assorted abrasions, lacerations, and bruises. Considering the number of free shots that sucker had at me, I was in a lot better shape than I had any right to be.

They charged Aubrey Lee Williams Jr., a thirty-five-year-old ex–Green Beret, with assault with a deadly weapon, the weapon being his shoes. The prosecution called three or four witnesses who all told the same story. They could have called fifteen more. The jury convicted Williams of felonious assault, and the judge sentenced him to one hundred days in jail, a $500 fine, and three years' probation.

I'd never taken a beating like that, and it was hard to swallow. But the worst part of the whole deal was when his attorney called me a liar on television. A reporter asked him if there were "discrepancies" in my story, and the lawyer said, "Garner isn't telling the truth." The best part was the outpouring of love and support. I got thousands of cards and letters from all over the world, and flowers from people in show business I'd never even met.

But the warm glow didn't last long: while I was still in the hospital, MCA/Universal filed a $1.5 million lawsuit against me for failing to complete the *Rockford* season.

I became an actor by accident, but I'm a businessman by design. My company, Cherokee Productions, produced *The Rockford Files.* I took less money up front in return for a 37.5 percent share of the profits. I was personally paid about $30,000 per episode, which was and still is a lot of money, but it could have been several times that. But I figured once *Rockford* went into syndication, the profit sharing would be my real reward, an annuity for my old age.

Early in 1979, someone at Universal mistakenly sent me an accounting sheet showing that *The Rockford Files* had lost $9.5 million in its first five years on the air. It shocked me. I thought we were doing well.

It's demoralizing to break your neck bringing a show in on budget and on schedule only to find you've been wasting your time and effort because they've been bookkeeping you to death.

Lew Wasserman was known as "the King of Hollywood" for good reason. As head of MCA/Universal, he was both feared and admired. As an agent with MCA, Wasserman had made groundbreaking deals for his clients. He incorporated Jack Benny and sold the entity to a radio network so Benny paid less than half the taxes he would have as a salaried employee. Wasserman somehow got Warner Bros. to pay a B actor named Ronald Reagan a million dollars a year in the 1940s. Reagan returned the favor when, as president of the Screen Actors Guild, he secured favorable treatment from the Guild for MCA. In the 1950s, Wasserman got Jimmy Stewart a percentage of the gross for *Winchester '73* and made him rich. Before that even the biggest stars got only a percentage of the elusive net, not "points" off the top.

Wasserman's hard bargains for his clients had helped bring down the studio system. As head of Universal, he created the thing that replaced it, a diversified entertainment company with tentacles in all areas of the business.

Wasserman was smarter and tougher than the original Hollywood moguls and he had more power. Say what you want about Jack Warner, Sam Goldwyn, Louis B. Mayer, and Harry Cohn, they were moviemakers first and businessmen second. Wasserman never much cared for movies and never pretended otherwise. He was fixated on the bottom line. He shunned publicity (other than for his art collection) and stayed in the background while cultivating connections with big labor unions, elected officials, and underworld bosses.

MCA bought the failing Universal Pictures and turned it into the industry's biggest supplier of television programs. Universal independently produced television and radio series, pioneered made-for-TV movies, and bought the Paramount film library and rented the movies out to TV stations. In 1975, Universal invented the summer blockbuster by releasing *Jaws* in hundreds of theaters across the US while saturating the TV airwaves with commercials.

Wasserman sold Universal to Matsushita Electric in 1990 for $6.6 billion and walked away with $300 million for himself.

I n the summer of '79, Bill Saxon and I were in Thailand playing golf. When it came time to leave, we wanted to buy gifts for our girls—we both have two daughters—and we heard about a department store in downtown Bangkok where they sold a special pin made from an orchid dipped in gold, and we asked our driver to take us there. We'd no sooner entered the store when someone shouted, "Rockford! Rockford!" Before we knew it, we were swamped by people wanting autographs and trying to touch me or tear off a piece of my clothing. It took a police escort to get us out of there. When we were safely back in the car, I said to Billy Dee, "And Universal tells me that *Rockford* hasn't paid out yet! If people in Thailand know me, how can the show be doing so poorly?"

Of course, *Rockford* wasn't doing poorly; it was earning millions of dollars in syndication. It was playing all over the world, morning, noon, and night, dubbed or subtitled in dozens of languages. *The Rockford Files* was one of the most successful television series ever, yet I wasn't getting a dime.

I can't stand big people hurting little people. Especially me. So I sued Universal for breach of contract and fraud for withholding my rightful share of the profits. I'd decided I wasn't going to put any more paintings on Lew Wasserman's wall.

As soon as the legal papers were filed, I began hearing the same things I'd heard when I sued Warner Bros. twenty years before: "You'll never beat them," "They'll draw out the litigation until you're bankrupt," and, of course, "You'll never work in this town again."

Lew Wasserman and Universal didn't invent "creative accounting," they just made it a science. Creative accounting is too polite a term for what Universal was doing, it was flat-out larceny. They systematically inflated the expenses to reduce—to *wipe out*—the net profit. They had all kinds of tricks. They double-dipped and triple-charged, they tacked on expenses unrelated to the actual production. It was a shell game with the net as the shell, a clever, intricate way of stealing money.

In one *Rockford* episode, we drove a car into a lake. Universal charged us full price for the car, and we had to repair it before we returned it to them. In another episode, there was a crash, and we had to buy the same damn car from them . . . and repair it again.

If the Universal set department bought something for us for $100, the studio arbitrarily multiplied it by 3.3, so it cost $330. After we used the item, they charged us another third of the stepped-up cost to take it away. Now we were at about $450. The studio added another third for its "generic account." To this day, I don't know what that means, but now we're up to $600. Then they tacked on another 20 percent for "overhead." In the end, a $100 item was charged to the series at over $700.

Universal also charged us a $50,000 "distribution fee" for each *Rockford* episode. We discovered that "distribution" consisted of having two Teamsters drive the film from Universal in North Hollywood to NBC in Burbank, a distance of five miles. Fifty thousand dollars per episode amounted to more than $6 million over the life of the series. Universal also charged us interest on the pretext that they could have taken the money spent on production and invested it in certificates of deposit.

Universal tried to tell us that despite taking in $120 million in revenues from syndication and foreign sales, the show had earned less than $1 million in profits. And it wasn't an isolated case. I didn't know it then, but that was standard operating procedure for Universal. It had been happening to an awful lot of actors, writers, and producers for a long time, prompting Steve Cannell to joke that Universal's definition of "net profit" was that "everyone in the universe gets something before you do." In those days, the studios would rather steal than do it right. They might have made even *more* money if they'd played it straight, but it wasn't in their nature.

If you had the nerve to complain, they pretended not to know what you were talking about. If you persisted, they shrugged their shoulders and told you to sue them. Few people did—it was too expensive. And if anybody had the money to hire a battery of lawyers and the guts to risk his career, Universal would drag out the litigation for years. It was like being in business with the Mafia, only Universal didn't need a gun, just a pencil.

Well, I had the money in the bank—over $5 million. I'd put it there just in case, and I didn't care about hurting my career. I was in it for the duration.

In December 1988, after seven years of filings and depositions, Universal sent me a check for $607,000. It was an insult. A few months later, they offered $6 million. I declined. We'd found out something Universal didn't want us to know.

Universal's salesmen went to TV stations and pitched reruns of popular series, those that had attained the magic number of one hundred episodes. My lawyers discovered that Universal was syndicating *The Rockford Files* as part of a package. Station managers were told they could have *Rockford* cheap, but only if they'd also take the less popular *Quincy*. Universal would bill *Quincy* at twice the rate of *Rockford*. In other words, on paper, *Rockford* earned only a fraction of the income it should have commanded, cheating me out of millions of dollars in profits.

When we confronted Universal with this knowledge, they immediately offered to settle out of court if we would seal the record. They didn't want this practice revealed, and they certainly didn't want to open their books.

On the day we were scheduled for trial, Universal offered me a huge settlement. I didn't want to take it. I wanted to tell my side of the story to a jury. And I wanted to expose Universal's bookkeeping tricks.

My lawyer warned me that we'd be rolling the dice. "Anything can happen in a trial," he said. "You could wind up with nothing, and you'll be out millions in legal fees."

I told him I was willing to take that chance.

Everybody around me told me I was crazy. Except Lois, who said she'd be fine with whatever I decided. But everyone else said, "Don't snatch defeat from the jaws of victory." My manager, Bill Robinson, told me, "Let it go; you've won!"

I chewed on it, and I finally realized they were right.

On March 23, 1989, we settled the case "on the courthouse steps." As part of the settlement agreement, I promised not to reveal the amount Universal paid me. I'd sued them for $22.5 million—$7.5 million in compensatory damages and $15 million in punitives. My legal fees were about $2.2 million. It's been reported that I walked away with anywhere from $9 million to $20 million. I can't legally comment on that, but I can say that for a week or two afterward, Lois had to keep telling me to wipe the grin off my face, and that she drew a big "V" for victory in lipstick on our front door that stayed there for a year.

The studios have always tried to get whatever they can by any means necessary. Their attitude is, if you want what's yours, you'll have to come and take it from them. They get away with it because people don't complain. If more actors and independent producers fought them, I think the practice of creative bookkeeping would be far less pervasive. So my advice to anyone in a similar position is to *fight them*. What's yours is yours, and you should go after it. My lawsuit proved that you *can* beat the system if you're determined enough. I think it also sent a message to future business partners that I will not be diddled, and to that extent it may have discouraged some people from doing business with me. They figured, "I don't want to get with him because if we try to steal, he's going to catch us." Well, good riddance.

I'll tell you something funny, though: not two weeks after we settled, a messenger arrived at the house with two scripts, and one of them was from Universal.

No hard feelings, I guess.

When I was making *Rockford* episodes, I used to love to get up and go to work every day. I was awake before the alarm went off. I was always the first one on the set in the morning and the last one to leave at night because I enjoyed it so much. And I wanted to experience that again.

Making TV movies is a little like formula car racing, where you have strict limits on the engine, transmission, suspension, aerodynamics, even the tires. The idea is to get everybody competing on a level playing field and then see who's smart enough to develop a winning formula. Compared to feature films, TV movies have lots of restrictions, too. They run as long on the screen as features, but you have to make them in a fraction of the time at a fraction of the cost. I loved that challenge. I wanted to see if I could shuffle all the elements and produce good films under the circumstances. That's why I decided to make the two-hour *Rockford* movies.

And for the money.

Beginning in 1994, we made eight *Rockford* movies. I tried to keep my production company as far away from Universal as possible. I told the studio people when we were negotiating that if I had to drive onto that lot every day, it would be like sticking a knife in my ribs. There were no accounting problems because it was cash and carry: they gave me the money, I gave them the film. In that order.

We chose CBS over NBC because CBS promised us the time slot after *Murder, She Wrote* on Sunday nights. We figured Angela Lansbury's audience would stick around for us, and we were right: the first *Rockford* movie, *I Still Love LA,* was the highest-rated TV movie of the 1994–95 season.

Rockford did to the television detective what *Maverick* did to the TV cowboy: back in the 1950s, there were fifteen cowboy shows and Bret Maverick knocked them all off. Then Jim Rockford came along in the '70s with his tongue in his cheek and wiped out all the detective series.

I guess I have a knack for killing genres.

The Polaroid instant camera was invented in the 1950s by Edwin Land, a physicist who was inspired when his three-year-old daughter asked him why she couldn't instantly see a photo he had taken of her. The camera was popular all through the 1960s and '70s. In 1977, Polaroid introduced the One Step, the latest in a line of cameras with self-developing film. In those days, it was a big deal to get a photo in sixty seconds rather than waiting days to get film developed.

I was doing *Rockford* when Polaroid approached me. I'd had several offers to do commercials, some for more money, but I chose Polaroid because they did things right and weren't stingy with production dollars. And I wanted to see if, later in life, I could have a hit television series, do the occasional movie, and make commercials as well.

And for the money.

I had a lot of fun doing them.

I've been asked a hundred times about the "stigma" of doing commercials. Well, I'm an actor. I hire out. I'm not afraid of hurting my *image*. I figured if Henry Fonda, Laurence Olivier, John Wayne, and Orson Welles could do commercials, so could I.

If you do it right, you don't demean yourself by selling a product, and you can be just as good in a commercial as in a feature film. I was selective: I wouldn't do commercials for beer, bug spray, or underarm deodorant. I did Mazda commercials, I was the spokesman for the Beef Industry Council ("Beef: It's what's for dinner!") until I had heart surgery to relieve blocked arteries. In a Chevy Tahoe commercial, I recited a poem called "Nobody Knows It but Me" that sounded like Walt Whitman or Robert Louis Stevenson but was actually written by copywriter Patrick O'Leary. I didn't want to be a pitchman because I don't believe in the hard sell. With Polaroid, I didn't want to get into technical details, either. I just wanted to entertain the audience and leave them with a good feeling about the camera.

I wanted the commercials to be at least as entertaining as the programs they interrupted, and I told the Polaroid people that I didn't ever want the humor to wear thin. That's why we made so many of them, about 250 over a five-year period. I didn't want viewers to see a given commercial more than a few times.

The first one with Mariette Hartley was in 1977, and our collaboration would last for almost six years. Jack Dillon, from the Doyle Dane Bernbach ad agency, wrote all the scripts. Mariette and I may have occasionally added something or moved things around a little, but for the most part the writing was so good we didn't have to change a thing. (Jack was a fiction writer as well, with over a hundred short stories and half a dozen novels to his credit.) Jack's spots were short and sweet.

We had a good thing going. Mariette is a wonderful actress and we got along well. They'd hired her for one day and we clicked immediately. With her deadpan delivery, we fell into a kind of "Bickersons" back-and-forth banter. She'd say it's black and I'd say it's white and she usually had the last word:

> JG: Polaroid's One Step is the simplest camera in the world. You just press one button.
> MH: How many does it have?
> JG: One.
> MH: Then that's all you *can* press.

> JG: This is Polaroid's new Time Zero One Step.
> MH: Pretty. Why is it black?
> JG: So you'll know it's the Time Zero One Step. And here's the world's fastest developing color [takes her picture]. You see it in seconds now, not minutes.
> MH: Look at that color! But why a "Time Zero" One Step?
> JG: It comes with a pack of Time Zero Supercolor film in this made-for-each-other pack.
> MH: Certainly are made for each other.
> JG: Just like coffee and cream . . .
> MH: Rolls and Royce . . .
> JG: Or me and you.
> MH: Try ham and cheese.

The chemistry was so great, in fact, a lot of people thought we were married in real life. Probably the ones who thought I was really Maverick. (The same thing happened after the success of *Mrs. Miniver* in the 1940s. The studio got thousands of letters urging Walter Pidgeon and Greer Garson to divorce their respective spouses and marry each other.) It got so bad that Mariette had a T-shirt made that said, "I am NOT Mrs. James Garner." When Mariette's daughter Justine was born, she got another T-shirt saying, "I Am NOT James Garner's Baby." Then I saw a woman on the street wearing one that said, "I Am NOT Mrs. James Garner, Either." The whole thing didn't make Lois too happy, so I got *her* one that said, "I'm the REAL Mrs. James Garner."

After a year, they were still paying Mariette scale. I felt they needed to make a better deal with her, because it just wasn't right for me to be making so much more than she was. So I did a naughty thing: I called her and told her all about it. Then *she* did a naughty thing and stuck it to them pretty good. But Polaroid sold a ton of cameras and everybody wound up happy.

Making those commercials with Mariette was a wonderful experience. I consider them a high point in my acting career. During that period, Mariette also did a *Rockford* episode. We were at Paradise Cove shooting a scene in which we kiss, and a photographer hiding in the bushes with a long lens snapped us and sold the photo to the tabloids, which passed it off as a real kiss. It caused a commotion at home for both of us, I can tell you.

I was never a photography bug, but when Polaroid introduced an instant movie camera, I brought a prototype with me on a golfing trip to Scotland. I took movies of everything I saw and did over there, thinking we might use them in future commercials. But none of the movies came out. The film speed was so low, everything turned out dark and blurry, so Polaroid never did well with the camera. And as digital photography made the instant camera obsolete, the company filed for a series of reorganizations and finally went out of business.

CHAPTER EIGHT

Golf

————————

The first time I played golf was in Texas, in the snow, while on tour in *The Caine Mutiny Court Martial*. Playing town after town on our way across the country, we did a lot of short hops in the bus. During the day, we'd go out and play the local muni course, sometimes in deep snow, with a red ball. We were just goofing around.

I didn't start playing seriously (only a golfer would put those two words together) until the late 1950s, after I'd signed with Warner Bros. I played every day I wasn't shooting a picture or making a *Maverick* episode, usually at Griffith Park, one of LA's busy public courses.

I didn't take lessons; I learned to play by observation. When my brother Jack moved to California, he helped me with this and the other, and I got better because of him. Years later John Cook gave me some pointers as well, and Gary Player once gave me a great putting tip. That's about the only real instruction I've ever had. Of course, like most golfers, I always kept my ears open for tips about the golf swing, what Bel-Air pro Eddie Merrins calls "bootleg lessons."

Golf is the most competitive game I know. You're playing against yourself as well as your opponents. It's an endless quest for perfection that you'll never achieve. It can be a punishing game, especially for a pessimist like me.

Mac Davis loved to kid me about it, and I admit my attitude wasn't the best. Whenever I'd hit a shot that looked like it *might* be out of bounds, I was always *certain* it was, and I'd say, "*Shit,* it's OB!"

"Be positive!" Mac would say.

"Okay, I'm *positive* it's out of bounds!"

Mac and I started playing golf together at the Bel-Air Country Club in Los Angeles in the early 1980s. Both of us were five or six handicappers, and we got to be pretty much a pair around the club. We played four or five days a week in a regular match with a bunch of other guys. We'd square off into foursomes, so Mac and I would be opponents one day, partners the next.

Mac's wife, Lisë, a former nurse, is one of the nicest people I know. I didn't meet her through Mac, though; she and I met when they took me to Cedars-Sinai with twelve broken ribs. I'd been filming a scene on a mechanical horse for an episode of *Bret Maverick.* The guy who was running it hadn't done it before and he threw me fifteen feet. I managed to duck my head before I hit, but landed on my left rib cage and broke 'em all.

In addition to being sweet, Lisë is gorgeous. When I woke up in the hospital, the first thing I saw was her radiant face, this beautiful angel looking down at me. I *literally* thought I'd died and gone to heaven.

One of the great things about golf is the camaraderie. In addition to my friendship with Mac Davis, the game really glued Bill Saxon and me together and gave us something to do besides sitting around talking about the old days in Norman. Since Lois didn't like to travel, whenever I'd get an invitation for me and my wife, I'd say, "My wife can't make it—can I bring my friend?" (Lois loved that I played golf because it got me out of the house. She never complained that I played too much or that she was a "golf widow." She doesn't play. I wouldn't let her.)

When we started playing together, I had to give Bill Saxon two strokes a side. His swing wasn't great, but he's strong, like an old country boy, and he hit the ball far. He improved steadily and we ended up playing even. Now that I no longer play, I sit on the sidelines cheering him on as he shoots his age every other day. As of this writing, he's done it almost two hundred times.

I shot my age when I was seventy, and it was one of the biggest thrills I've had in golf. I can't prove it, but I bet it's rarer than making a hole in one. It takes skill, good luck, and, of course, *longevity*. (It's the one athletic accomplishment I can think of that *requires* it.) But mere life span isn't enough, because shooting your age, like getting old, isn't for sissies. Most of those who do it are good athletes who've been playing golf for decades. They've managed to avoid major injuries and illnesses and have learned to play through the minor ones. Most of the golfers who consistently shoot their age were good players in their younger years.

During the 1970s, Bill Saxon and I must have played in a hundred PGA Tour pro-ams. I'd get an invitation and would ask to bring Billy Dee along and we'd hop in his jet. My brother Jack would often join us. He taught Bill a lot about the game and sometimes caddied for him.

We played a lot with "super seniors"—guys like Dow Finsterwald, Tommy Aaron, Gene Littler, Bobby Nichols, Don January, Phil Rodgers. I got to meet and spend time with Byron Nelson, one of the nicest men I've ever known.

One of the most memorable rounds was at Champions Golf Club in Houston with Jackie Burke and Jimmy Demaret. Jimmy was a great player, but he was also a snappy dresser, a singer, and a raconteur who entertained in clubs along the tour. He was one of the first golfers to become a TV commentator, on *Shell's Wonderful World of Golf.* Oh, and he somehow found time to win thirty PGA Tour events, including three Masters titles. All the more remarkable when you consider that he rarely practiced because, as Dan Jenkins said, "it cut into his party time."

"Mister Dee-muh-ray," as I called him, had a wonderful disposition, was fun to be with, and was something of a philosopher: he once pointed out that "golf and sex are about the only things you can enjoy without being good at."

In the early 1960s, golf was beginning to take off on television, mostly thanks to Arnold Palmer's dashing style of play. The networks began broadcasting tournaments live, the pros were beginning to make more prize money, and it was the dawn of the age of endorsements.

Charles Coody, Gene Littler, and Tommy Aaron were among the first endorsers. They rigged a deal to wear a goofy hat with the Amana appliance logo in the middle of it. They got fifty bucks every time they appeared on television wearing it. It didn't seem to matter to anyone that appliances had nothing to do with golf. The Amana company would also fly the pros to Iowa to play in a tournament in return for a discount on freezers.

Arnold Palmer was the first to have his own brand, with the umbrella logo on everything. Look what blossomed from that: now PGA touring pros are covered with almost as much advertising as NASCAR drivers.

In the early 1960s, I played against Sam Snead on a TV show called *Celebrity Golf.* Each week Snead took on a different entertainer in a nine-hole match. Some of Snead's other opponents on the show were Perry Como, Dean Martin, Bob Hope, Robert Wagner, Randolph

Scott, and Ray Milland. Though our match was on a course I'd never played before, Brentwood Country Club in Los Angeles, I managed to make four pars and two birdies to tie Snead. Or rather, he tied me. He had to eagle one hole and sink a forty-foot putt on another to do it. He wasn't happy about that, I can tell you. Snead was a curmudgeon and full of himself. I think he had the first nickel he ever made. But he could play.

Bill Saxon and I once played with Dan Jenkins in an LPGA pro-am in Las Vegas. Bill took a practice swing and accidentally hit me in the head with his driver. It didn't hurt me, but I played it to the hilt, dropping to the ground, pretending to be unconscious. It gave Dan quite a start until he realized I was acting. Said he thought he'd witnessed James Garner being murdered by his best friend.

When we were making a *Rockford* episode in the mid-1970s, Tom Selleck reminded me that we'd first met years before, at Joe Kirkwood's nine-hole golf course in the San Fernando Valley. I used to jump over there from the studio when I was doing *Maverick*. One day Tom, then still in his teens, was playing the course and he almost hit me with a golf ball. I'd forgotten the incident, but Tom told me I slowly turned and said, "I believe the expression is 'Fore!'"

One year Saxon and I played in a tournament in Tucson where we each won a gross of Ram golf balls. Forgetting the tournament was sponsored by Ram, I asked if I could have Titleists instead. Bill pretended he didn't know me.

I played with President Clinton at Congressional Country Club in Bethesda, Maryland. Someone had presented him with several drivers made of metal from a Russian satellite, of all things. The president gave me one of them, and I was of course honored to receive a gift from the president of the United States. I was leaving town the next morning, so I took the driver back to my hotel, packed it in my golf bag, then zipped up and locked the outer travel bag.

While lying in bed watching TV that night, I received a call from the president. He asked me if I'd remembered to take the driver. I said I was sure I had, but I told him to wait a minute while I looked. I put down the phone, went to the closet, unlocked and unzipped the bag and confirmed that the driver was there. As I returned to the phone, I realized I'd just put the leader of the free world on hold. I got back on the line and told him I had the driver. I thought that would end the conversation, but the president kept talking, and we chatted about this and that for what seemed like twenty minutes until it dawned on me that he'd called just to chew the fat. I don't know what came over me, but I blurted out, "Pardon me, Mr. President, don't you have anything better to do than talk to *me*?" He had a good laugh at that. Luckily. I never used the satellite driver, by the way. I think it's still in the garage.

Golf has been berry, berry good to me. It's taken me around the world. In the fall of 1995, Lois and I flew up to Canada and had dinner with Stuart Margolin and his wife Pat—at the time they lived off the coast of Vancouver—then we all caught a late-night train to the Rockies. The next afternoon we were in Jasper, Alberta, one of the most beautiful places I've ever seen. We stayed in a lodge, and Stuart and I played golf every day. At night, there were elk outside our rooms. On the course one day, I hit a ball that landed underneath a big buck elk. We were playing with a native Canadian who said, "I think you'd better leave your ball there." It was getting near rutting season so you didn't fool around with them.

Most of my golf travels were with Bill Saxon. We played in the Hawaiian Open on Oahu and at the opening of the Kapalua Village Golf Course on Maui with Bill's son Steve and Arnold Palmer. We flew to Japan in the early 1970s, when golf was just getting popular there, and played several rounds with Japanese pros and celebrities to promote the Lobo golf club. We'd invested in the company along with Charles Coody and Johnny Unitas. The trip was a success: we sold a few hundred sets of Lobos and got to play four or five of the best courses in Japan. Now they have about three thousand courses, by the way, second only to the United States, with more than fifteen thousand.

In 1978, Bill and I flew to Scotland and stayed at the Gleneagles Hotel. From there we went by car each day to play some of the major golf courses in Scotland: the King's and Queen's courses, Turnberry, Muirfield, Gullane No. 1, North Berwick, and St. Andrews, the cradle of golf, where we played with Keith Mackenzie, the secretary of the Royal and Ancient Golf Club, and his friend Stewart Lawson. After a guided tour of the old clubhouse with all its little rooms, we engaged in a preround ritual: in a small locker room in the basement, we all downed a dram—and not a *wee* dram—of Scotch, which our hosts assured us would take care of us for at least nine holes.

We played a match: Scots against Yanks, no strokes, a golf ball to each winner from the losers. Bill made par on the seventeenth, the famous "Road Hole," to put us two-up with one hole to play. Our Scottish opponents declared the match over, gave us each a ball (an *old* ball), and started walking in. Bill and I wanted to finish the round, so we played number 18. After which Mr. Mackenzie invited us to join the R&A Club. Not appreciating what an honor it is, we said, "No, thanks. We already belong to too many clubs." Brilliant. We went over to Scotland again a year or two later with our wives. We were guests at the British Open and were flown by helicopter to Muirfield for the final day of the championship.

While Bill and I were playing on the southern coast of Spain in the fall of 1999, we dropped by Valderrama to watch the World Golf Championship. Tiger Woods was in the field and Bill wanted to meet him, so I offered to perform the introduction, even though I'd never met Tiger myself. We stood near the tenth tee waiting for Tiger, and as he passed within two feet of us, I said, in my best James Garner voice, "Well, hello, Mr. Woods!" Tiger blew right past us without turning his head. Never even blinked. I don't think he was being rude; I think he was so focused on golf that he was oblivious to everything around him.

In Singapore, we teed off at 5:00 a.m. and by 8:30 it was so hot I had the dry heaves. On the last hole you had to walk down into a ravine and then up the other side to get to the green. I didn't think I'd make it to the clubhouse. In Thailand, we played the "Army Course" with two generals amid very tight security: armed troops lined the fairways and Jeeps with mounted machine guns escorted us.

For many years we played in the Darrell (Royal) and Willie (Nelson) Golf Tournament in Texas with the greats of country music in attendance. Darrell is the winningest coach in University of Texas football history, having won three national championships. He's also a good friend. Willie Nelson is, well, Willie Nelson, as much a character as anyone I've ever met. Willie is one of the wittiest people I know, and probably the most tolerant: He accepts everyone on their own terms, rich or poor, young or old.

The golf was fun, but the entertainment at night was outstanding. I love country music, and the musicians were bigger-than-life personalities, guys who were up and down, in and out of love, lying, cheating, drinking, always looking for a "hook" for the next song. The biggest "personality" was Waylon Jennings. We became good friends, and I actually toured with Waylon for a few weeks. If it had been more than that, I don't think I'd be alive today.

After great performers like the Gatlin Brothers, George Strait, Alex Harvey, Vince Gill, and Mickey Newbury did their sets on stage, they'd go off to separate rooms for "pickin' 'n' grinnin'" sessions. There'd be a picker here and a picker there. That's where I met Ed Bruce, the guy who wrote "Mammas Don't Let Your Babies Grow Up to Be Cowboys." I later cast him in *Bret Maverick*.

I had an awful temper on the golf course, and I threw clubs when I got mad. I think one of them is still in the air. I threw so many clubs I finally had to heed Tommy Bolt's advice. "Terrible Tommy," aka "Thunder Bolt," was a good guy and a great PGA Tour player who won a lot of tournaments, including the US Open. But he was more famous for his temper. He advised always to throw the club *down the fairway*. That way you don't have to go back for it. That valuable tip saved me a lot of steps over the years, because I was a world champion club thrower. But what I could *really* do was bury it. Give me some damp ground and I could sink an iron *that* deep. Just *try* to get that sucker out.

I'd get so mad playing golf . . . it was a side of me that most people never saw. I'd get especially angry over missing a short putt. I realize now that my temper caused me to do things that made people want to go hide.

In the mid-1970s, Bill Saxon and I played a money-raiser in Orlando, Florida, for returning Vietnam POWs. A good-size crowd turned out to watch and support men who had sacrificed so much for the country. Our foursome included PGA Tour pro Charles Coody and a former POW, a major, as I recall. The format was best-ball of foursome. On the third or fourth hole, the other three had all hit into the water and I was the only one left who could make par for the team. I had an uphill putt of about three feet. As I settled over the ball, Coody said, "Okay, Jim, keep your head down and stroke 'er in there." Well, I missed it, and with a couple hundred people watching, I hurled my putter into the swamp. The crowd gasped. I stomped off the green, ranting and raving: "I've been playing golf for twenty years and I don't need *Charles effin' Coody* to tell me to keep my head down! *Nobody* tells me to keep my head down!"

Of course, that was my excuse for missing the putt. I stormed to the next hole, a par three, and grabbed any old club out of the bag and promptly hit the ball in the water. I kept going to the next tee and hit my drive before the rest of my foursome arrived. Still steaming, I sat down on a bench to wait for them. Bill's wife, Wylodean, whom I'd known since grade school in Norman, had been in the gallery and witnessed my outburst. She came over and sat down beside me. I glared at her and said, "*NOW* WHAT?"

"Well, excuse me!" she said.

The look of hurt and surprise on Wylodean's face snapped me out of my tantrum. I apologized profusely. I told her I hadn't meant to be so rude and that I realized I'd made an ass of myself. She was gracious and never mentioned it again. That's when I hit bottom. From then on, I was more aware of my temper and more in control of it, and as I got older, the outbursts were fewer and farther between.

I'd get angriest when I missed a putt, maybe because I was usually a pretty fair putter. I have a different approach to it than most people: I close my eyes.

Gary Player taught me that. He said, "Jim, how far is that putt?"

"Twenty feet."

"Okay, now how much does it break?"

I did my little calculations, plumb bob, whatever. "Eight inches."

"Okay," he said, "Now line up, you close your eyes, visualize the roll, and hit that ball exactly eighteen feet, eight inches."

It went right in the center of the hole.

I used that method until I quit playing three years ago. I've turned around and taught it to other people, and it worked for them, too. It isn't one of those, "I've got the secret now" things; it's mental.

There are some pretty good golf courses in and around Los Angeles: Riviera, Bel-Air, Rancho Park, Lakeside, Los Angeles Country Club North, Wilshire Country Club. I was a member at Riviera for twelve years. Had a regular game there with Bill Saxon, who was also a member, and Pat Harrington Jr., a talented actor-comedian who'd played Guido Panzini, the Italian golf pro, on *The Steve Allen Show* in the 1950s and Dwayne Schneider on the 1980s sitcom *One Day at a Time*.

There were lots of entertainers at Riviera, including Dean Martin, Vic Damone, Donald O'Connor, Jim Backus, and Jack Ging, a good golfer and fellow Oklahoman who'd starred as a halfback at OU. The best golfer in the showbiz lot was an actor named Bob Wilkie, a big man who usually played heavies.

The sportswriter Jim Murray was also a member at Riviera. Jim wasn't an exceptional player, but he loved the game. When he made a hole in one on the 230-yard fourth hole, someone asked him what club he'd hit. "I cut a little driver in there," he said.

In 1988, the family that owned Riviera sold it to a Japanese businessman who made it harder and harder to get a tee time. Bill Saxon joined Bel-Air and suggested I do the same. I didn't think I could get into Bel-Air because Lois is Jewish, but it wasn't a problem. It was the best move I ever made.

A good caddie is indispensable. He calms you down when you need it and thinks for you when your brain goes fuzzy. To say nothing of his knowledge of the course. My regular caddie at Bel-Air was New York Mike, whose real name is Michael Loughran and, yes, he's originally from the Bronx. Mike is a good caddie and a pal. He knows what he's doing. He'd help me read putts, and I'd either agree or overrule him. (I knew those little bitty greens at Bel-Air just about as well as anybody.) You play better when you have a caddie who knows his business, and it enhances your enjoyment of the game. I took Mike with me to the Crosby whenever I could.

Bing Crosby started a tournament in 1937 at Rancho Santa Fe, near San Diego, in which entertainers, athletes, and businessmen joined the best golfers in the world for a week of golf and fellowship. Bing was a pretty fair golfer in his own right. In 1930, carrying a two handicap as a member at Lakeside, he won several club championships and competed in the US and British Amateurs. After World War II, Bing moved the tournament to the Monterey

Peninsula, an area Robert Louis Stevenson described as "the most felicitous meeting of land and sea in creation." The golf courses there are so spectacularly beautiful, with breathtaking views wherever you look, it's hard to concentrate on your game.

In those days, Bing's tournament was played on three courses, Spyglass Hill, Cypress Point, and Pebble Beach. At Spyglass, the newest of the three, I always felt I was walking uphill. Cypress Point is one of the most exclusive clubs in the world and the golf course is uniquely beautiful and punishing. The par-three, sixteenth hole is probably the most difficult, and most scenic, par three in the world. But Pebble Beach is the star. It's a public course, though you have to pay a $500 green fee and book well in advance to play it.

Bing personally selected the amateurs for the tournament but let the pros choose their partners. A lot changed after he died, but the AT&T, as it is now called, is still a unique format on the PGA Tour. While most pro-ams are a separate contest played on the Wednesday before the four-day professional tournament, the AT&T pro-am is three days of play—Thursday, Friday, and Saturday—concurrent with the pro tournament. The amateurs, who get their full handicap, team with professionals and play all three courses. Amateurs who qualify in the low ten pro-am teams get to play on television on Sunday at Pebble Beach.

Rain and wind are usually a problem, so much so that Jim Murray suggested that if Bing and Bob Hope ever wanted to do a road picture about the Crosby, they could call it *The Road to Pneumonia*. But I always felt that the worse the weather, the better chance I had to win, because it didn't bother me as much as it did higher handicappers like Jack Lemmon, who carried an 18 from Hillcrest.

Jack loved golf and played in the Crosby/AT&T thirty-four years in a row . . . but never made the cut. Jack's professional partner, Peter Jacobsen, affectionately nicknamed him "the Human Hinge" for his terrible swing. Byron Nelson once analyzed it in slow motion and identified eleven major flaws. On top of that, Jack was terrified of playing in front of a crowd. Said he'd rather play *Hamlet* with no rehearsal than play golf on television.

Golf spectators are knowledgeable, quiet, and respectful (but not always—more about that later). They are so polite, in fact, that their silence can be intimidating. You swear you can feel every set of eyes on you. But galleries didn't bother me, and I developed a little trick for playing in televised tournaments. It's humiliating to hit a bad shot on national TV. The good news is that the camera stays on the golfer, not on the flight of the ball, so when I hit my shot, even if it was a shank or a snap-hook, I just held my finish, smiled, and strode briskly down the fairway. I used the technique more than once with excellent results. The only time it failed was when my ball hit the camera lens.

Jack Lemmon wanted to make the cut and play on Sunday more than anything else in the world, and we were all pulling for him. But he couldn't seem to get out of his own way. To give you an idea, on the long, par-three seventeenth at Pebble Beach one year, we had a breeze at our backs and Jack nailed a driver right at the flag. Unfortunately, the ball sailed forty yards over the green. It was the only good shot he hit all day, but it was in the ocean.

Another year Jack and Peter Jacobsen were only a few shots behind the lead and looked certain to make the cut when the pro-am was canceled because of heavy rain. And then there was the time Jack shanked one into his hotel room at the Del Monte Lodge. His wife Felicia was in the john at the time. She said the ball ricocheting off the walls sounded like a machine gun and she thought terrorists were attacking Carmel.

Jack always accepted defeat gracefully. His perseverance and good humor were inspirational. I think that's why he had so many golf fans rooting for him. They could relate to his tribulations on the course, like when he'd take three strokes to get out of a bunker. Maybe even non-golfers identified with his struggle. It became an annual story line—a quest that became ever more urgent with each passing year. Peter Jacobsen said he would rather see Jack make the cut than win the tournament himself. But it wasn't to be.

Contrast Jack Lemmon with Bill Murray, whose behavior at the AT&T is a disgrace. He thinks he's mocking the whole thing by dressing like a slob and putting with the wrong end of the putter, but he's only making an ass of himself. He should have been banned from the tournament years ago after he tried to dance with that old lady in the bunker and she fell down. I don't care if *she* didn't mind, *I* did. I'm glad I was never paired with him, because I would have refused to play.

Clint Eastwood fell in love with the Monterey Peninsula in the 1950s, while in the army stationed at Ford Ord. He promised himself he'd settle there if he ever earned enough "crumbs." Well, Clint wound up with the whole bakery, and not only does he live on the Monterey Peninsula, he was elected mayor of Carmel in 1986, owns his own course there, Tehàma, and a piece of Pebble Beach Golf Links to boot. Clint played his first Crosby in 1965, when he was playing Rowdy Yates on the TV series *Rawhide*. He'd been interviewed on television and asked whether he'd be playing in the upcoming Crosby and he said, "No . . . I guess they don't like cowboys." Bing heard about it and sent Clint an invitation with a note, "See, we do like cowboys." Clint's been playing in the tournament ever since.

The Clambake, as Bing liked to call it, was one of the highlights of my golfing year, but in 1964, I almost didn't play. I'd banged up my ribs shooting the beach scene in *The Americanization of Emily*. I went to the hospital for x-rays and the doctor said they weren't broken, so I went back to work, though they were really sore. That night I drove to Pebble Beach for the tournament. The next day, Monday, I played a practice round and the ribs were still hurting. When I got back to the hotel there was a call from the hospital—they'd misread the x-rays and several ribs were broken after all. I didn't have to play until Thursday, so I went to a doctor in Monterey. He told me I couldn't do any more damage to my ribs or lungs by swinging a club, so I figured out how to play without worsening the pain: I just blew all the air out before swinging. I played okay that way and my team made the cut.

Bill Saxon and I were often in the same foursome at the Crosby, and in 1981, Nick Faldo was Bill's pro and I was paired with young John Cook, whom I'd known since he was a boy. My brother Jack was Bill's caddie. We usually played at Pebble Beach on Saturday, the big TV day, but the weather had been so bad, the tournament was shortened to three days and we finished at Spyglass. We'd played the back nine first, so the ninth hole was our eighteenth and final hole. I hooked my tee ball into the skinny pines in the left rough. The ball hit a spectator and knocked him down. I felt terrible and went over to make sure the man was okay. Then I said, "The hell with it, I'm not playing the hole." I always tried to stay out of the pros' way. If I didn't have a chance to help the team on a given hole, I'd pick up.

At that point in the tournament, John Cook was individually tied for the lead. A win would have been a big career boost and a windfall in prize money. As I walked down the fairway, I heard a shout from the gallery: "HEY, ROCKFORD! HEY, ROCKFORD!" Some jerk had been heckling me all day. I'd done my best to ignore it, but when he kept it up, I motioned him to be quiet because John was trying to putt out to win the tournament. John missed the putt, triggering a five-way playoff.

We signed our cards, and as I walked through the gallery, I said, "Who's that loudmouth?" The crowd parted and there were two guys in their twenties who'd obviously been drinking. I told the guy, "You shouldn't yell like that. It doesn't make any difference to me, but the pros are playing for a lot of money. John Cook would have won the tournament if he'd made that putt."

He didn't say anything, but started picking at my sweater, just below the neck.

"Don't do that!" I said.

"Or what? You'll deck me?"

Before he could finish saying, "deck me," I decked him.

The next thing I knew he was on the ground and Bill Saxon was trying to keep me off him.

"You want some more?" I said.

"I'm a big fan of yours, and my dad, who died of cancer, just loved you," he said.

Then he started crying.

Oh, man.

I'm happy to say that John won the tournament when he made a birdie on the third hole of the playoff. It was his first win and it launched a successful career on both the PGA Tour and now the Champions Tour.

I thought the incident was closed, but someone had snapped a photo and sold it to the tabloids. The next day it appeared all over the world. The heckler brought a case against me for assault and battery, claiming irrevocable harm because he was a recovering alcoholic and drug addict, and I had intentionally inflicted emotional distress on him.

I had no such intention. I only wanted to beat the crap out of him.

The complaint alleged $2 million in damages. The trial was in Monterey a few months later. I took the stand and told my side of the story. When the jury came in after deliberating for all of half an hour, the judge asked if they'd reached a verdict. The foreman said, "Yes, Your Honor, we have two statements: One, Mr. Garner's not guilty, and two . . . we'd like to have our picture taken with him."

With Bill Saxon's airplane at our disposal, we'd fly to Greensboro, Charlotte, Atlanta, Asheville, and Tampa to play in pro-ams and other golfing events. We didn't miss too many in that part of the country.

Bill was an oil operator for most of his professional life. His company, Saxon Oil, would search out prospects and then round up investors to finance drilling. Arnold Palmer had been one of Bill's early investors and they became friends. They bought a golf course together near Orlando called the Bay Hill Club, and during the winters they had a regular game there at eleven o'clock every morning. When *Rockford* was on hiatus, I'd stay with Bill and join them. It was a great time and I got to meet and play with a lot of interesting people, including Arnold. I've never met anybody who enjoys golf more or plays harder to win a two-dollar Nassau than Arnold Palmer.

I've never been much of a gambler. I never bet the ponies or the lottery, and I don't care for casino games, but in the early 1950s, I used to go to Las Vegas on weekends. I'd take only one or two hundred dollars, because I wasn't making any money. I had a golfing buddy there, a blackjack dealer named Montana. Before I'd leave town he'd say, "How ya doin'?"

"Oh, I'm down about two hundred bucks."

"What time are you leaving?"

"Eleven o'clock."

"Okay, come in around ten thirty."

I'd sit down at his table and in half an hour, I'd have my two hundred back. But no more.

I played a lot of backgammon with Luis over the years, but never for money. I played poker, mostly in home games, though I did play in the World Series of Poker in 2006. Got knocked out in the first hour by a guy with a bigger full house than I had. Ordinarily my hand would've kept me going for a while.

I'm not a *bad* poker player; I just draw bad cards.

I learned the game around the kitchen table with Uncle John Bumgarner, who was a good player. He'd say, "We used to be wealthy; it cost me a lot of money to get this good."

If you're wondering whether being an actor helps at the poker table, yes and no. Yes on offense, like when you're bluffing, no when it comes to reading "tells." I'm terrible at that.

I don't bet on football games, but I love the NFL. I've been an Oakland Raiders nut since the 1970s. The late Dr. Robert Rosenfeld, who was my orthopedic surgeon, was also the Raiders' team doctor. I'd fly up to Oakland with him and sit on the sidelines with the players. There was a long stretch when the Raiders won whenever I showed up for a game and lost when I wasn't there. Soon if I wasn't there and they lost, they blamed me! When the Raiders moved to Los Angeles, I had season tickets at the Coliseum.

In the glory years, the Raiders had great players and a great coach in John Madden. George Blanda played until he was pushing fifty. Kenny "the Snake" Stabler could burn you at thirty yards; Fred Biletnikoff was as clutch a receiver as ever played the game; Jim Otto never missed a game—he never missed a *play*. Art Shell, Ted Hendricks, Gene Upshaw—I loved those guys.

There's an annual tournament at Bel-Air named for the swinging bridge across the ravine that bisects the tenth hole. It's a tough format: The first day of the tournament is better-ball of partners and on the second day, play is from the back tees and both balls count. On the third and final day it's alternate shot, which can be tough because you feel like an idiot when your partner hits a great drive and you screw up the next shot.

The bad news about the Swinging Bridge Tournament is that it draws a huge field and rounds take five hours. But everybody wants to play in it because it's so much fun. And hard to win.

In 1998, my regular partner couldn't play, so Bill Saxon suggested I team with John McKay, a friend of his from Dallas. John is a good player and he knew the course after having spent twenty years in LA with CBS Television. He'd played in the Swinging Bridge Tournament many times before.

On the first tee I told John, "I only ask two things: one, we never say we're sorry, and two, we never say, 'We really need this one, partner.'" (John later told me he's used that with partners ever since.)

John and I played well enough the first two days to stay in contention. On the last day, it all came down to the eighteenth hole. John hit a good drive, and after I put our approach shot to within three feet of the hole, John needed to sink the three-footer, which had a six-inch break, to win the tournament. With a crowd watching, John lined up the putt, hunched over the ball, and calmly stroked it into the cup.

I. Went. Crazy.

I was so thrilled, I didn't even mind going to the awards ceremony—I'd never gone in all the years before. When they handed me the trophy, I said, "I think I'd rather have this than an Oscar, because with an Oscar, you just go out and work and if you're lucky, it happens. But I went out to win this tournament." It was a moment I'll always remember.

Arthritis keeps me from playing golf now, and I miss it. Looking back, like all golfers, I had my strengths and weaknesses. I drove the ball pretty far, with a little fade. My irons were okay, except from about a hundred yards out. That shot was my Achilles' heel. My short game was pretty good, especially putting. Sometimes I didn't do what I was supposed to do on the golf course, but it wasn't because I choked. Spectators never bothered me, but my temper was a problem. I think I could have been a better player if I'd controlled it. I had a love/hate relationship with the game: I got frustrated when I didn't play well and I'd make myself miserable. If I hadn't been so hard on myself, I'd have enjoyed the game more. But golf took me all over the world and introduced me to many wonderful people. Bottom line, I've taken a lot more out of golf than golf has taken out of me.

CHAPTER NINE

Act-ing!

I didn't particularly want to be an actor, but by the time I reached my mid-twenties, I *really* didn't want to be a roustabout. Watching movies in the Sooner Theatre in Norman as a boy, acting was the last thing I could imagine. But after a hundred odd jobs, I was looking for clean, well-paid work, and I'm glad I found acting, because it pays the best and it's the most fun of all.

I was awful at first, stumbling around, hoping to get lucky. I didn't care about acting, I just wanted to support my family. I'd gotten married to Lois and had an instant family. Our daughter Kim was just out of the hospital, weak with polio. I had to get serious. The responsibilities of life made me pay attention to what I was doing on the screen.

I'm a Methodist, but not as an actor. I'm from the Spencer Tracy school: be on time, know your words, hit your marks, and tell the truth. I don't have any theories about acting and I don't think about how to do it, except that an actor shouldn't take himself too seriously, and shouldn't try to make acting something it isn't. Acting is just common sense. It isn't hard if you put yourself aside and just do what the writer wrote.

I don't have the background a lot of actors have. For one thing, I've never taken acting lessons. That's not true: in 1954, while playing a silent judge in *The Caine Mutiny Court Martial,* I briefly studied at the Herbert Berghof Studio in New York. When I say briefly, I mean one class. I couldn't see the point. When Warner Bros. put me under contract, I took one or two classes with their drama coach, Blair Cutting. All I remember about the whole experience with Blair is if the wind was strong, his hair would blow off.

In those days people kept telling me I needed a "foundation" in the theory and technique of the great acting teachers. I wondered about it at first, but then realized that my foundation was the life experience I'd had by the time I was twenty-five. I'd been all over the world and seen a lot. I figured I knew at least as much as someone who'd been to acting school. Let's face it: Anybody can be an actor. There are no qualifications. The only other profession like that is politics.

I learned my craft doing *Maverick*. Natalie Wood and I were both under contract to Warners at the time, and we worked together in *Cash McCall*. One day on the set, she said, "Jim, now that you've established yourself, you need to take some acting classes."

"Why would I want to do that?" I said. "I've got the top show on television. If and when things start to go south, I'll consider taking lessons, but until then I don't want to mess with a good thing."

I never thought acting was frivolous, though I thought some actors were. It's a worthy vocation if practiced right. But I have to laugh when I hear actors talking about their *art*. Hey, it's a *movie*. Just say the lines.

I could never teach anybody to act because I don't have a clue myself. The class would last about thirty seconds, because I'd tell them to just be yourself. Put yourself in the situation the character is in. How would *you* react to it? That's all I know.

I'm a very structured actor. I like to have the whole script in front of me before I shoot. I like it solid and I like to stick to it. (Some directors work without a script, but I don't think they're very good.) You can put the best actors and the best directors in the world out there, but they're nothing without the written word. The script is sacred. I don't improvise, because the writers write better than I do. So my first instinct is to leave the script exactly like it is. Actors like to tinker because it's easier that way. If they don't understand it the way it's written, they assume they know better than the writer. But the writer has a point of view that the actor does not. He's looking at the whole picture, not just one character.

The late writer-producer Larry Gelbart once said it's rare for a writer to find someone who wants to serve the material. "Not Gable," he said, "who refused to go down with the submarine, because Gable doesn't sink." Well, I'll sink. I'll do whatever's necessary to tell the story. That includes doing off-camera lines with fellow actors. It's a courtesy to a colleague, but it's also a service to the piece. You get better results from the actual person because it's consistent: If I do a scene with *you* and then read lines in my close-ups to *him* off-camera, the audience is going to see a difference.

I don't act—I *react* to what someone else does. Give me a "reactor" over an actor every time. A reactor is sensitive to what's going on around him. If you don't have something to react to, you're just out there chewing the scenery.

If you listen carefully, you remember your words. You hear what the other actor is saying and you get *involved*. I try to listen to every word—even if it isn't directed at me—and see the reaction to it. I try to stay with the dialogue and not anticipate it, to be in the action and react to it rather than just observe it. When you approach acting that way, you don't learn lines, you learn *thoughts*. When I can't remember a line, it's usually because it doesn't flow with the rest of the script.

You put on a face for the public. The face isn't false; it's just another side of you. If it were false, you couldn't last. People want something real and natural, and if they catch you acting, you're dead. It has to look real. In order to look real, it has to *be* real, and I've always thought of the characters I played as real people.

People think it's easy for me to make it look easy. "That's just good ole, easygoing Jim," they say. Well, Lois can tell you I ain't no "easygoing Jim." People think I'm "playing myself." Well, I'm not myself on the screen. I'm playing a character, but I try to put myself in his position. I work hard at not seeming to work too hard. I try to make the audience think it's the first time I'm saying it. That's not always easy, especially after the twelfth take. I'm basically a three-take actor. After that, it's all downhill. (I get bored when I have to do a lot of takes. And if I have to do a lot of takes, you can bet it isn't my fault.)

Gene Hackman is my favorite actor, though I've never worked with him. Never even met the man. (We were in the same movie, *Twilight,* but didn't have any scenes together.) I'd watch Gene do anything on the screen. I love the way he delivers his lines, the choices he makes. I also love Robert Duvall. He immerses himself in research for a role and then makes it look effortless. I don't know if he considers himself a Method actor, but if he is, it works for him.

I'm the opposite. I don't do much preparation for a part. I purposely don't read the books of movies I might make, because I don't want to be disappointed by what they might change or leave out. I don't do research, and I'm not interested in delving into the character's hidden facets. I don't care about his "backstory" or what kind of toothpaste he uses. For me, too much analysis takes the fun out of acting.

When we were making *36 Hours,* George Seaton told me a story about his friend, the British character actor Edmund Gwenn. You may remember him as Kris Kringle in the original *Miracle on 34th Street.* Seaton and Gwenn had a running argument about which was harder to do, comedy or drama. Seaton said drama; Gwenn insisted it was comedy. Well, Gwenn got sick, and when Seaton heard he wasn't going to last long, he went to say good-bye. He found Gwenn in a hospital ward. After some small talk, Seaton said, "Dying must be hard."

"Dying is easy," Gwenn said. "*Comedy* is hard."

That's right. You can create drama with lighting, with scenery, with music. You can heighten it with editing. But you can ruin comedy with those things. You can't fake humor. It had better be funny or you're dead.

I draw a line between comedy and humor. Comedy is slapstick— slipping on a banana peel and all that stuff. Humor is more subtle. Humor is cerebral and pure. It lasts. Either the joke is there or it isn't, and if something isn't funny, you ain't gonna make it so by falling down.

I do humor, not comedy. If I'm funny at all, I try to be *slow* funny. I tend to look at everything from the side, and I'm more interested in character than flash, because flash hits quick and leaves quick. It takes a little longer to know a character, but character builds and builds, and it's funnier.

You can do comedy alone, but you can't do humor without a good partner. You have to have somebody to bounce off. To play humor you need a "sense of humor," which means you have to know what's funny and what isn't. And you have to have comic timing. You can't learn that; you have to be born with it.

Robert Montgomery was a wonderful comic actor, but he didn't get much credit because he made it look easy. You never saw him acting. The actors who get the credit are the ones you do see acting.

I like a happy set, and I think it shows in the finished product. I like to laugh. But I also like to work. I enjoy going to the set every day with my fellow actors and the crew and the director. But I don't take it home with me. When they yell, "Wrap!" I don't think any more about it. I don't even worry whether it'll be a success or a failure, because I know I've done my best and have no control over how it'll be received. But I can't wait to get back to work the next day.

When young actors want advice, I ask them: "Do you really, truly, *have* to be an actor?"

"Yes, I *have* to!"

"Okay, tell you what you do: Get a decent job. Make sure you have as much financial security as you can. Then go to your little theater and act your heart out. Forget about trying to make a living as an actor, because the odds are way against you."

It's a tough business. There's no security. Last I heard there were twenty thousand members in the Screen Actors Guild in Los Angeles. Of those, only about a thousand make a living. That means, year after year, nineteen actors out of twenty have to work a day job to survive. If you want to be an actor, don't do it for the money.

A lot of film actors go back to the theater periodically to "sharpen the saw." They say they miss it. I don't, because I've always been frightened of live audiences. When I was in *Caine Mutiny Court Martial* and *John Loves Mary,* the only two stage plays I've ever done, I had to pretend there was no back door in the theater or I would have used it. To this day, I'd be a wreck if I had to work in front of a crowd.

I was always nervous at the start of a picture, and often before shooting a *Maverick* or a *Rockford* episode. I'd get flustered doing TV interviews: I have a bad memory for names and it embarrasses me when I've just worked with a great director and I can't think of his name. I'd go on talk shows to plug something, but I didn't like it.

I never enjoyed working on the stage the way some actors do. There were never any plays I wanted to do. Some actors want to do Shakespeare. I don't give a damn about Shakespeare. (He never calls.) The same thing night after night gets old, and applause doesn't turn me on. Never had that particular addiction. Some actors are devoted to The Theatah, but I couldn't care less. Maybe that's why I don't bother with acting superstitions. Stage actors say, "Break a leg" and all that stuff. They call *Macbeth* "the Scottish Play" because they're afraid to say the name. Doesn't concern me. I say, "Good luck" to fellow actors all the time.

I promised myself in Paul Gregory's office in 1953 that I'd give acting five years to see if I liked it and could make a living at it. My goal was to keep working. After five years I was starring in *Maverick,* so I thought *Okay, I'll go for another five.* After that, I went for another five, then another. It wasn't until my fiftieth birthday that I believed I could last in the business.

Throughout my career, I've gone back and forth between television and movies. I started in TV in the 1950s, did movies in the '60s, went back to television in the '70s, and did both from then on. Clint Eastwood, Steve McQueen, and I were the first to make the leap from TV to movies, but it was unusual. Television was a second-class medium for a long time. When we started, being on television carried a stigma. There was a pecking order: stage actors were next to God, film actors were right up there with the angels, TV actors were beneath them, and commercial acting was the dregs. If you were a television actor, you weren't allowed to do movies; if you were a movie actor, you didn't dare do television, and if you were a stage actor and you did a movie, they said you had "sold out." In the old days, a movie actor got more respect in the industry than a television actor. Today if you have a hit on TV, you get just as much respect, maybe because there's so much competition on television. The biggest stars can do an HBO movie or even a TV series and not lose their clout. Theater, movies, television, even commercials—it's all the same. We're actors.

Well, not completely. There are some differences. I always felt movies were easier. The pace was slower and the pay was better. Television was more demanding, both mentally and physically. The budgets for movies were bigger and you had more time to shoot them. That's why the product was usually better. That's changed.

Now the big movies are all action and special effects. The better stories are on television. In movies, the director has final cut; in television, it's the producer. It's hard to be a television director. You never have the time or the money to do what you want.

Acting for television, you don't have to project yourself like you do in a movie because the TV camera is looking right down your throat. It does your projecting for you. There's a difference in the way the public treats you because TV is a personal medium. When I was doing *Maverick*, I was part of the family. I'd been in their living room like an old piece of furniture. If I ate in a restaurant, people would invite me to sit at their table: "Hey, Jimbo, come meet the wife and kids!" Would they say that to Cary Grant? (After I'd been doing *Maverick* for a couple of years, I was at the Beverly Hilton for some big function. Cary Grant came over, introduced himself, and told me how much he liked my work. I was so flabbergasted, all I could manage was something dumb like, "I like *your* work, too.")

When I was on television, our mailman would want to bring his kids over to meet me. He felt he knew me because I was on a small screen in his living room every week for free. As soon as I started doing movies, fewer people came up to me in public. You were up there on the big screen and they were in awe of you, so they kept their distance.

In 1963, I was in four hit pictures: *Move Over, Darling; The Thrill of It All; The Wheeler Dealers;* and *The Great Escape.* I was advised that an all-out publicity campaign could make me number one at the box office. I said, "Why would I want to do *that*? Once you're number one, there's nowhere to go but down." I wanted to avoid the highs and lows and have longevity. I thought I'd be better off hanging in there at a solid number five or six and let the other guys fight it out for the top spot.

In Hollywood, you have to "defend your quote"—keep your fee as high as possible and never accept less. Lee Marvin raised his quote to a million dollars a picture after he won an Oscar for *Cat Ballou* and had trouble getting parts.

I never worked with Lee, but I thought that as an actor he was very colorful. As a guy, he was a pain in the ass. He just didn't care. He was a bad drinker. One night in a limousine on our way to some function, he made moves on my wife. That's a little more than I can handle and I almost decked him.

Anyway, Lee wanted to work but couldn't take a salary cut. I didn't want to fall into that trap, so I never let my quote get too high. Actors are paid more than they're worth anyway. Producers are idiots for paying the ridiculous prices we ask. We make so much money, the majority of pictures never make a profit. I think movies would be a lot better if more actors waived their big salaries in order to do worthwhile pictures.

I don't think actors today are well served by their agents and managers, who aren't as good as they used to be. They just want their 10 percent and let their clients do things they shouldn't. They have one hit and three flops and their careers are over.

By the late 1960s, I'd done one film after another and was burned out. I told my agent I was taking a year off and didn't want to read any scripts. After a few months of golf every day I said, "If there's a *really* good script out there, I'll look at it." Nothing came my way. A couple months later I said, "If there's a script out there, I'll look at it." Nothing. A few months later I said, *"Get me a script!"* Producers forgot me. I wasn't on their radar, so they didn't think of me for a part. The lesson is, never be off the screen for long. The industry is fickle. They forget you quickly. You have to keep working.

On the other hand, you can't make film after film. There aren't enough good scripts, and sooner or later, you're going to do some stinkers, which will disappoint the audience, and they'll stay away, and your value will drop. It's better to do good work in fewer projects. I think you make more money in the long run that way. Most of the bad pictures I've made, I did for the money. *The Pink Jungle, A Man Called Sledge, One Little Indian*—any one of those could have ruined my career.

The anxieties of this business are incredible. You can get away with a few bombs, but suddenly they catch up with you and you're looking for work. You never feel secure. Henry Fonda was one of the great movie actors, but one day at the height of his career he told me, "I just finished a picture and it'll probably be the last one I'll ever do." *Henry Fonda* was worried about whether he'd work again. I had those doubts all the time. The old Hollywood cliché is true: you're only as good as your last picture.

I never tried to analyze the secret of being popular. Ratings never meant a thing to me. Never even looked at them. Now and then, somebody would walk up and say, "Look at these demographics," and I'd be polite and say, "Good, okay." I was too busy doing what I do, which is making film. I do my best and I have no control over what happens after that, so I don't worry about it. I never get too high after a success, or too low after a failure. I don't worry if it's going to succeed or fail, because I have no control over that. I do the work and forget about it. The only way I judge my work is by how much it embarrasses me when I see it. Not *whether* it embarrasses me, but how much. I'm never satisfied with a performance, because I know what I was trying to do and realize I fell short. I don't like how I look or how I sound. I look at my performance and think, *Why'd I do* that? That's why I don't watch myself. I don't look at my movies and I don't watch old *Maverick*s or *Rockford*s. I'm not a fan of me.

One of the keys to longevity as an actor is choosing roles carefully. I turned down so many scripts, my manager Bill Robinson always says he'd rather have 5 percent of what I turn down than 10 percent of what I do. When I get a script and I understand the character— which doesn't happen that often—my next question is, How's the movie as a whole? I look at the writer, director, producer, and other actors involved. Then I make up my mind. The industry wants blockbusters, but I like pictures about relationships between people. I don't watch action-adventure or sci-fi movies, and I don't want to do any. I don't understand them. A reporter once asked if I would ever do a nude scene. I told him I don't do horror films.

I've never regretted losing or passing on a role, because I always figured something as good or better was right around the corner. The only two pictures I ever went after were *Sayonara* and *Grand Prix*. Otherwise, I just waited for the right part to come along and it usually did.

I don't like movies that glorify violence. That's why I passed on *Rambo*. He had a bad attitude. He killed a bunch of Americans— National Guardsmen and police. I wanted nothing to do with him. I guess the violence in my early life made me partial to characters who try to avoid it.

Audiences are influenced by what they see on the screen, and I think it's wrong to bombard them with violent images. Why does the hero have to kill thirty people in the first reel? I don't think it's exciting or entertaining.

I'm no do-gooder; I just like to do good movies. I consider myself an average American, and I think I have a duty to other average Americans. As an actor and a producer, I try to exercise a certain amount of restraint. I feel I have a moral responsibility to the audience, particularly a television audience. After we did a *Rockford* episode showing how to get a phony driver's license, we learned that the boys who hijacked the Chowchilla school bus in 1976 and kidnapped those children had watched our show and used the information to get licenses to help them commit the crime. I felt awful about that.

I prefer clean over dirty. I saw an episode of *Deadwood* on HBO and was embarrassed by the foul language. They didn't talk like that in the Old West! I like the old-fashioned way, where the language is clean and sex scenes are done tastefully, not graphically. And I don't like to glorify gangsters. I think it influences people to imitate them. I thought *Bonnie and Clyde* was beautifully done, and I know that the real Bonnie Parker and Clyde Barrow were folk heroes, but in fact they were cold-blooded killers, not a couple of lost little lambs.

It's gotten much worse. Now we have formula pictures that appeal to the lowest common denominator. Everybody's wrong and nobody cares enough to point out what's right. These movies are all about special effects without much story content. They don't deal with people and their problems. The characters have no redeeming qualities. It's violence for its own sake.

I turned down the Richard Burton part in *The Night of the Iguana*. It was way too Tennessee Williams for me, and I didn't care for the film they made. I was offered the role Jack Nicholson played in *Terms of Endearment*. I met with the writer-director, James L. Brooks, but had no idea what he was talking about. I couldn't communicate with him and didn't understand what he was trying to do with the movie. When I asked point-blank how he was going to end it, he couldn't tell me. I guess I just couldn't get on his level. So I walked out of his office and told my agent the part wasn't for me. (I found out later that Burt Reynolds and Harrison Ford turned it down, too.) Jack Nicholson did a much better job than I'd have done, and it turned out to be a great film.

There was a Brian Forbes movie at Columbia from a James Clavell novel that I wanted to do called *King Rat*. I loved the script. But George Segal got the part, I think because he was under contract to the studio and was a lot cheaper than I'd have been. In other words, George did to me on *King Rat* what I'd done to Roger Smith on *Sayonara*. Fair enough. I assumed it wasn't meant to be and never looked back. I was signed to play Gus McCrae in the *Lonesome Dove* miniseries but had to drop out because I had surgery for an aortic aneurysm and couldn't ride a horse. Robert Duvall took it and did such a fantastic job, I can't imagine anyone else in the role, including me. Ten years later, I played Captain Woodrow Call in the sequel, *Streets of Laredo*. It all evens out over time . . . if you hang around long enough.

As far as I can tell, the secret to having a long career is, above all else, you've got to be lucky. No substitute for that. Call it *timing* if you like. You have to have the right thing for the public at the right time. A little talent helps. You have to pick and choose scripts according to what you do best. And always try to maintain your dignity.

If I didn't want to be an actor, I certainly didn't want to be a star. Fame is a trap. It comes and goes in a flash. Ever heard of the four stages in an actor's career?

1. Who is James Garner?
2. Get me James Garner.
3. Get me a James Garner type.
4. Who is James Garner?

I wanted fortune, but never fame. Not only is fame fleeting, it's also deceiving. People are constantly telling you how wonderful you are. Your ego blows up like a balloon. You get sucked in by your own publicity and lose your grip on reality. It's a drug; you need more and more of it. It's also a bargain with the devil: you win fame and lose anonymity. It sounds like a fair trade. It isn't.

I didn't appreciate my anonymity until it was gone. You can't do simple things like shop in a department store, take in a ball game, or stroll in the park. When you lose your anonymity, you also lose your privacy. It's important for an actor to observe behavior, and I was always a people watcher. But once you're famous, you can't be inconspicuous. After *Maverick,* people were observing *me.* I remember standing in the vestibule of a New York hotel waiting for a car to pick me up. I stood there for half an hour watching people. Nobody bothered me because I could see out but they couldn't see in. That was in 1960, and it was the last time I could do that in public.

While we were making *The Glitter Dome* in Annapolis, Maryland, the secretaries in the building across from my hotel would watch me with binoculars. They said I smoked too much. (Didn't say anything else.) While I was staying at a hotel in Madrid, a female "fan" broke into my room and stole a sports jacket as a souvenir. Once, as I walked through a hotel lobby in Las Vegas, two women approached and one put her hand up to my face like she wanted to stroke it or kiss me. Instead, she felt behind my ear and said to her companion, "See Mary, I told you he never had a face-lift!" Then there are the folks who confuse you with the character. They actually think you're Bret Maverick or Jim Rockford in real life. These people need to *get* a life.

During one dinner in a Palm Springs restaurant, I brought the fork to my mouth three times but never got a bite. My daughter Gigi says she can't remember a meal in a restaurant that wasn't interrupted. She says, "It goes with the territory," but I know she didn't like it. Neither did Kim or Lois. It ruined our time together as a family whenever we were in public.

I couldn't go anywhere without someone around me. Guys would follow me into men's rooms for autographs. Paul Newman told me he stopped signing them forever the night he was standing at a urinal in Sardi's and a guy shoved a pen and paper at him. Paul didn't know whether to wash first before shaking hands. Clint Eastwood said that when the *Dirty Harry* pictures were in release, people would ask him to autograph their *guns*. Gary Cooper wrote checks for everything—gasoline, cigarettes, groceries, meals in restaurants—because he knew most of them wouldn't be cashed. Coop figured he might as well get paid for signing his name.

In the early 1980s, Bill Saxon and I flew to Southeast Asia to play golf. When we landed in Sri Lanka, the customs people rushed out to our plane as soon we touched down. They didn't suspect us of smuggling, they just wanted my autograph.

I hate giving autographs but do it anyway. In fifty years, I've probably signed a hundred thousand. I try to be cheerful about it because it takes only a few seconds and it's easier than turning somebody down and hurting their feelings (or, worse, having them get nasty). So I smile and write my name on little scraps of paper.

While we were doing *Rockford* on the beach at Paradise Cove, I had a leather director's chair with saddlebags that I'd sit in for hours with a little pad that said, "From the Desk of Jim Rockford" and sign autographs all day. I'm sure 95 percent of them got thrown out or wound up forgotten in a drawer.

I wasn't always polite to autograph seekers. One year after a round at the Greater Greensboro Open, Billy Dee and I were being taken back to our hotel in a courtesy car driven by a female volunteer. The car was parked next to the putting green where a bunch of pros were practicing. It was a tight parking spot and the lady was having a hard time maneuvering it out. She was going back and forth in small increments and I had my head out the window directing her. At that moment, a woman approached, stuck a paper and pen in my face, and asked for an autograph.

"Lady, could you just wait a minute? We're trying to get this car out of this space," I said.

"Well excuse me, Mister Movie Star!"

I did a slow burn and said, "Lady, how would you like to kiss a fat man's ass?"

The pros on the putting green, who had stopped to watch, all applauded.

There are a few perks. You get special treatment here and there, but it isn't worth it. If America suddenly got amnesia and forgot who I was, that would be fine with me. I just don't get it. On one hand, I know that some people like my work, but somehow that doesn't get through. I've never thought of myself as anything special, and I don't like to be the center of attention, but there wasn't much I could do to prevent it. I'd have worn a disguise in public if I thought it would have done any good, but I figured they'd know who I was the minute

I opened my mouth. It was once reported that I paid the seller of a map to the stars' homes to take me off the list, but that's not true. I may have threatened to give the guy a shot in the mouth, but I didn't bribe him.

I hate everything about show business but acting. Publicity doesn't interest me. I don't read anything they write about me—articles, reviews, whatever. (Well, I do read reviews, but only the good ones.) I never liked making personal appearances or having my picture taken. That goes back to my days as a model.

I'd rather dig a ditch than do an interview, let alone a press junket where you sit in a hotel room all day while a hundred reporters work you over one by one. I've never liked premieres or entourages or anything associated with celebrity. I'm not too crazy about limousines, either. I can't stand Hollywood parties; when Lois and I went out, it was usually for dinner with close friends.

And I don't give a damn about awards. When *TV Guide* named me the best dramatic actor in television history, I didn't even get a free copy of the magazine. That's okay: I didn't like *TV Guide* anyway because the owner, Walter Annenberg, used it as a platform for Nixon, Reagan, and Bush.

There was an English actress who said, "The Americans are famous for giving presents for acting." Exactly. I don't like trophies, especially for acting. I have no interest in Oscars. Though I'm a member of the Motion Picture Academy, I rarely see the nominated movies, so Lois does the voting.

I didn't get into the business to be better than anyone else. They give too much credit to actors, and I don't think they should be singled out. It's the writing. When it's done right, acting isn't a competition, it's a collaboration. The better my fellow actors are, the better I am. If I get an acting award, I think I'm stealing it from somebody who deserves it more than I do. They should just nominate five people, give them all a trophy, and go home.

I couldn't stand fan magazines. Even as a teenager, I knew they were bullshit. I'd look at *Photoplay* and think, *What a bunch of phonies!* All those supposedly candid shots of the stars in "real life." You could see them posing. I never understood the whole fan thing, because I've never been a fan of anybody. How can you care so much about someone you never met? I didn't want to be part of that. But when *Maverick* became a hit, I did those same stories, to my shame. The fan magazines were so sleazy, they weren't saved in libraries like old issues of *Life* or *The Saturday Evening Post*. I'm glad.

I hate *Hollywood*. You say "Good morning" in this town and they say, "What did he mean by that?" Maybe that's why they never understood me; I always said exactly what was on my mind. The industry is like it's always been, a bunch of greedy people. You have to watch 'em every minute. I once got into a movie deal with a producer who said he had all the elements lined up, but when it got down to the wire it turned out he never had them. When I asked what happened he said, "I lied. It was the only way I could get you into the deal." He thought that made it okay.

I never got along with studio executives. Most of them have been to business school or law school, sometimes both, but as far as film goes, they have no creative talent at all. Their opinions aren't worth a damn, so they go with the numbers. They're in constant fear of losing their jobs, which makes them indecisive. In negotiations, their goal is to get the best of you, not to make a good deal for everybody involved. I've never understood that.

I was careful not to get friendly with studio executives, because then I'd have to be nice to them. I wanted to be able to say whatever I wanted without worrying about harming a relationship.

Hollywood is dishonest, it's petty, and it's ageist. Late in his life, Fred Zinnemann, the Oscar-winning director who gave us *From Here to Eternity, High Noon,* and *A Man for All Seasons,* had a meeting with a young producer who didn't know who Zinnemann was.

"Well, Mr. Zinnemann," said the young man, "What have you done?"

"You first," said Zinnemann.

It's worse for actresses. Women come into their own in middle age—they're smarter and more attractive. I thought Lana Turner was much more interesting at forty than she was at twenty. Producers don't seem to realize that you still have the drive and most of the energy. You don't look young, but you've *lived,* and that makes you a better actor. William Goldman was right: in Hollywood, nobody knows anything.

Nope, there's nothing I like about fame. Except for the ten-foot-tall, bronze statue of me as Bret Maverick that was unveiled in Norman on April 21, 2006. It's near the train station, on a corner where I used to hang out when I was a kid. The town also changed the name of a street to James Garner Avenue.

Norman was a great place to grow up, and I'm proud and happy to be from Oklahoma. I've always stayed loyal to my home state. People in the rest of the country don't know what a wonderful place it is. The Rodgers and Hammerstein version of Oklahoma has nothing to do with reality. When I saw the movie, I thought to myself, *Well,* they're *having fun*.

Though I haven't lived in Norman for a long time, my friends and relatives there have been very supportive. A group of them—committee members Roy Hamilton, Bill Cobb, and Bob Goins—along with Bill Saxon and Lee Allan Smith, were responsible for putting up the statue. They raised the money and hired the sculptor, Shan Gray. I went to the unveiling ceremony. We had a family reunion and there was a reception at the old train depot. Old friends and perfect strangers came to wish me well. It was an unforgettable day.

Funny how it worked out: the statue is right across the street from the Sooner Theatre, where I'd watched movies as a boy, never dreaming anything like this could ever happen to me.

CHAPTER TEN

Producing

This is immodest, but I think *Support Your Local Sheriff* is one of the better Western spoofs ever made. It's comedy, not humor. It's very broad, with puns, slapstick, finger-in-a-gun-barrel kind of stuff. It's the old story about a gunslinger who drifts into town—in this case, "on his way to Australia"—becomes sheriff, and takes on the powerful family that runs the town. When they hand him the badge, there's a dent in it from a bullet. "This must have saved his life," I say.

"It would've . . . if it weren't for all those other bullets."

Bill Bowers wrote the script and wanted a producer credit, so I gave it to him. The first day on the set, he wanted to know what to do, and I said, "See that chair over there with your name on it? Sit there and be quiet. We'll holler if we need you." (Never hollered.)

Burt Kennedy had wonderful actors to work with: Joan Hackett, Jack Elam, Walter Brennan, Bruce Dern. Burt had directed some real Westerns, including *The War Wagon* with Duke Wayne. He was a good director, but for some reason he didn't want Joan Hackett. I think he may have promised the role to Stella Stevens. Stella would've been fine, but I loved Joan. She was in the Jean Arthur league of comedic actresses. Just a *funny* woman. Burt kept complaining about her until I finally said, "You can reshoot anything you like, but we're not getting rid of her." I think Joan did a wonderful job in the picture and audiences and critics alike applauded her performance.

Jack Elam was one of the nicest guys in the world and a lot of fun. Loved to gamble. He'd bet you the sun wouldn't come up if you gave him the right odds. He'd been an accountant in charge of disbursements at one of the studios, but he really wanted to act. Some producer came in with a script he wanted to do and Jack said, "Look, I'll see that you get the money if you give me this little part here." That's how he became a movie actor. Though it was his first comedy, Jack was easy to work with and he did a great job as my drunken sidekick.

Walter Brennan was a marvelous old poop. He was well up in his seventies—I think it was the last picture he made. He'd won three Oscars. Walter was the first actor I'd ever seen use cards. He knew the dialogue cold and never flubbed a line, but I guess he just needed to know that his words were there as backup. He put a card up here and another down there and just kind of glanced at them to make sure. You couldn't tell, though.

Bruce Dern was a fine young actor and I think this was his first comedy. He went on to do great work in a long series of movies.

Support Your Local Sheriff was my first producing job. I'd noticed that, though actors make a lot of money, somebody has the money to pay *them*. Producers. I'd also noticed that producers weren't smarter than me, they just made more money. *I* wanted to make more money. And have more control. So I formed Cherokee Productions.

That's when I learned there's a reason why producers make the big bucks.

Most people don't know what a producer does. It's not an easy job. They have to secure financing, commission a script, and hire everybody else to make the picture. They even have to come up with a title.

It was originally called *The Sheriff*. I was with Burt Kennedy and Bill Bowers in an office on the second floor at MGM. I told them I thought *The Sheriff* was too dull. But we couldn't think of anything better. I left the meeting early because I had to go home, and as I walked downstairs, there was a time clock with a sign over it: "Support Your Local Police." I turned around, walked back up the stairs, poked my head in the office and said, "I've got it: *Support Your Local Sheriff*." Didn't even wait for a reaction. When I got home, there was a message from Burt: "Great title!"

People had warned me that comedy Westerns weren't commercial, but I went ahead and made it anyway, for $750,000, which was nothing even then. It opened for a week and didn't do any business. The studio wanted to shelve it. I said, "Tell you what: You put up ten thousand dollars and I'll put up ten thousand dollars, and we'll run it in one theater." We put it on Wilshire Boulevard for a month and they lined up. We rereleased it and it did great business everywhere. I'm still getting checks.

Nichols was my first TV work since *Maverick* more than ten years earlier, and my first foray into television producing. My agent, Meta Rosenberg, was our executive producer. As far as I know, she was the first woman to hold such a high position in television. The writer-director Frank Pierson had created the character and served as our producer. Frank had already written successful movies, including *Cat Ballou, Cool Hand Luke,* and *Dog Day Afternoon*. We had directors like John Badham and Paul Bogart, and writers like Buck Houghton, Marion Hargrove, and Juanita Bartlett.

Juanita had been hanging around town writing spec scripts without making a sale until she took a job as Meta's secretary. One day Juanita asked Frank Pierson if he needed a script for "Bertha." Frank said he wasn't aware of a character named Bertha in the show. Juanita explained that the saloon on the *Nichols* set was named

Bertha's, and that she had a story idea for an episode featuring Bertha. Frank told Juanita to go ahead and write a script. She did, and we all liked it so much, we made Bertha an ongoing character, cast Alice Ghostley in the role, and hired Juanita as a staff writer.

But Juanita was still very shy and unsure of herself. She cried for a week and didn't want to leave her secretary's desk. She thought the whole thing might be a fluke and kept on making coffee for Meta until we convinced her that the new secretary could do that. After doing a rewrite of another script, Juanita finally relaxed. She went on to a long career as a writer-producer. She isn't shy anymore.

Nichols is a turn-of-the-century Western set in a small town in Arizona. I love that era. Right after World War I, before industrialization and world leadership, the country was just waking up. New inventions like the telephone and the automobile were making life better and more exciting, but the old values still hadn't given way.

Nichols—we never gave him a first name—retires from the army and returns to his hometown of Nichols, Arizona, named for his grandfather, who'd founded it. He takes the job of sheriff but doesn't carry a gun, not because he's afraid of them, but because he's sick of violence. In short, Nichols isn't much of an authority figure. He's more interested in making a quick buck than enforcing the law.

Maverick and Rockford are basically the same character, but Nichols is different. He's a free spirit and an independent thinker struggling to keep up with a fast-changing world. He has his own style, with jodhpurs, cavalry boots, and a goofy little cap. He drives a 1914 Chevrolet and a belt-drive Harley-Davidson.

I'd run the Baja 1000 and driven fast cars in *Grand Prix,* but I was scared to death of that rickety old bike. It was uncomfortable and dangerous. Though the bike had been restored and strengthened, the handlebars were weird and it had no suspension, so it was hard to control. We built another one out of a modern motorcycle and fitted it with tanks and fenders to make it look like the original, but in some shots, I had to drive right into the camera, so they couldn't double for me or the bike.

To make *Nichols* work I needed a sidekick who was a shifty-eyed, back-stabbing rat, but also lovable. Tall order. We'd made screen tests but couldn't find what we were looking for until one day I saw a clip from *Love, American Style*. It wasn't a scene that should have gotten a laugh, but the actor was so good, he broke me up. I knew he was the one for the part.

The actor was Stuart Margolin, and we cast him as my deputy sheriff, Mitch. Stuart and I were on the same wavelength from the start: in our first scene together, we met on a staircase and improvised a side-to-side bit that came off beautifully. It set the tone for our future work together. Mitch was the forerunner to Angel Martin, the character Stuart played in *The Rockford Files,* and later to his slippery Native American, Philo Sandeen, in *Bret Maverick*.

Neva Patterson plays Ma Ketchum, whose crooked family has taken over the town. Nichols's only friend (and love interest) is Ruth, a barmaid played by a very young Margot Kidder. We also had John Beck and M. Emmet Walsh as recurring characters.

There was great social and political turmoil in the country in 1971. The civil rights and women's movements were in full swing and the Vietnam War was still sending Americans home in body bags. We slipped in a little commentary here and there—*Nichols* was antiviolence, pro–civil rights, and pro–women's rights—but we kept it gentle and never got preachy. And always tried to keep it funny.

Chevrolet was our sponsor. When we screened the pilot for them in Detroit, the wife of one of the executives said, "It's not *Maverick*!"

I knew we were dead then and there. The folks at Chevrolet thought they were getting *Maverick* and, by golly, they wanted *Maverick*. They picked up half the show and sold off the other half.

Nichols never got the chance to find its audience. We were preempted eight out of twenty-four shows by the presidential election campaign, and NBC switched us from one night to another in midseason without telling us, so it was pretty clear they had given up on the show. They renamed it *James Garner as Nichols* but it didn't help

NBC put us up against *Marcus Welby, M.D.,* the top-rated show on television at the time, and we ran even. The critics liked us, and our ratings were better than a lot of shows that got picked up by the networks in those days. But the network canceled us anyway.

I was so angry and disappointed, I decided to kill Nichols off in the last episode. In the opening sequence, Anthony Zerbe pulls a gun and blows me away. There's a funeral and they bury me. But I come back as my twin brother, Jim Nichols, to avenge the killing. In the last shot, as I ride out of town on the Harley, the camera pans up to a sign: "You Are Now Leaving Nichols."

In my mind, *Nichols* is right up there with *Maverick* and *Rockford*. It lasted less than a year, from September 16, 1971, to March 14, 1972. I made a profit on it, though it ran for only twenty-four episodes and was never rerun. I think *Nichols* was ahead of its time. It was different and creative, and we had such wonderful people working on both sides of the camera. The cancellation about broke my heart.

The Hallmark Hall of Fame, a television anthology series that began in 1951 with *Amahl and the Night Visitors,* has become an American entertainment institution. Hallmark has high standards and they stick to them. Over the decades they've done programs with strong performances and excellent production values—Shakespeare, the classics, biographies—plus original material with top-notch writing, directing, and acting. It was an easy decision for me and my producing partner, Peter Duchow, to join forces with Hallmark.

The Hallmark Hall of Fame production of *Promise* originally aired on December 14, 1986. With wise, sensitive direction by Glenn Jordan, a magnificent script by Richard Friedenberg, and inspired performances by Piper Laurie and James Woods, *Promise* won five Emmys (Best Actor, Best Special, Best Direction, Best Teleplay, Best Writing), two Golden Globes, a Peabody Award, a Christopher Award, and the Humanitas Prize, given to the writers of television programs that "probe the meaning of human life" or supply "enriching human values."

I play Bob Beuhler, who'd promised his mother when he was twenty-one that he'd look after his emotionally disturbed younger brother D.J. When the old woman dies thirty years later, Bob is faced with the prospect of caring for a "crazy man" for the rest of his life.

I couldn't have played the character five years earlier. I'd have thought he was too unsympathetic. I was always reluctant to play heavies. People have told me that this was a mistake, that I should take on a wider variety of roles. But I never wanted to be a bad guy on the screen. I didn't want to be a superhero either—didn't want to go to either extreme. That's why I hesitated. Not that Bob is a villain, he just never grew up.

James Woods had been in the first episode of *The Rockford Files*. When we hired him for *Promise,* I called to say how happy I was to have him. He said, "I bet you don't remember me," and I said, "You bet I do. I'm not gonna forget *you.*" In case you haven't noticed, Jimmy is very bright, extremely articulate, and a brilliant actor.

Jimmy researched the part of D.J. by spending time at a halfway house in Santa Monica called Step Up on Second. It was founded by Susan Dempsay, whose son, Mark Klemperer, was schizophrenic.

People in their late teens or early twenties—usually men, but it happens to women, too—can suddenly develop schizophrenia. Their odd behavior is often misinterpreted and they go undiagnosed. They self-medicate with alcohol and illegal drugs, and many wind up homeless, strung out, muttering to themselves.

Susan Dempsay envisioned a place where these kids could at least get off the streets. It's not that she didn't want to take care of Mark herself, but he'd do erratic things like suddenly jump out of a car and disappear for weeks. She'd find him eating out of a Dumpster. So she created a refuge where people like him could relax, maybe learn about government assistance programs, be reminded to take their meds, and connect with others like themselves.

I had no idea what schizophrenics have to endure. I learned that they inhabit a terrifying world of hallucinations and inner voices that seem completely real. Even when they're well, they have the burden of knowing they can lose control in an instant. I've never forgotten what one of them said: "When I was awake, I seemed alone, even when I was with people. My life was narrated by thoughts that weren't mine."

Jimmy's D.J. is very intelligent. But he's crazy. In lucid moments, he knows he's crazy and can talk eloquently about what it's like to be schizophrenic. Those moments make his suffering even more heartbreaking. But most of the time, D.J.'s behavior is exasperating. He sits for hours in front of a television set, chain-smoking and watching commercials, obediently sending for useless products because he takes the words "order now" as a command from a higher authority. He digs up the backyard on a ridiculous whim, makes embarrassing scenes in public, washes his hands compulsively. He has violent mood swings from despondency to euphoria.

One day at Step Up on Second, Jimmy Woods met "Sam," who gave a beautiful, eloquent description of what it's like to be schizophrenic. Richard Friedenberg put it in the script:

> D.J.: Do you want to know what it's like, Bobby? It's like, all the electric wires in the house are plugged into my brain. And every one has a different noise, so I can't think. Some of the wires have voices in them and they tell me things like what to do and that people are watching me. I know there really aren't any voices, but I feel that there are, and that I should listen to them or something

will happen. That's why I send for all those ads on the TV, because I feel the voice in the ad is talking to me. I hear him talking to me. He tells me to buy the things and that . . . well, I'm afraid if I don't . . .

I can remember what I was like before. I was a class officer, I had friends. I was going to be an aeronautical engineer. Do you remember, Bobby?

BOB: Of course, I do.

D.J.: I've never had a job. I've never owned a car. I've never lived alone. I've never made love to a woman. And I never will. That's what it's like.

You *should* know. That's why I'm a Hindu. Because maybe it's true: Maybe people *are* born again. And if there is a God, maybe he'll give me another chance. I believe that, because this can't be all I get.

Accepting the Emmy for Best Teleplay, Richard Friedenberg said he hoped the film would help schizophrenics by calling attention to their plight. I'm sorry to say that twenty-five years later, schizophrenia is the worst mental health problem facing the nation. Asylums have been closed, and government spending on mental health has been cut to the bone. There are new medications for schizophrenia, but though more expensive, they're not much more effective than the old ones. And there is still no cure.

After *Promise* had wrapped, Peter Duchow and I were sitting in a coffee shop in Salem, Oregon, talking about the Bill Wilson story. Jimmy Woods was eavesdropping (as usual) from a couple of booths away. I'm not going to say he *lobbied* for the part, but he ran over and announced, "I *am* Bill W.!"

My Name Is Bill W. is the story of the founding of Alcoholics Anonymous. Few American films had dealt with alcoholism seriously. Aside from Billy Wilder's *The Lost Weekend* in 1945, *Come Fill the Cup* in 1951 with James Cagney as a recovering alcoholic newspaper editor, *The Voice in the Mirror* in 1958 with Richard Eagan and Julie London, and *Days of Wine and Roses* (1962, written by J. P. Miller and directed by Blake Edwards), drunks and drunkenness were played for laughs in films.

If alcoholism was treated seriously at all, it was portrayed as a character flaw rather than a disease. Which mirrored the general attitude. People thought that if you were a drunk, it was because you lacked willpower. The only help for alcoholics was in the form of a hot meal and a sermon, or a trip to the drunk tank, sanitarium, or psycho ward. If you were a drunk, you stayed a drunk until you died.

My family history had sensitized me to the problem, so when my producing partner, Peter, suggested doing a serious film about Alcoholics Anonymous, I welcomed the idea. I wanted to tell the story of how two men came up with a simple way to deal with alcoholism and help millions of people lead decent lives.

William Griffith Wilson was a World War I hero and a hotshot securities analyst through the 1920s. When the stock market crashed in 1929, his already excessive drinking spun out of control. After several alcohol-related trips to the hospital, Bill had an epiphany and swore off booze. But sobriety didn't bring him the peace he'd hoped for, and his battle to stay sober put a strain on his marriage.

On a business trip to Akron, Ohio, craving a drink and terrified of falling off the wagon, Bill asked a local minister to put him in touch with another alcoholic, just to talk. That's how he met Robert Holbrook Smith, MD, a barely functioning alcoholic surgeon.

At first, "Dr. Bob" was reluctant to talk with Bill and planned to spend only a few minutes with him. But after Bill told him, "I'm not here to help *you,* I'm here to help *me,*" Bob got interested. The conversation kept going until they both realized that if they could talk it out, they could make it, one day at a time.

The two men gave each other a safe harbor from "the stormy sea of booze," as Dr. Bob put it. Their decision to share their "shaky little fellowship" with other drunks resulted in Alcoholics Anonymous, one of the most successful self-help movements in history.

We struggled for five years to bring the story to the screen, going through four or five scripts. We didn't hit on the right approach until MaryAnn Rea in my office plucked an unsolicited script out of the slush pile from an unknown writer named William Borchert and suggested that Peter and I read it. As usual, MaryAnn was right.

We'd been focusing on AA the organization, and it didn't click until we read Bill Borchert's script, which centered on the love story between Bill Wilson and his wife, Lois. It was the first script Bill had ever written, though he'd been a successful producer. Once we decided just to tell a great story, everything fell into place. Daniel Petrie directed with great skill and insight, and we got fine performances from JoBeth Williams as Lois and from Gary Sinise as Bill's friend and drinking buddy, Ebby.

I think Bob Smith and Bill Wilson are among the great men of the last century. They got together to help each other, but the organization they founded in 1935 has helped millions of people around the world by giving them a way to share their experiences without being judged or preached at or psychoanalyzed. AA's twelve-step program really works. It provides an option for dealing with alcoholism besides death, insanity, or incarceration.

But we weren't proselytizing, we were just trying to tell a story that hadn't been widely known about how AA got started. Members of AA couldn't break the tradition of anonymity, but *we* could. Nor could AA endorse the film; however, individual members let us know they were pleased that we told their story in a sensitive and effective way.

Lois Wilson gave her blessing to the project before she died in 1988 at the age of ninety-seven. Lois had been a loving and loyal wife, but she couldn't save Bill. He had to save himself, with the help of another drunk. Confronted with a different husband when Bill got sober, Lois founded Al-Anon, a self-help organization for the families of alcoholics. In 2010, she was the subject of another Borchert/Hallmark movie, *When Love Is Not Enough: The Lois Wilson Story*.

Jimmy and I were temperamentally suited for our respective roles. Like Bill Wilson, Jimmy is hyperactive, fast-talking, and driven, while I'm more of a plodder, like Dr. Bob. While Bill W. was the go-getter, the front man, Dr. Bob was the anchor, the one who insisted on keeping everything simple and anonymous. (Bob once persuaded Bill to turn down the cover of *Time* magazine.)

Jimmy carries the film on his shoulders. My part isn't very meaty. It's really just a cameo. It was the first part I'd done since heart surgery and I was still shaky. I told Jimmy, "I don't think I can make it." He assured me I could, and he was right, but I couldn't have handled much more at the time.

Jimmy had researched the part of Bill W. by going to AA meetings and talking to recovering alcoholics. He'd never had a problem with alcohol, but I had. I started drinking as a teenager and I was a nasty drunk. Under the influence of alcohol, I couldn't control my temper. Somebody would say something and I'd deck 'im. I drank beer, whiskey, vodka—anything they put in front of me. I drank to get plastered. Did I have a "drinking problem"? No, I didn't have a problem at all. I just went right ahead and drank.

Oklahoma was a "dry" state in those days, but there were plenty of bootleggers around Norman. Mark Fisher was the king of them. He started in the 1930s, when the only legal drink in the state was 3.2 beer, and he stayed in business until liquor by the drink became legal in 1984.

The South Canadian River separates Cleveland County from McClain County to the west. The riverbed is probably a mile and a half across, but the stream of water is only fifty yards wide, so there are trees, bushes, and sand dunes in the flatland called the "river breaks." That's where Fisher had his shack, an area that everyone thought of as a no-man's-land belonging to neither county. I guess that's why the law left Fisher alone. Or maybe he was paying somebody off.

Mark sold to drinkers from both sides of the river, including college kids from OU and us high school kids, no driver's license required. There was easy access down to the river, but you had to know how to find Mark's shack. We were scared to go in. You never knew who might be sitting inside with a shotgun on his lap. It was always after dark, and we had to get up the nerve to walk up to the door and shout, "Whatcha got tonight?"

You could get "Green Label" bourbons like Jim Beam or Jack Daniel's for about fifteen dollars a pint, but we bought "Red Label" blended whiskey like Four Roses or Three Feathers at ten bucks a pint, mixed it with Coca-Cola and poured it down till we threw up.

I was a binge drinker until sometime in my early thirties, when I realized that I didn't like the way alcohol made me feel or behave. It also occurred to me that the liquor industry could produce more bottles of the stuff than I could down. I said to myself, "Something awful is gonna happen if you keep doing this. You'll end up killing somebody."

So I quit. Just like that. I've been a light drinker ever since—very little beer or liquor, but I did learn to enjoy a glass of wine with dinner and built up a pretty decent wine cellar. At one point, Lois and I even had a small vineyard that produced wines under the private labels White Rhino and Chateau Jimbeaux.

My father was a full-time drinker, and I think I really quit booze because I didn't want to follow him. He'd go on epic binges. In the early 1920s, he was in a group of men in Norman who fancied themselves cowboys. They rode horses and wore cowboy boots and hats. They had a "roping club" on the edge of town where they'd all get together and rope calves. The wives knew it was just an excuse to get together and drink moonshine. My dad was a different person when he was drinking. For most of his life, booze brought a lot of misery on him and on the people around him.

My real addiction was to nicotine. I smoked my first cigarette when I was eight. It was a Chesterfield, because that's what my dad smoked. Later I switched brands: in my seventh-grade class picture, I'm standing behind a girl, holding a pack of Lucky Strikes next to her shoulder. (My first endorsement.) Though I was partial to Luckies, I'd smoke any brand I could bum. I loved to smoke. When I started we didn't know what we do now about the medical effects, but we knew it wasn't right.

I didn't care.

When I started doing The Rockford Files, in 1974, I smoked on camera whenever I felt like it. After a while, I realized it was a bad example, so Jim Rockford quit. But I didn't. I used the standard excuse, "I don't want to gain weight," plus an original one: "I'm not gonna let C. Everett Koop tell me what to do!" I was a hard case. I kept smoking even after heart surgery in 1988. I finally quit in 2005, with more than sixty "pack years" under my belt.

I started smoking marijuana in my late teens. I drank to get drunk but ultimately didn't like the effect. Not so with grass. Grass is smooth. It had the opposite effect from alcohol: it made me more tolerant and forgiving.

I did a little bit of cocaine in the 1980s, courtesy of John Belushi (we'd met through a mutual friend and hit it off right away), but fortunately I didn't like it. I discovered that it never got better after the first time you did it.

I smoked marijuana for fifty years. I don't know where I'd be without it. It opened my mind to a lot of things, and now its active ingredient, THC, relaxes me and eases my arthritis pain. After decades of personal research and observation, I've concluded that marijuana should be legal and alcohol should be illegal. But good luck with *that*.

The reaction to *My Name Is Bill W.* was almost all positive. People in AA were happy with it. As far as I recall, we got nothing but praise from that community, including the people on the set who were in the program. Of all the things I've ever done as an actor or producer, I think *My Name Is Bill W.* has had the greatest impact. It was certainly one of the most gratifying experiences I've ever had as a professional. People came up to me and said, "I got sober because of your movie" or, "My husband joined AA because of your movie." You need only one of those to make it all worthwhile.

When Jimmy Woods and I were on the *Donahue* show promoting *My Name Is Bill W.,* a guy called and said, "I'm a drunk. I'm drinking right now and I'm alone. I have a gun and I'm going to use it on myself." Jimmy twelve-stepped him right on the air: "You know, you really want to think about what you're going to do," Jimmy said. "If you could push a button and make it okay, would you do it?" The man said yes. "Well," Jimmy said, "AA is the button. Just give it a try, then do whatever you want." The man hung up. We were told that a few months later he called *Donahue* back and said he was in recovery.

CHAPTER ELEVEN

Love Stories

———————

M urphy's Romance is one of my favorites, as much for the
people I worked with as the film itself. It was easy to do. Everything
went smoothly on the set and everybody liked each other. It was a
pleasure to go to work every day.

Martin Ritt was a wonderful man and a fine director. He made
movies that said something. I'd known Marty for a long time—we
played softball in the park together, and my daughter Gigi and his
daughter Tina were school friends. I'd always admired his films but
hadn't worked with him, so when *Murphy's Romance* came along, I
jumped at it.

Like me, Marty had grown up during the Depression. He came out
of the WPA and the Group Theater in New York to become a
successful television director, and he went on to direct such movies as
Hud, The Great White Hope, Sounder, Conrack, and *Norma Rae,* to name
a few of his two dozen features.

The studio wanted Marlon Brando for the part of Murphy Jones.
Marty and Sally Field loved Marlon, but they thought he just wasn't right
for it. The studio was adamant, but Sally and Marty went to bat for me.

Sally told them, "If *Garner* doesn't do the picture, *I* don't do the picture."

Sally is a wonderful girl and we got along great. It's a cliché, but we had great chemistry on the screen.

I could certainly identify with my character, Murphy Jones, a kindly but slightly eccentric small-town druggist who befriends Sally's character, Emma Moriarty, a confused divorcée come to town with her young son to start a horse ranch. Murphy is the kind of liberal who puts a "No Nukes" sticker on his antique Studebaker and battles city hall to replace the parking meter in front of his store with a tree.

We shot the picture in and around Mesa, Arizona. I have fond memories of that area: for one thing, *best tamales I've ever eaten*. The mother of the assistant pro at the local golf course made them. *God,* they were good. When I left town she made two dozen and we put them in the freezer. Plus I shot my all-time best round there, a 65.

Murphy's drugstore was actually in nearby Florence, Arizona, and all we needed to do was dress it up a little. But we had to build Sally's ranch from the ground up. It was on land next to a state prison and we'd see chain gangs on our way to and from the set.

Marty Ritt is all about substance over flash. His films reflect his strong social conscience. He was one of Hollywood's most prolific and successful directors, despite having been blacklisted during the McCarthy era. He was easygoing and supportive of everyone on the set and was especially encouraging to writers and actors. I considered him a dear friend and colleague. (A few years after *Murphy's Romance,* when it was announced that Marty would be doing *Nuts* with Barbra Streisand, I knew his heart wasn't good, so I called him and said, "Don't do it Marty. She'll fucking kill you." Afterward, Marty told me she damn near did.)

———

Murphy's Romance is honest and low-key, with straightforward cinematography and a quietly brilliant script by the husband-wife team of Harriet Frank Jr. and Irving Ravetch, who'd worked with Marty on *Hud* and *Norma Rae*. There's a scene in the picture that exemplifies their talent, "the hat bit," in which Murphy explains the significance of the different ways of wearing a cowboy hat:

> MURPHY: It doesn't matter how you bend it, it's how you wear it. You wear it back on your head like that, well, that means you like people, your digestion works, and you've got all day. If you wear it tipped over on the side, like that, it means you're a rooster and you're looking for a young lady or a fight, whichever comes first. But if you wear it square on your head and low down on your forehead, well, that means get off the sidewalk and clear a path because you're cocked and ready to fire!

I asked the Ravetches, "How'd you guys *know* that?" They said, "We just did, that's all."

And I think the last scene in the picture is one of the great love scenes ever:

> EMMA: Good evening, Murphy.
> MURPHY: Good evening.
> EMMA: It's gonna be a lovely night, isn't it?
> MURPHY: Yes it is.
> EMMA: Did you have a nice ride?
> MURPHY: Yes I did. It's gonna be a handsome moon tonight.
> EMMA: Think it's gonna rain?
> MURPHY: Nah, it's dry this time of year.
> EMMA: Are we talking about the weather?
> MURPHY: You are.

EMMA: That's not what I want to talk about.

MURPHY: Take a different tack, Emma.

EMMA: I don't know what tack to take.

MURPHY: I'll help you. Separate the men from the boys, Emma. I show some wear, I don't deny it. But fruit hangs on a tree long enough, it gets ripe. I'm durable. I'm steady. I'm faithful. And I'm in love, for the last time in my life.

EMMA: I'm in love for the first time in my life.

MURPHY: So?

EMMA: So! Stay to supper, Murphy?

MURPHY: I won't do that unless I'm still here at breakfast.

EMMA: How do you like your eggs?

Breathing Lessons is a Hallmark TV movie, from Anne Tyler's Pulitzer Prize–winning novel of the same name. Tyler is a wonderful writer, and though I don't usually read the books my movies are based on, I didn't hesitate in this case because I thought it would be as good as the script, and it was. That's not always the case. On the other hand, even if you have a good book, you may not be able to make a good movie from it because they're two different mediums.

Breathing Lessons is about a day in the life of two people, with no violence and no real action. It's a leisurely paced, simple story about Maggie and Ira Moran, an old married couple who don't seem to have much in common. Maggie is flighty, Ira is a realist. Maggie's a nonstop talker, Ira is a man of few words. Maggie will share the intimate details of their personal lives with anyone who'll listen, which never ceases to make Ira cringe. She doesn't think he appreciates her, and vice versa. But it all works out because they love each other dearly.

Joanne Woodward and I hadn't worked together before, but I quickly discovered that she's not only a great actress, she's a good person, and we hit it off right away. We had a week's rehearsal, which made us comfortable enough to try things. I've done pictures where you go in the first day and they want you to do a love scene. That's hard because you really don't know the person.

Joanne gave me so much to work with, I knew it was going to be good. She has guts. She'll do stuff. For instance, the scene where she tries to straighten out a dented fender with her bare hands wasn't in the script.

Playing Ira wasn't a stretch, because I understand him and I like him. At the time, Joanne and I had each been married for over thirty years, so we both knew the territory. I saw a lot of Lois in the script, and Joanne said she saw a lot of her husband, Paul Newman. We'd make wry little comments to each other as we filmed. She'd say, "Yup, that's Paul!" and I'd say, "Uh-huh, that's Lois."

Somebody once said that marriage consists of two people, one who wants the window open and the other who wants it shut. Lois lives on the phone. I hate phones. I'd throw them out of the house if I could. Lois has no sense of time. If she says she'll be there in thirty minutes, you're lucky if she shows up in an hour. Whereas I'm extremely punctual. If I tell someone I'll be there at a certain time, I'm there ten minutes earlier. On paper, Lois and I don't seem to have much in common. But, like Ira and Maggie, if either one of us gets in trouble, we're going to come to the other's defense. (Lois is one of the most eccentric people I've ever met. You know the patches of saggy skin you have on your elbows? Lois once asked a plastic surgeon to get rid of those. The surgeon said, "Sure, if you won't mind walking around with your arms permanently outstretched, like Frankenstein's monster.")

When I read the script for *The Notebook,* I thought it was a beautiful story, but I didn't appreciate its scope. I called my agent and said, "Is this a TV movie or a movie movie?"

"Movie movie."

I read it again and realized that anyone from ten to one hundred can enjoy it. It made sense to me because it's about undying love. I believe in undying love, and I think the film is a success because the audience believes in it, too.

I play Noah Calhoun, a man trying to break through to an Alzheimer's-stricken woman by reading to her from a notebook. I'm trying desperately to make her remember the past. I found it refreshing to see two older people in a romantic situation. This man loves her passionately; people can still have passion in their relationship after many years.

Noah is the kind of person that people think I am. He's stubborn and he's determined to break through, and he does, though only briefly. As I read to her from the notebook, we flash back to the story of two young lovers, played by Ryan Gosling and Rachel McAdams.

I've had personal experience with Alzheimer's: my aunt Emma suffered from it. I loved listening to her stories, but it was bittersweet: She could remember everything that happened when she was a girl, but didn't know my name. Not being able to recognize my loved ones is the thing that scares me most about aging.

Nick Cassavetes did a beautiful job of directing. When you consider that his parents, John Cassavetes and Gena Rowlands, used to shoot films in their apartment when Nicky was a boy, he's been in the movie business all his life. He was our guiding light. He knew what he wanted and got it, because he knows how to talk to actors. He took the Jeremy Leven screenplay (from the novel by Nicholas Sparks) and turned it into a powerful film.

Nick did something that impressed me. He'd envisioned a shot where ducks surround the young lovers in a boat. He *had* to have that shot, so he hired a wrangler to train hundreds of ducks for six months for something that would be on the screen for twenty seconds. When I saw the finished film, I thought it was magnificent. Then I found out it was all special effects because, despite all the effort and expense, the real ducks wouldn't do what they were supposed to. But that didn't diminish my admiration for Nick's commitment..

Nick and Gena were so tender and respectful of each other, I loved watching them. On our first shot of the picture, Nicky called out, "Okay, Mom—action!" It broke me up and I ruined the take. (But what else was he going to call her, "Ms. Rowlands"?)

I hadn't met Gena before we started the picture, but I loved working with her. Not only is she a wonderful lady, she's never given a bad performance in her life. The climactic scene near the end of the picture had worried me. I couldn't decide what I was going to do. In the end, I just let Gena set the tone and I reacted to what she did. Sure enough, she tore my heart out. I think Nick used the first take.

The rest of the cast is perfect: Rachel and Ryan took risks and tried things that would never have occurred to me. Sam Shepard, Joan Allen, James Marsden, Kevin Connolly—they're all in service of the story. I don't usually go on like this about films I'm in, but this one is extra-special.

The story goes from teenage to old age. It's love found, love lost, love found, love lost. Some critic called it "schmaltzy." It *is* a tearjerker, but there's nothing wrong with sentiment if it's honest. We don't need to apologize for anything. It's as touching a love story as I've ever seen, and I'm proud to be in it.

Lois and I don't have a "Hollywood marriage." Out here, people don't take marriage seriously. They don't seem to value loyalty and commitment. They vow to stay together "till death do us part," but a lot of them never get to the "D" in "death."

The secret to a long marriage, I think, apart from the physical side of it, which is very important, of course—you have to have respect. Lois and I have always respected each other. I think that's why we've lasted so long. You have to think of how everything you do will affect your partner. I've had chances to go crazy, but I asked myself, "What'll that do to Lois?" And I said, "No, I'm not gonna do that."

But it wasn't all roses. Lois and I went through an eighteen-month separation starting in 1979. We weren't angry at each other, and the marriage was never in real danger. It wasn't *us,* it was *me.* Lois was smart enough to know that I just needed some time alone because I was physically and mentally exhausted from the demands of doing *Rockford.* I was ready to quit acting. I fell into a deep depression. I was so edgy that the smallest thing would set me off. I started seeing a psychiatrist.

I moved out of our home and rented a house in the Valley. I spent a couple weeks on the road with Waylon Jennings. It was wild. He even brought me on stage one night to sing, but I was so nervous I don't remember it.

Lois had a lot of people saying, "Divorce his ass," and she had every right. But she had the patience to hang in there with me. You don't really know someone until you've lived with them. You have to accept the things about them you don't like, and they have to do the same for you. It's give and take. Unless you're willing to do that, don't get married.

Lois knows me better than anybody in the world. Just like the couple in *The Notebook,* we'll be there for each other forever.

Now, if I could just get her off the phone.

Sportswear ad,
circa 1948.
(mptvimages.com)

With (left to right)
Robert Gist,
Charles Nolte,
Henry Fonda, and
John Hodiak in
*The Caine Mutiny
Court Martial*
(1954). *(Eileen Derby
Images)*

With (left to right) Reiko Kuba, Marlon Brando, Miyoshi Umeki, and Red Buttons in *Sayonara* (1957). *(mptvimages.com)*

Cigarette break in costume as Bret Maverick, circa 1960. *(Joe Shere/mptvimages.com)*

LEFT: With Jack Kelly on the set of *Maverick,* 1958. *(Gene Trindl/mptvimages.com)*

BELOW: With fellow Warner Bros. TV cowboys, circa 1960. Left to right: Will "Sugarfoot" Hutchins, Peter "Lawman" Brown, Jack "Maverick" Kelly, Ty "Bronco" Hardin, Wayde "Colt .45" Preston, and John "Lawman" Russell. (Missing: Clint "Cheyenne" Walker.) *(Bison Archives)*

My greatest talent: making one eye look at the other. *(Leo Fuchs/mptvimages.com)*

Rare photo: practicing my swing, circa 1958. *(Sid Avery/ mptvimages.com)*

The Children's Hour (1961), with Fay Bainter, Shirley MacLaine, Audrey Hepburn, and Karen Balkin. *(Al St. Hilaire/mptvimages.com)*

With Marlon Brando and Diahann Carroll at the March on Washington for Jobs and Freedom, August 28, 1963. *(Eliot Elisofon/Time & Life Pictures/Getty Images)*

On the set of *The Great Escape* with (left to right) James Coburn, Steve McQueen, and director John Sturges, 1963. *(Corbis)*

Manhandling Doris Day in *Move Over, Darling* (1963). *(Corbis)*

With Julie Andrews in *The Americanization of Emily* (1964). *(Everett Collection)*

ABOVE: Rehearsing the beach scene in *The Americanization of Emily*. Note the gaffer's leg in the background. *(Don Cravens/Time & Life Pictures/Getty Images)*

LEFT: With Lois at John F. Kennedy airport, 1964. *(Getty Images)*

LEFT: With Yves
Montand in *Grand Prix*
(1966). *(Everett Collection)*

BELOW: A close call
filming *Grand Prix*.
*(Keystone Archives/Heritage
Images/Imagestate)*

With Sidney Poitier in *Duel at Diablo* (1966). *(Kobal Collection/Picture Desk)*

In my little blue Mini Cooper, 1966. *(Gunther/mptvimages.com)*

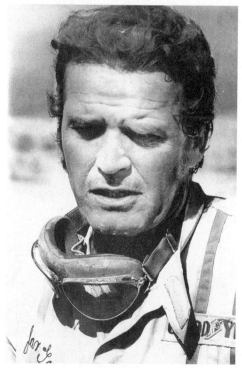

ABOVE: Driving the Baja 1000 with Scooter Patrick, 1968. *(Ron Johnson)*

LEFT: Having fun at the Baja 1000, 1969. *(Ron Johnson)*

Congratulating
AIR racing team
driver Lothar
Motschenbacher
after he finished
second in the
1969 24 Hours at
Daytona. *(Courtesy
of Louis Galanos)*

With Paul Newman in the pits at the 1985 Indianapolis 500. *(Indianapolis Star)*

LEFT: My "homage" to Henry Fonda, seen here in *My Darling Clementine*. *(Photofest)* ABOVE: In *Support Your Local Sheriff* (1969). *(akg-images/The Image Works)*

As "Nichols," 1970. *(Everett Collection)*

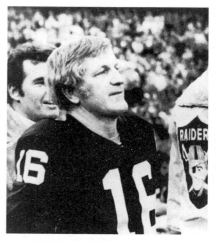

On the Raiders' sidelines with George Blanda on December 22, 1975, just after he'd kicked an extra point against the Kansas City Chiefs that made him the first player to score 2,000 points. *(Getty Hulton Archives/Getty Images)*

With Noah Beery, Jr.—
"Pidge"—on the set of *The
Rockford Files,* 1978. *(Gene
Trindl/mptvimages.com)*

On the set of *The Rockford
Files* with Charles Floyd
Johnson, Stephen J.
Cannell, Meta Rosenberg,
David Chase, and Juanita
Bartlett, 1979. *(Gene Trindl/
mptvimages.com)*

With Julie Andrews and Robert
Preston in *Victor/Victoria* (1982).
(Corbis)

With James Woods in *Promise*
(1986). *(Everett Collection)*

With Jack Lemmon in *My
Fellow Americans* (1996).
(Photofest)

As Captain Woodrow Call in *Larry McMurtry's Streets of Laredo* (1995). *(historicallycorrect™)*

With (left to right) Tommy Lee Jones, Donald Sutherland and Clint Eastwood in *Space Cowboys* (2000). *(Corbis)*

With Gena Rowlands in *The Notebook* (2004). *(Everett Collection)*

Maverick statue in Norman, Oklahoma.
(Courtesy of Robert Howe)

CHAPTER TWELVE

This Is My Life

I n the 1950s there was a live network television show called *This Is Your Life*. Every week the host, Ralph Edwards, would ambush some unsuspecting individual, usually a celebrity but sometimes an "ordinary" person who'd done something extraordinary, and review his life in front of a studio audience. There was a reveal at the top of the show where Ralph would tear the wrapping off the *This Is Your Life* book and say, "Joe Zilch, *This . . . is . . . your . . . life!*" The music would swell and poor Joe would be a dead duck. For the next half hour, they'd trot out old friends, relatives, and former teachers for little reunions. The camera would push in tight on the victim's—I mean, the subject's—face for his reaction as each guest was introduced.

One afternoon in June '58, Jack Kelly and I were on the *Maverick* set at Warner Bros. shooting an episode directed by Richard Bare. Dick, who was in on the surprise, pretended to be ill, so we wrapped for the day. Someone from the publicity department came over and said, "Jim, since you have the rest of the afternoon off and you're still in costume, would you mind shooting some stills with Jack over at NBC?"

I think I grumbled something about being under contract and having no choice.

They took us over to NBC, and while they were supposedly setting up the lights for the photo session, Ralph Edwards burst in and sprung the trap. I pretended to be surprised and a little annoyed—the way I'd seen others react to "Mr.-This-Is-Your-Life-Himself."

I *was* annoyed, but not surprised. That day, probably for the first time in my life, I was late for work and was still home when the car came to take Lois and the girls to the *This Is Your Life* set. When I realized what was going on, I pitched a fit. I dreaded the prospect of having my personal history exposed on national television. For that matter, at age thirty, I wasn't ready to review my life under any circumstances.

"No *way* am I gonna do that," I said.

Lois tried to persuade me, but I stood firm. I was about to lock myself in the bathroom when she said the magic words: "They flew your whole family in from Oklahoma. Do you want to disappoint them?"

That did it.

Both my grandmothers were there, along with my father and Mama Grace, Uncle John and Aunt Leona, my brothers, Bum and Jack, plus Jim Paul Dickenson, Henry Kaiser, Paul Gregory, and Captain Horace West, my commanding officer in Korea.

They had me.

Once the show began, I got into it and was happy to see everyone. I enjoyed the after-party at the Hollywood Roosevelt Hotel even more. But if you ever happen to catch the video, watch my face when Ralph Edwards says, *"James Garner, this . . . is . . . your . . . life!"* See my expression? That's *ACT*-ING!

I've been lucky to have worked with many talented actors, and gotten along with most of them. The only coworkers I've ever had problems with were the ones who didn't do their jobs. I've worked with good directors and gotten along with them, too: William Wellman, Joshua Logan, William Wyler, George Seaton, Arthur Hiller, John Sturges, John Frankenheimer, Norman Jewison, Paul Bogart, Blake Edwards, Richard Donner, Martin Ritt, Glenn Jordan, Clint Eastwood.

But I've never wanted to direct. That should be worth *something*. (Never made a record album, either. Too many actors have.) I directed one *Rockford* episode, "The Girl in the Bay City Boys Club," written by Juanita Bartlett. The director dropped out at the last minute and I had to step in. Not something I enjoyed. It's hard to act and direct at the same time. You have to prepare a scene, make sure everybody knows what they're supposed to do, then switch hats and step in front of the camera. I'd rather concentrate on acting.

I've had other chances. Steve Cannell always wanted me to direct his *Rockford* scripts, but I've never been comfortable telling people what to do. Sure, I'll make suggestions here and there, but I generally let the people I hire do their jobs. They're happier, I'm happier, and we all work better that way.

In 1988, I had two open-heart operations and discovered I'm a fatalist. Lois was beside herself with worry, but I decided that since it was beyond my control, I'd just accept my fate, whatever it might be. If I can't change or influence something, I'm not going to think about it two seconds.

If archaeologists dig up my bones a thousand years from now, they'll wonder what in the world I was. I've had broken ribs, broken knuckles, a cracked coccyx, dislocations, sprains, and torn ligaments. I stopped counting the number of stitches I've had at two hundred. I broke my right kneecap twice. I've had nine knee operations, including three knee replacements (the right one twice). After one knee operation, I got a staph infection that laid me up for three months. I've had ulcers, diverticulitis, an aortic aneurysm, a quadruple bypass, and a hemorrhagic stroke. I had surgery to remove an arterial blood clot I got when my trainer held my leg up too long. (The poor guy felt awful about it.)

I've been in constant pain from arthritis since the 1960s. Disintegrated disks in my back and neck have made me a couple of inches shorter than I used to be. Now the pain keeps me from playing golf and driving a car. Though I've taken a lot of pain medication over the years including Vicodin and Percocet, I can't remember what it's like to be pain-free.

What's the old line? "If I knew I was gonna live this long, I'd have taken better care of myself." I didn't take care of my body while I was working. Most of the tears and sprains and breaks resulted from doing my own stunts. I didn't eat properly, I didn't get enough sleep, and I was usually out of shape. The only time you'd catch me jogging was if someone was chasing me, and he had to have been big or I wouldn't have run.

And I smoked.

But the truth is, even if I knew I was going to live this long, I almost certainly would *not* have taken better care of myself. You have to live your life. What's the point of being here if you don't *live*? That may be the only point!

What have I learned? I learned, at the age of fourteen, that I had to fight my own battles. That's when I made up my mind that nobody would ever step on me again.

If you survive combat, you think of every day after it as a gift. I don't think people appreciate life as much as those who've gone through that.

You have to take risks to get rewards. When you're standing on the edge of a cliff trying to get up the courage to jump off and fly, it always looks a lot farther down than you think.

People ask me what I'm proudest of, careerwise. They expect me to name a movie or a television show, but the thing I'm proudest of professionally is that I never kissed anyone's butt.

Success doesn't change people. If they get difficult and arrogant, they were that way before and just weren't in a position to show it.

I don't believe that nice guys finish last. I've known too many wonderful people who finished first because they had lots of help. The best way to accomplish your goal is to have other people pulling on the rope with you. If you have a team where everyone embraces the same general principles and tries to help one another, you have a much better chance of winning.

Is the audience always right? Nooo! Look at all the trash out there.

I've been married to the same woman for over half a century and the list of my leading ladies is a Hollywood Who's Who, but I don't claim to know anything about women. Half the time you *think* you know them, but you don't. All I know is, I love them. I love them all. But I'm afraid of them.

I think there's something out there bigger than we are, but I don't have a clue what it is.

Something funny happens as you get older. You loosen up. You get a little freer and a little braver. You don't hold back so much. You try not to get too high or too low. When your feelings go up and down that's called *stress,* and it's a killer. And you're not so insecure. Believe me, I *am* insecure.

At the end of the day when you put your head on your pillow there is only one person you had better please: yourself.

People who don't know me think I'm easygoing and lighthearted, but I'm a pessimist by nature, maybe because I was always disappointed when I was young. I'm really an old curmudgeon. A guy who says he's an expert on curmudgeons tells me it isn't curmudgeon-like to proclaim yourself one, but I don't care. MaryAnn likes to say, "You're not a real curmudgeon, you're a curmudgeon wannabe." We argue about it:

"I am too a curmudgeon."

"You are not."

"Am too!"

"Not!"

A lot of my characters are curmudgeons. Jim Rockford's a curmudgeon: he pretends to be tough, but it's only a front. I guess I've played more and more curmudgeons as I've gotten older: Murphy Jones in *Murphy's Romance,* Albert Sidney Finch in *Decoration Day,* Ira Moran in *Breathing Lessons,* Jim Egan in *8 Simple Rules.*

Deep down, curmudgeons are good people. They try to do the right thing. They have a sense of humor and a sense of proportion. They speak their mind and devil take the hindmost. They have principles and they don't run from a fight.

Curmudgeons know that some things are worth fighting for, that we all need boundaries that we're ready to defend no matter what. If you don't make an enemy or two along the way, you're not doing it right.

But I'm not a macho guy. I don't *like* macho guys. I'm a marshmallow. No, a Tootsie Pop: hard on the outside, soft on the inside. I don't go looking for trouble, but I've never backed down from a fight, because if you back down, you lose right then, and *I don't like to lose.* I try to get along with the world, but when big ones start treading on little ones, those who can't defend themselves—I'll get in there and do something. I might get stomped on, but that's okay. I can't help it. I guess that's why Frank Wells used to call me "Crusader Rabbit." I believe there's justice out there if you fight for what you know is right. The pain you have to endure is worth it.

If I give you my word, that's it. If say I will do something, you better believe I'll do it. I'm loyal: if I'm your friend, it's forever. The only thing you can do to change that is lie to me, because I can't stand dishonesty. Lie to me just once, and you're in trouble. Well, I might let you get away with it *once,* but the second time it's all over.

I'm a big fan of the "crimson and cream," the University of Oklahoma football team. Oklahoma is known as "the Sooner State," and the OU football team adopted "Sooners" as their nickname. The University's fight song is "Boomer Sooner," sung to the tune of "Boola Boola." If you've followed OU football as long as I have, you've heard it at least a million times. I've always had affection for OU, having grown up around its campus. Anyone who's lived in a college town knows what I'm talking about.

When I was asked to give the OU commencement address in 1995, the year of the Oklahoma City bombing, I could not believe they wanted *me.* I immediately declined because of my stage fright, but they wore me down, and I finally agreed to do it eight months before. It was the worst eight months of my life.

Bill Saxon and Steve Cannell helped me write the speech. They gave me pages and then I worked the material my own way. But I still worried I'd say something stupid and make a fool of myself.

I've got to be the most unlikely commencement speaker OU ever had. I didn't graduate with my class at Norman High; I got my diploma from tests in the army while I was in Korea. I spent about twelve minutes at OU, yet over the years I've had dozens of people tell me they had classes with me there. They must've looked quick.

At a dinner the night before graduation, OU president David Boren introduced me as "Doctor Jim Garner" and everyone stood up and applauded. By the time I reached the podium, I was crying.

For a country boy, I've been to a lot of places and done a lot of things. I have a wonderful family and great friends. I've had a long career, made some money, and had the greatest gift of all: I found something I liked to do. I don't feel I've left anything on the table. I don't regret not having done this or that. *I've had a good time!*

I like people and I think I'm a good judge of character. I go by my gut and haven't been disappointed very often. I've been criticized for picking up strays. I've been told I'm too kindhearted for my own good, that I'm a "pigeon." I don't think so. It's just that I've had a few broken wings in my life and wished somebody would pick me up and dust me off.

I've been asked again and again, "How do you want to be remembered?" I usually say I don't care, but that's not true. I want to have accomplished something, to have made a contribution to the world. It would be wonderful if just one person looked at my life and said, "If he could overcome that, maybe I can, too."

Beyond that, I think an actor can contribute by making people forget their troubles for an hour or two. Call it relief, escape, diversion . . . I think one of the greatest gifts is being able to make people happy. I *like* to make people happy.

So, if anybody asks, "How do you want to be remembered?" I tell them:

"With a smile."

Outttakes

Family, friends, and colleagues weighed in for this book, and since their stories sound better directly from them, here they are, in their own words.

Jim and I "met cute." He tells everyone it was at a Stevenson-for-President rally, but it was actually a week before, at a barbecue one Sunday afternoon at Toni and Jess Kimmel's house in Studio City. Jess was the head of the talent department at Universal. At the time the studios nurtured young actors, gave them drama classes, etc. James Bumgarner had just gotten his contract at Warners.

At that moment in my life, I was an emotional wreck. My daughter, Kim, was in the hospital with polio. Her esophagus was paralyzed and she couldn't swallow. I'd just been fired from my job as a receptionist at Foote, Cone & Belding because I took so much time off to be with her.

Jim made quite an entrance. All of a sudden, shooting into the backyard like an arrow, this gorgeous man runs across the lawn, smiles, says, "Can I go swimming?" and dives straight into the pool! My first thought was, *Wow, who* is *this man? He's too beautiful to be alive!*

The Kimmel children were in the pool and Jim started playing with them. I thought it was somehow odd to see such a young, good-looking guy playing with kids like that, so I watched him. He was pretending to be a monster. He'd pick up the kids and throw them back in the water, and they'd come out screaming for more. *Adorable!* I said to myself, "Forget it. He's too beautiful. He's not going to look at you," and I dismissed him from my mind.

A little later, he sat down at our table still wet and proceeded to tell jokes. One of his favorite things in those days was pretending to be gay. Here's this masculine man putting on this attitude. We fell down laughing. He was so adorable and so funny I thought, *He's too good to be true.*

About a week later, the Kimmels called. "Do you remember Jim Bumgarner?"

"Yes . . . "

"He'd like to see you again. Come to a Stevenson-for-President rally at our house this weekend."

There were lots of guests at the rally, but pretty soon I saw Jim, all by himself in the kitchen. The first thing he said was, "Would you like to have dinner with me tonight?" Before I could answer, an attractive young woman came in and said, "Jim, are we having dinner tonight?" and Jim said, "No, just made other plans." The woman had a Scotch in her hand and she threw it in Jim's face—ice cubes and all—and stormed out. He was dripping wet, with Scotch running down his face onto (I found out later) the only suit he had. But he didn't lose his composure. As he calmly dried himself with a dish towel he said, "You know, I've got a girlfriend."

"That one?"

"No, another one, BarBara Luna."

She was a well-known young actress in town. I wasn't thrilled to hear that he had at least two other women in his life.

After he'd dried himself off, we left the party. On the way to dinner he stopped the car and said, "Do you mind if I kiss you?"

I was stunned, but I let him kiss me. Willingly.

Then he said, "So, will you marry me?"

Still joking, I said, "Of course!"

We went to Frascati, on Sunset. It happened that Gene Shacove, my hairdresser, was there. (He's the guy they modeled *Shampoo* on— Warren Beatty lived with him to watch how he operated.) Gene said, "Who are you with?"

"That boy over there."

"Oh, really? What's going on with you two?"

"I don't know, I just met him."

"I'll bet you marry him."

"Really? As a matter of fact, he just asked me to marry him!"

Jim and I saw each other every day and every night for the next week. One night we were up on Mulholland "talking" in his car when he again asked me to marry him. I could see he was serious and I said yes without hesitating. By then I was serious, too.

Jim won't like me telling this, but a tear ran down his cheek when I said yes.

"I never thought anybody would ever love me," he said.

Jim didn't have any money and I didn't have any money, but he'd met Kim and she liked him. We'd gone to an ice cream parlor, and while Jim was getting the cones I said, "Kim, what do you think? Should I marry him?" I always asked Kim about the men I dated. I'd considered marrying a man I didn't love who had money and was willing to adopt my daughter because I was worried about what would become of us.

Kim said, "Yes, Mom, marry him. He's perfect and you're perfect together."

We got married two days later. It all happened so fast, it was like a dream.

And a miracle.

—LOIS GARNER

I was a young girl when my dad Jim created a new kind of TV magic based on his wry delivery, self-deprecating wit, and the brightest smile I've ever seen. He was an instant sensation as Bret Maverick and I was proud of him. One of my fondest memories of those days is of a tour of the Warner Bros. studios with him. We visited various sets where we were shown all the cameras, lights, and equipment. Then I got to ride a horse and meet actors in costume, including some delightful cowboys and Indians. I even had my hair "done" by a makeup artist. And I met Gary Cooper. I didn't know who he was at the time, but I could tell he was a very nice man. The whole experience made me think I was in a magical place. I had the sense Jim was showing me off, which made me feel part of a family with him. I was proud of both of us.

—KIMBERLY GARNER

The most frequently asked question during the course of my life has always been, "What was it like growing up with him?" My answer has always been the same: "He was just my dad, and like most kids, I was not paying that much attention to the fact that he was all that different."

However, I did notice that we never made it through a meal in public without tons of people coming over to ask for an autograph. He was always very gracious, but occasionally I needed an attitude adjustment because I didn't really understand it. I was always naturally protective of him and still am. I remember one incident when we were in England trying to do some normal family sightseeing at the Tower of London and we were literally mobbed by hundreds of fans running toward us. We barely escaped without being crushed.

Like many other fathers, he was gone quite a bit and often worked odd hours. It didn't seem that different from most of my friends' fathers, except that my dad usually came home with makeup on!

He really made a concentrated effort to stay connected to me, no matter where he was or what he was doing. Any time I ever needed to talk to him, he was accessible. If he was going to be away for a long time, we would meet him on location to break it up a bit. He worked in some of the most beautiful places in the world. I remember on one trip in particular, he bought "me" a slot car racetrack and set up this elaborate obstacle course, winding under and around all the furniture in our gigantic sitting room in our hotel suite. I don't think the poor hotel staff were thrilled with our crazy indoor mini Grand Prix, but we both loved every second of it! We had to keep going back to the toy store to buy more cars because we kept wearing them out!

My dad was always the kind of parent who would get down on the floor and play with the kids. He never met a child he could resist. If he saw a baby, he had to say hi no matter where he was or what he was in the middle of doing.

He was always very hands-on, completely present and totally involved. All my friends adored him, too, and not because he was some big "Hollywood star," but because I had the most fun dad! If we wanted to jump off the balcony into the pool, he would do it first just to make sure it was safe enough for us to try.

I am blessed in many ways to have a father like him, but, unfortunately, I was often too young to fully appreciate some of the wonderful privileges I enjoyed because of him. I can remember flying in the Goodyear blimp while my dad was piloting it, riding around the racetrack at Brands Hatch in the Formula One car he drove in *Grand Prix,* riding a horse *inside* a sound stage, going to the Academy

Awards, sitting in the front row of a Beatles concert in Italy, flying on a private studio jet full of celebrities, walking through the pits before the Indy 500, staying on the Matterhorn at Disneyland twelve times in a row, being flown into the center of a racetrack by helicopter, meeting the president in the Oval Office, dining with royalty, et cetera. What a lucky kid!

All fathers are special, but as a child, I just did not realize how special mine was, but I certainly do now!

My dad would always take me to work with him whenever it was possible. He would usually leave the house while it was still dark. I remember thinking that the only people who were up before the crack of dawn were people who worked in the movie industry and milkmen.

I'll never forget the morning of the Sylmar earthquake [in 1971]. My dad happened to be in the shower when the house started shaking so violently that he was literally thrown out of it. Since I was going to work with him that day, I was already awake and was paralyzed with fear, watching the books fly off the shelves. But as soon as I heard him running down the hallway to my room, I knew everything would be all right. My dad was there to rescue me, as he went on to do many times throughout my life.

Since my dad was always the consummate professional, he was going to work that day come hell or high water. He was always overprepared and extra early. He *never* wanted to make anyone wait for him. So we started out for the Disney Ranch, which happened to be near the epicenter of the quake. The few cars left on the freeway when the quake struck had all pulled over, and sure enough, there were some cast and crew members on the side of the road trying to decide what to do next and where to go. My dad said, "Hey, let's go to work!" He was their fearless leader and they all followed him just as they usually did.

My dad is not a wishy-washy, "I-don't-want-to-get-my-hands-dirty" type. He is definitely the kind of guy you want around in an emergency. In 1961 we lived in Bel Air and our next-door neighbors were an elderly couple who had recently adopted a baby.

The Bel Air fire was one of the worst on record and everyone in the surrounding area was evacuated, but my father stayed and hosed down our roof and our next-door neighbors' roof until the danger had passed. Our neighbors were stunned to find their house still standing. Almost every house on our street had burned to the ground, and the only things left standing were their brick fireplaces.

It took great courage for my dad to risk his life that way, and I have always been proud of him for being that kind of person. He is one of these rare people who actually lives by the golden rule, who stands up for the underdog and believes wholeheartedly in the principle of the matter.

Over the years, I have heard countless stories about his absolute professionalism, his many acts of kindness, his immense generosity, all the while remaining completely humble and never seeking anything in return. It is mystifying that any actor could create this kind of longevity in Hollywood, construct a lifetime of classic work, and never have a bad word said against him.

My father has never let any of this "Hollywood" hype go to his head. He has never forgotten where he came from. It does not matter to him if you are the head of the network or you are a grip, he is going to treat everyone with the same amount of respect and kindness. Actually, truth be told, he would probably treat the grip a little better. ;)

—GIGI GARNER

Jim and I were driving on Interstate 10 out to a golf course somewhere. Jim was in the fast lane, but he wasn't speeding. Some guy got on Jim's tail, and he was gonna show him how *he* could drive. He really got close and was tailgating Jim. So Jim stomped on it and got ahead of the guy and let him go by. Then Jim slipped back in behind the guy and just laid on his rear bumper. He kept tapping his bumper—this was at 65 miles an hour—and then he pushed him! That guy lost his nerve real fast. Jim scared the hell out of him. Scared the hell out of me, too.

—JACK GARNER

Our high school basketball team was in overtime against Capitol Hill from Oklahoma City. We were one point down and Jim was fouled with one second left on the clock. He had two free throws but missed both of them, costing us the Mid-State Conference championship. "Bird Dog" Coleman never misses an opportunity to jab Jim about that. The last time Jim was in Norman, Bird Dog said, "Hey, Jim, remember when you missed those two free throws?" Jim said, "Bird Dog, if you ever, ever say that to me again, I'm gonna hit you right in the face!"

—ROY HAMILTON

Jim and I met through mutual friends in the early 1950s. Our senses of humor melded right away; we both saw the ridiculousness of everything, and we laughed like crazy.

We were an unlikely pair of buddies, but fun was always easy for us. We put on little shows at parties and played a game called In Plain Sight, where you had to look for camouflaged items that people planted around. I remember us switching jackets at a party once. And we always had good dinners at our mutual homes.

And then I played Billy the Kid on *Maverick*. It was even more fun working with him. Everybody loved him at the studio because he made their lives easier. All the actors I know who've ever worked with Jim adore him. He's very generous on the set, and smart.

Jim is one of the most intuitive people I know, but he's complicated. I think he always seemed happiest when working. I'm not sure why, but I suspect it's something deep. Although he's very private, we have had, I guess you could say, an *intimate* relationship over the years, sharing very confidential and personal things. But I'm not so sure that's his usual way.

I know Jim was thrilled with his success in television (I always thought he could have become a serious movie star, too), but he never gave himself enough credit as an actor and an artist, and he is both of those things for sure. There's an enigmatic aspect to him that most people never see. They accept the image he wants to portray. But I think he has his secrets. Maybe something like the cat who ate the canary? . . . but always with a big smile to go with it.

—JOEL GREY

When Jim and Steve worked together on *The Great Escape,* it was a tenuous relationship. They liked each other—at least Steve liked Jim—but Steve was wary of him, I think because Jim was so incredibly good looking. Of course, so was Steve in his own way, but he just felt that Jim was tall, dark, and handsome, while Steve was more of the rough-and-tumble kind of guy.

In 1963, just before Steve and I went to Taiwan to film *The Sand Pebbles,* Paul Newman, James Garner, Steve, and I went to the car races at Riverside. On our way home, the men got annoyed because I insisted on stopping at the next service station restroom. When they did stop, I discovered to my dismay that there was a long line of women ahead of me. I couldn't stand the delay any longer, and I knew the men were probably getting angrier by the minute, so I came up with a brilliant idea. I said to the girls standing there, "Hey, do you know there's a car full of movie stars around the bend?"

"Who?" they cried in unison.

"Why, there's Steve McQueen, there's Paul Newman, and there's James Garner!"

The girls looked at each other and ran like crazy, leaving me in sole possession of the facilities. I never did tell the fellas how a swarm of females suddenly discovered them!

—NEILE McQUEEN TOFFEL

August 28, 1963, was an exhilarating day. Those of us from the West Coast who came to the March on Washington were grateful to be there and thrilled to be united in such an important common cause. We understood there was possible danger but we put our fears aside.

I was the only woman in the group, and that day I received brotherly attention from some of the most beautiful men in the world. Especially James, who was always chivalrous and caring about women.

Later, when I came to town to do my own television series, he was the first to welcome me to the community. I have a vivid memory of a car pulling into the driveway and Jim getting out and saying, "Welcome. This is a crazy town, there's lots of good and lots of bad." It was just the advice one needed coming to a strange land. "I'm a big brother," he said, "if you need anything, call me, I'm not far away."

Soon after that, I was on a tennis court with Jim, Sidney Poitier, and Dennis Weaver. Naturally, I was wearing my most provocative little white shorts. A bee flew into the shorts and I panicked. I was screaming and yelling, all the while thinking, on the one hand, I should take the shorts off to allow the bee to escape, but on the other hand wanting to preserve my modesty. The men were trying to distract me from being terrified by this little bee, especially Jim, who was so sweet and so funny. He said things like, "I don't know, that bee might never come out of there" and "I think that's the happiest bee in town." When the bee suddenly fell onto the ground of its own accord and sort of hopped around in circles, Jim flashed that famous grin and said, "Look, he's drunk!"

—DIAHANN CARROLL

Jim and I worked together only twice, in *Move Over, Darling* and *The Thrill of It All*. He's so good at what he does . . . I felt married. We didn't see each other much over the following years, but we've stayed friends because we talk on the phone regularly. I don't know how, because Jim *hates* the telephone. *I* usually have to call *him*. "Can't you pick up a phone?" I say, but he just grumbles.

We had fun. He's a marvelous actor. He's very real when he talks to you. He's so funny and so nice, I just love him. Even though he broke two of my ribs. *Jim, if we don't speak for a while, I forgive you for breaking my ribs. Both of them. Don't give it another thought.*

—DORIS DAY

Talk to anyone who has ever worked with Jim, and the word "family" will emerge almost immediately. In many cases, their association with Jim lasted several decades. No wonder they consider him, and he considers them, like family.

Roy Huggins was never part of that extended family—which seems odd at first, considering how integral Roy was to Jim's two greatest successes. Roy cast Jim as Bret Maverick, a character he created in 1956 when he was under contract as a producer at Warner Bros. Television. The success of *Maverick* made Jim a huge star, enabling him to make the leap to feature motion pictures in the 1960s.

Jim and Roy shared many traits, but they were also wired differently. Roy was a writer first and foremost, so he was often reclusive by choice—a mentality that, in many ways, reflected his approach as a television producer, particularly during his eighteen years at Universal. Though he oversaw the entire production of *Rockford* during the show's first season (as he did on every TV project for which he was "show runner"), Roy devoted most of his energy to two specific areas: the development of stories and scripts, and the editing of the film. All other aspects of day-to-day production, he entrusted to the likes of such capable lieutenants as Jo Swerling and Stephen J. Cannell. With regard to story and character development, Roy's focus was so singular that he would often isolate himself for days at a time—usually in the form of one of his patented "story drives," where he would embark on a long drive in his car, accompanied only by his tape recorder, and dictate several full-length stories for his shows. (On one such excursion, he dictated a sixteen-page single-spaced story that served as the basis for the *Rockford Files* pilot.)

Roy was also unusual in his choice of working hours. He often arrived at the studio at five or six in the evening (when most shows wrapped up production for the day) and worked well into the early-morning hours. As a result, an actor working on a Huggins-produced show was not likely to see him on a daily basis. So as well as he knew Jim—and came to understand him throughout their long association together—if Roy were alive today, I believe he would cite his modus operandi as a producer as one factor that would've prevented him from becoming part of Jim's extended family.

I respect and admire both men. Whatever personal differences kept them apart, their professional collaborations changed the face of television in two genres. Along the way, they each left their own distinctive mark, for which we should all be grateful.

—ED ROBERTSON, author of
Maverick: Legend of the West and *Thirty Years of The Rockford Files*

I worked with Jim on *Rockford* for six years and he never changed a line. He did the lines exactly as written. And not only that, if we had a guest star on the set who was bending the dialogue or doing approximations of the lines, Jim would listen to it in the camera rehearsal and then he would go over to that actor and in the nicest way he'd say, "You know, I think we have the best writers in

Hollywood working on this show, and I never change a line, and it would certainly mean a lot to me if you didn't either." So he was down there protecting the words.

I remember once, in the fourth year, David Chase, who as you know is the creator of *The Sopranos* and is one of the best writers I know . . . David was one of the producers on *The Rockford Files* for four of the five years, and in the fourth year, we got a call that Jim was having trouble with one of the lines in a script that David had written. Jim was always good with his dialogue and hated to be the guy holding up the company because he couldn't remember a line. Occasionally he would have a line he couldn't remember, and it would just drive him nuts, and apparently, this line was completely baffling him and he couldn't get it out. And one of the things about David is that he writes soliloquy-type speeches—they're this long on the page—and that was part of the problem. And so I get a call from an assistant director who says, "You'd better get down here, he's throwing furniture, he's so upset." So I grab David and we're walking down to Stage 12 or wherever it was and I'm saying, "Well, you know, this is the exception that proves the rule: here we are five and a half years into this show and never rewritten a line for this guy and here's the one time that it's going to happen."

And David's kind of upset because he liked the line. Well, we get down to the set and the red light's turning on the door and we have to wait until it shuts off and we walk into the soundstage and you can hear Jim screaming. He'd blown the line again. David's kind of standing in the background—he's like a little miffed because we'd never changed any of our dialogue.

I walk over to Jim and I go, "Hey, I'm down here with David and we can break this line up and throw one of the lines to Pidge [Noah Beery Jr.] and it'll take us five minutes."

Jim looked at me and he said, "Change this line? Steve, this is a *great* line. I just can't remember the goddam thing!"

So we never changed it. And we were perfect: never changed a line on the show.

—STEPHEN J. CANNELL

I was thirty years old. *The Rockford Files* was looking for a new producer, and this was going to be my big chance. The show had been on the air for two years and I was not a watcher of it, so they sent me to a screening room to see a couple of episodes. I'd never produced—I was a story editor—and I think I watched three in a row and got the feeling that *Rockford* was the only show I'd ever seen that didn't exist just in its own time slot. It was in Los Angeles, and Los Angeles is a real place and these are real people. I'd never felt that way about anything else I'd seen. I think that has changed since, but at the time, there was something generic about television. Place didn't matter. But *The Rockford Files* was very much about the place where it was set. And the people.

Jim taught me that good acting involves listening. When you have to do fifteen takes of the same scene, by the second or third take, an actor has heard what the other person is saying so it no longer registers. He's only thinking about getting his line out. Jim is really good at listening and making it fresh every time. He told me that was because his first job was as one of the jurors in *The Caine Mutiny Court Martial* on Broadway. He had no lines, so he had to sit there for three hours trying to stay awake. The only way to make it work for him was to listen like it was brand new. That's easier said than done. It's not real when you've already heard it a million times.

I also learned about camera. I began to understand how film translates words into images. There was something about the way Jim worked that made me see that very clearly, maybe because there was no nonsense on the set. It was all about the work, and the work stood there very clear for you to see, without the Sturm und Drang. On Jim's set, everyone was treated with kindness and respect. There was no bullshit, no Hollywood slithering going on. Compared to the experiences I'd had before, working on *Rockford* was an upgrade to first class.

Every Christmas Jim gave each of the writers their scripts bound in beautiful red leather with gold lettering on the cover. We'd have a party at a Mexican restaurant near the Burbank Studio. We'd be sitting there dipping chips in guacamole and drinking beer and I'd suddenly think: *What am I doing here? What am I doing here with* James Garner? *With* Maverick! *How did this* happen?

—DAVID CHASE

When *The Rockford Files* debuted back in 1974, we were living in Michigan. I was the series's biggest fan. It became sort of a religious experience, and friends knew not to call me on Friday night between nine and ten because I wouldn't pick up the phone.

When we moved to Southern California in '78, one of the first things I did was try to find Jim Rockford's trailer. I knew it was at a place called Paradise Cove in Malibu, so I jumped in the car and headed for the beach. I was cruising up the Pacific Coast Highway when I saw two semi trucks with "Rockford Files/NBC" on the side. I couldn't believe it!

I parked near the trucks and got out of the car. The first person I ran into was Luis Delgado. I told him I was a huge fan of the show and asked if Mr. Garner was there and he said, "Yeah, he's here, do you want to meet him?" Just like that! I could have been *anybody*! (I *was,* actually.) Luis took me over to a motor home, opened the door, and there was Jim, sitting in a chair. Luis said, "This young man would like to meet you," and Jim said, "Come in, son." Jim always makes everybody feel welcome.

—ROB HOWE

Garner says he's easygoing, but he's lying. He's angry and desperate, just like I am. That's why *Rockford* has always worked so well, because Jim is coming from a very passionate, driven place.

—JOE SANTOS

The relationship between Jim Rockford and Beth Davenport was never explicit, just implicit. On purpose.

The character was created by Juanita Bartlett in the first *Rockford* episode she wrote. Beth was the first intelligent and attractive female character on television. There had been smart women before, but they usually wore big glasses and were fat or old. To have a young woman who actually had a brain in her head was something quite extraordinary at that time.

Working with Jim was like getting a little acting class every day. I learned a lot about camera angles, lenses, lighting. One of the hardest things to do as an actor is to walk and talk at the same time, especially when you have a lot of dialogue and there are about fifty people moving along with you off-camera. I always had a lot of lawyer shit to say. Jim helped me get my bearings so I'd know where the camera was at all times. He knows all that stuff because he's been doing it all his life. He looked after me.

In addition to the technical things I learned from Jim, I also learned a lot about being a leader. Everybody loved him—but he took care of not only the actors and me but the whole crew. He knew everybody's name, he knew everybody's kids' names. He had an enormous generosity toward everyone on the crew. And so of course they were all completely devoted to him in return.

I think Jim is such a good actor because he actually leaves his actor at home and he brings himself to the screen. That kind of ease in front of a camera takes time. He's also a very appealing human being. Both men and women feel safe with him, they feel like they *get* him.

—GRETCHEN CORBETT

I had a term contract at Universal, a serious development deal, and had done two pilots that hadn't sold. Universal got a script for a new show called *Magnum* and assigned it to me.

Well, I didn't like the script. It was very James Bond–like and the guy did everything right. He was a superhero with a woman on each arm, and he was too perfect. I told them, "I don't think I should play guys like this. I really don't like him." I probably said, "I want to do a character like Rockford." We got into a big thing. My whole future was on the line. Most people didn't know who I was and the studio said, "Who the hell do you think you are? You've never even been on the air!" It was a big dilemma for me because I did not think I fit in that kind of show.

I didn't know what to do. If I stood firm and refused to take the part, whether or not they could have legally won in a courtroom, two things would have happened: (1) they could have tied me up forever, (2) I would have gotten the reputation of being difficult and may never have worked again anyway.

I talked to Jim about it and he said, simply: "Do you want to do the show?" I said no. He said, "Well, Tom, I'm not going to tell you what to do, but I'll tell you this: if they want you, you'll never have more power than you do right now. As soon as you sign on, you're going to have no power and no position and no one's going to have to listen to you. Maybe if the show's a raging success you'll get that power back in the second or third year, but if you're going to make a stand, now's the only time you can make it."

It occurred to me that this is not a guy who's just throwing advice off the top of his head. This is a guy who's taken those kinds of risks.

It was not a precious discussion, not "Jim, I have to talk to you . . ." We were sitting around waiting for the crew to come back from lunch and it came up. Then we went on to something else. In fact, if I had sat him down and said, "I have to talk to you, I need some advice," I probably wouldn't have gotten any. We were just talking.

I took Jim's advice and it worked. "Okay," Universal said, "how 'bout if we give you a choice of three pilots? *Magnum* would be one of the three and we'll bring in somebody new who can rewrite the show more to your liking."

And that's what happened. And it changed my life. In the new script, Magnum was not a superhero. He's a tough guy, as Rockford was, but he was reluctant. That's all from Jim.

I've had a couple of mentors in the business. One was Ben Johnson, who gave me my introduction to Westerns. The other is Jim. I don't think he'd be comfortable being called a mentor, nor do I think he considered himself one, but he *was,* whether he likes it or not.

—TOM SELLECK

When I was working with James in *The Rockford Files,* he kept disappearing every day and I kept thinking, *I want to have lunch with my leading man—how often am I going to get to work with James Garner?* So one day I cornered him and asked if he wouldn't mind telling me where he goes every day, and couldn't we at least have one lunch at the commissary? He said, "I'm terribly sorry, I have to go for my acupuncture." He said that the only way he could survive was to go to his acupuncturist and get rid of the pain. I thought, *Wow, that's quite a testimonial.* So I went to his acupuncturist for years and the acupuncturist said to me, "You know, acting is very injurious to your health."

—ERIN GRAY

James Garner changed my life.

I met him in 1946, when we were both nobodies, and we grew up together. (We're the same age—only three days apart.) My relationship with Jim has given me all sorts of opportunities in the movie business beyond being a stunt man, but he's also done a lot of things for me that don't have a dollar sign on them.

Jim and I are like brothers. I can talk to him about anything. That kind of relationship between an actor and his stuntman is very rare. In fact I know of only one other like it: between Clint Eastwood and Buddy Van Horn. Jim is a stuntman's stuntman. He can drive with the best of them and he knows how to take a punch or a fall on camera.

Jim has always given me respect. He allowed me to speak on his behalf at production meetings and he entrusted me with hundreds of thousands of dollars of his money. We have a friendship beyond imagination. With Jim, I always know where I stand, and the standing is good.

—ROYDON CLARK

James Garner taught me how to cross my eyes, one at a time. It's a skill I have employed often to no advantage whatsoever.

—LEE PURCELL

It was television, starting in 1974 with James Garner in *The Rockford Files,* that really brought the investigative profession into the limelight. The show also had a major influence on people using the private investigator title.

No one in the country knew what a private investigator really did, or even what a PI was, until *The Rockford Files*. Jim Rockford accurately portrayed the gumshoe of the time: if you wanted to get information, you had to get out there and ruffle some feathers. Jim Rockford was real. He worked hard to make a decent buck, but he often got beat by clients, even though he was trying to do the right thing. Real PIs deal with that on a regular basis. Even the fact that Rockford didn't like to carry a gun is accurate: PIs are more likely to be packing a smart phone and a laptop than a gun.

Jim Garner is such a nice, down-to-earth person; he was a role model for me when I was coming up in the industry. He was representative of what the field was at the time and he portrayed it beautifully. The show made such an impact on the profession that we wanted to recognize James Garner for it, so we named him Television's Most Famous Private Investigator.

—JIMMIE MESIS, editor in chief, *PI* magazine

Going into a new *Rockford* season, say the director of photography wanted a raise. The studio said, "Get another DP." Jim quietly said, "Take the difference out of my money." He did that all the time with various crew members.

Actors don't make what people think they make. Here's the basic formula: All actors have an agent who gets 10 percent of the gross. If the actor is paid $1 million for a movie, the agent gets $100,000. When a studio pays an actor $1 million, it's required to deduct a 25 percent withholding tax. So the actor doesn't get $1 million from which to pay the agent $100,000, he gets only $750,000.

In addition to the agent who gets 10 percent, there's usually a business manager who gets anywhere from 5 to 7 percent of the gross and, frequently, a monthly guarantee. If the actor is out of work for a year, the business manager still has as much work to do as when the actor is working. He's managing investments, filing income tax returns, writing checks, paying bills, so he still gets paid month after month. Then there's the public relations person. The good ones used to work on percentages, but they don't anymore. Now they get a monthly fee, anywhere from $600 to $2,500, for the same reason: when the actor's not working, they're still doing their job; they're still arranging interviews, getting his picture on magazine covers, et cetera.

Managers have come into the picture in the last twenty years. Managers are permitted by the State of California to produce a movie and cast their client in it, so the manager can make whatever he can as the producer and commission his client for acting in it. Managers get anywhere from 5 to 15 percent of the gross.

So, if an actor is paid $1 million for a movie, his check from the studio is only $750,000 because of the withholding tax, he's paying $100,000 to his agent, say $50,000 to his PR person, another $50,000 to his business manager, and another $100,000 to his manager. He's left with $300,000 out of $1 million. It's not "poor actor"—movie stars are still paid astronomical sums, but it's not what people think.

—BILL ROBINSON

As Jim's business manager, I attended endless days of depositions and some very difficult face-to-face negotiations with Sid Sheinberg, president of Universal. I remember one session in which Sheinberg said to Jim, in order to induce him to settle the case, "I'll let you produce a picture. I'll give you a budget of x and you'll get all the profits."

I couldn't believe my ears. The whole lawsuit was about Universal's cheating Jim out of his rightful profits from *The Rockford Files* by making the net disappear, and here was Sheinberg offering the same deal.

"Let me get this straight," I said. "You mean net profits after 'overhead,' 'distribution fees,' 'advertising charges' . . . "

"Well of course!" he said.

I forget who walked out of the room first, but that ended the meeting.

We finally got a trial date. Universal had offered a payout over a number of years, which would work out very well for Jim. The one thing that would seal the deal was a check from Universal for a lump sum in addition to the payout, but they refused to raise their offer on the total settlement amount.

On the morning of the trial, which was scheduled to begin at 1:30 p.m. in downtown Los Angeles, Jim and I were sitting in the Beverly Hills office of Marvin Burns, our lead counsel, when Sheinberg called.

"I'd like to come over and take one more shot at settling this," he said.

Jim didn't even want to talk to him. He was ferocious: "These bastards tried to screw me and I'm going to get them," he said.

We almost pleaded with him: "Jim, what's the harm in letting him come over?"

After further attempts at persuasion by both Marvin and me, Jim reluctantly agreed to at least listen.

Sheinberg arrived a short while later and made his pitch: "Jesus, Jim, we ought to be able to resolve this. It's going to cost you a lot of money to try the case. I can't give you the figure you want, but close to it. Will you at least consider it?"

"No, we're not going to compromise."

Sheinberg left the room to let us confer. Marvin and I both urged Jim to accept what we considered an equitable deal and Jim finally said, "Well, I don't want to do it, but if you guys are so certain I should take it, I will."

We asked Sheinberg to come back in, but he suddenly got tough: "I want to settle this, but I can't give you the figure you want. It's not going to happen."

That made Jim angry all over again. "Absolutely not!" he said. "We're going to trial."

I was sure that killed our last chance to avoid a costly and risky trial. Just when I thought Sheinberg would get up and walk out, he reached in his pocket and pulled out a check already made out for the initial payment on the total we'd been demanding all along.

"Okay, we've got a deal," he said.

Sheinberg just wanted to see if he could knock us down that last little bit, but he gave up when he was finally convinced that Jim was willing to go all the way.

—JESS MORGAN

I didn't like to ride with Jim in the car. He was death-defying, and he loved to scare you on Mulholland on those curvy roads. Especially in that Mini Cooper. Here's a guy with terrible knees and a terrible back and he's bending into a pretzel to get into that Mini Cooper—that's typical Jim. It felt like a racecar. He's always had fast cars. I don't even like to ride in a golf cart with Jim. He scares the hell out of me. You hang on for dear life. I think he does that on purpose.

Jim could get angry on the golf course. I'd make these long putts—I was always a good long putter—he'd get so mad and I'd say, "Man, you're beautiful when you're angry" or "You know, your eyes flash when you're mad." He'd get even madder.

He was an expert club thrower—I've seen New York Mike have to climb a tree more than once—and he could slam his hand into the steering wheel of the golf cart hard enough to do some damage. I'd say, "Jim, one of these days you're gonna break your hand."

"I wish I would," he'd say, "then I wouldn't have to play this game."

He's a wonderful curmudgeon. That may be an oxymoron, but that's exactly how I'd have to characterize him. A wonderful curmudgeon. He never played good enough. If he made bogey, he should have made par; if he made par, he should have made birdie. He never admitted to hitting a good shot.

"Great shot, Jim!"

"Well, I hit it a little thin . . . "

One day we were on the eighth hole at Bel-Air. There's a stagnant pond in front of the green and Jim was backing away from the cup trying to line up a putt. Jim kept backing closer and closer to the pond until his foot slipped. He slid down a rock and went feetfirst into the foul water. He was completely submerged! The only thing sticking up was his putter, and his hat was floating on the water.

Frank Chirkinian was playing with us, so the two of us ran over and pulled Jim out. He looked like the Creature from the Black Lagoon, with algae all over him. He was so mad he couldn't even cuss, he was *sputtering:* "Gardn . . . dardn . . . mordn . . . fordn." We pulled him up onto dry land and put his cap back on his head. He was completely soaked. We said, "Come on, Jim, let's forget it—we'll run in and get you some dry clothes and play the back nine later."

"No, goddamn it, I'll finish the hole!" He putted out and stomped off to the ninth tee, at which point the water began to squirt out of the bottoms of his shoes like there were little fountains in his feet. I turned to Chirkinian and said, "Frank, I'm not gonna laugh, are you?" and he said, "Hell no!"

As soon as Jim got far enough away, we both fell down laughing.

Someday I'm going to put a plaque out there that says, "Rockford's Rock."

—MAC DAVIS

The curmudgeon in Jim came out on the golf course. He was negative about his game. But he was always courteous and complimentary to others, including me. It was always, "I hit it too hard," or "I'll never get that thing up and down from there." That was the way he played. Then he found a perfect companion in Mac Davis. Mac is just like Jim and he's also been a dear friend of mine for twenty-five years.

Jim, Mac, and I were part of an interesting group at Bel-Air that was a mix of all kinds of players. There were entertainers, businessmen, and other professionals, including the actor George Scott, comedians Bob Newhart and Dick Martin, the press agent Jim Mahoney, and Jim Middleton, an oil company executive. We'd meet at the club midmorning, have breakfast, and try to beat the lunch crowd onto the golf course.

Once, when I arrived at Bel-Air after a long absence, one of the guys in our group said, "Bill, you need to talk to your buddies, Jim and Mac. They're getting so cranky, no one wants to play with them anymore."

I rode in the cart with Jim that day, and before I could open my mouth he said, "Sax, you need to say something to Mac. He's getting so ornery, I'm the only one who'll play with him."

A while later, when Jim was out of earshot, Mac came over and whispered, "Billy Dee, you need to say something to Jim; he's such a curmudgeon, nobody will play with him but me."

The two of them are birds of a feather.

— BILL SAXON

In January of 1969, I was working the 24-Hour race at Daytona and, when not on duty, spent time in the pits taking pictures of the fabulous cars and legendary drivers. James Garner was there in his capacity as the AIR team owner. Mr. Garner was always very accommodating to folks who wanted to take his picture, get an autograph, or just talk.

A friend of mine who had a car entered in the race and his crew were on a tight budget for the event. They didn't even have enough money for hotel rooms, so they planned to camp out in the paddock at the Speedway, sleeping in and around their vehicles.

On one particular night, my friend was in his sleeping bag, which was on an aluminum lounge chair next to his vehicle. During the night a cold, damp fog rolled in off the Atlantic Ocean and by early morning my friend was covered in dew and he was cold to the bone. Mr. Garner was an early riser and left his trailer as the sun was coming up, drinking a hot cup of coffee to keep warm. He was on his way to the garage area when he noticed this fellow in the lawn chair who was just beginning to wake up.

Garner went back into his trailer and got another cup of coffee and gave it to my friend, who by now was awake and flabbergasted that this celebrity was bringing him a much-needed cup of hot coffee.

—LOUIS GALANOS

While Garner wasn't the world's most fearless driver, he had the best retention of any man who drove for me. On a prerun, if he hit a bump, he'd come back five days later and tell you where it was within ten feet.

—VIC HICKEY

As a brand-new nurse at Cedars-Sinai in Los Angeles, I got a call from a physician en route with a patient from a movie set. They were going to bypass the ER and bring the patient straight up to the floor. I'd never had an emergency floor admit—we normally didn't do that. Patients went to the ER, ICU, or the OR before being transferred up to us, so it had to be someone very special, and it was: James Garner.

Though I had no history on him, I was given several orders by the doctor. One of them was for a lot of morphine because they suspected multiple rib fractures. I called down to Medical Records—this was before we were computerized—and said, "Would you please send up the most recent admission of Mr. Garner? He's on his way in and I need it within the next ten minutes, stat." I wanted to see if he had any allergies before I gave him a heavy narcotic.

A few minutes later an orderly arrived wheeling a cart filled with charts. "Which one is Mr. Garner's?" I asked.

"They all are," he said.

That's when I went, *Uh oh!*

By the time I found the most recent admission and checked his history, they were coming down the hall. It was like something out of a *Peanuts* cartoon. He had such an entourage around him, the only thing missing was the dust cloud. All these men, and they were so *loud.* Well, they all followed us into the room. I got Jim into bed with the help of the techs and tried to take his blood pressure, but I couldn't hear anything because the guys were making so much noise. I walked around the bed and said, "Look, fellas, this is a hospital and you need to go home now. Mr. Garner's going to be fine, but I'm sedating him, so please leave. Here's the number if you want to call the hospital later to see how he's doing."

Jim had his eyes closed the whole time—he was in such agony. I rolled him over to take his vitals and it was just so darn cute: he had this little leopard-print bikini underwear and I remember thinking, *Well, look at you, Mr. James Garner!* (I didn't know then that Lois had bought them for Jim.) I turned him on his side and gave him an injection and then turned him on his back. I was standing there taking his vital signs, just quietly going about my business, when he opened his eyes, blinked at me, and said, "Did I die?"

"No, Mr. Garner, you certainly did not. You're at Cedars-Sinai and I'm your nurse and my name is Lisë. You're going to be fine. I just gave you some medicine."

He kept staring at me for the longest time and finally said, "I thought you were an angel."

Though Jim and Mac were friends, I didn't meet Mac through Jim, and neither of them was aware I knew the other because I didn't talk about my patients to Mac. One day a few months later Jim and Mac were on the golf course and Jim was telling the story of a nurse at Cedars named Lisë who he thought was an angel and Mac said, "I'm married to her!" Jim refused to believe it, so they called me from the club and I confirmed it. Mac said, "You never told me!"

"Well, honey," I said, "I don't tell you who my patients are—it's against medical ethics and they wouldn't appreciate me talking about them off the floor."

—LISË DAVIS

It was 1984, and I was working in the mailroom at the Burbank Studios. It was one of my first days on the job. I was on my bike, with a bunch of heavy scripts in the basket. It was raining. James Garner stopped me and asked where Producer's Building Number One was. I had no idea because I had just started, but I had a map, so I took it out and unfolded it and he held one end while I held the other. Meanwhile, I had the bike straddled between my legs, and with all the heavy scripts, it began to slip. I fell right onto him on my bike and got mud all over his pants. I felt horrible, but he was just so gracious and kind. He didn't make me feel bad about it at all. Later on that day, I was riding my bike around the lot and I heard, "Hi, Honey!" He was waving to me from Producer's Building Number One.

—MARILYN HECK

Everybody was stuffed into a condominium down there [in Florida, while shooting Robert Altman's *Health*]. Two- or three-room apartments for the cast, or at least the alleged illustrious members. We were all in Garner's room one evening—Betty Bacall, Carol Burnett, Glenda Jackson, James, and some others. Bacall said something like, "I forgot my glasses" or "Could you go get a book I left in my room?" and I volunteered to go get it. I went there, looked around, and found whatever the mysterious, negligible object was.

And there was her diary!

Looking back, a little too prominently placed on the bed—a red diary—one of those daily reminders. It was open and facedown. Somebody said, "Conscience is the voice of your parents," and I could hear either my mother or my father, I wasn't sure which voice it was, saying, "We do *not* look at people's private papers." (Who was the figure in British history who said he didn't want his spying done by saying, "Gentlemen don't read each other's diaries"?)

Anyway, I thought, *It can't hurt. I won't leaf through it, I don't have time—they're expecting me back.* I just took a glance. And it said in effect, if not precisely, "It's going well here. The hotel is okay. I like everybody here except Cavett. He dresses like a teenager and thinks he knows it all." I remember the scalding horror. That was enough. If there was more, I slammed the book shut. I went back up to Garner's room trying desperately to look unruined. Nobody ever did anything or said anything.

Months and months later, it was Carol Burnett who tipped me to it. She said, "Didn't they ever tell you that was a joke?"

"Are you kidding? No!"

I called Garner and he could not stop laughing. I thought we would have to call 911 to pick him up off the floor. They not only performed it perfectly but they waited it out perfectly. A long time later, I thought, *Garner is such a nice guy, maybe he joined in pretending that it was a joke because they felt all guilty about it,* but I don't think that's true. I think the whole thing was his idea.

—DICK CAVETT

While shooting *Health* for Bob Altman, we all stayed in condos at the Don CeSar Hotel in St. Petersburg. Everybody got along fine, but we were very cruel to Dick Cavett, who played himself in the movie. He took it gracefully and thought it was hysterical that we'd do those things to him.

Now, Dick is not very tall. One morning he came into the makeup room all oiled up wearing nothing but a bathing suit. (He had a cute little body.) The makeup room had a wall phone and Dick, who was always name-dropping, said, "I have to call Marlon," and we all said in unison, "Perkins?" Dick laughed at that, and then, when Dick reached for the phone . . . Jimmy lifted him up.

I was thrilled to play opposite Jimmy in *Health*—I had so much fun doing scenes with him. He was on my television show not long after that and he was very funny. Doing comedy in front of an audience can be intimidating if you're not used to it, but Jimmy has great comedy chops, as we say in the business. I was a little surprised at how comfortable he was, because he'd talked about his stage fright. If he was nervous, it didn't show. His timing was perfect and the audience ate him up.

—CAROL BURNETT

I was surprised and pleased to learn that Jim was working on a memoir. I never thought he would, because he's a very private person. He never talks much about himself, and you never felt you could ask him a bunch of questions. That's irritating, because you can't get any information on how he really feels about stuff, so he's very hard to figure out. Which, I guess, makes him more attractive in a way.

Jim is one of the most worthwhile people I've ever met. Everybody who ever worked with Jim is crazy about him. You can't not be. He's a most appealing creature: an adorable man and a funny and terrific actor. I don't think people realize that. Those of us who worked with him did, but I don't think he got the kind of attention his talent deserved, and he was kind of passed over as a leading man. But his legacy will not be forgotten because his talent is really big. As an actor, he knows exactly how to behave in every scene. He can make you feel what he's feeling. That's a great gift.

—LAUREN BACALL

I met my now ex-husband, Rick Tschudin, in 1981, when we were both working on *Bret Maverick*. I got the job after I'd been seriously injured in a car accident. Jimmy said, "Just do what you can on the set and make some money so you can get the physical therapy you need."

Rick was a second assistant director of photography, and when I told Jimmy we were getting married, he said, "You're engaged to a second assistant? You're marrying *below the line?*" I explained the backstory: Rick was my best friend's brother and I'd always had a crush on him. Had it not been for Jimmy's generosity in creating a job for me, I wouldn't have met Rick again. Without Jimmy, I wouldn't have my beautiful daughters, Hannah and Ashley. So to speak.

—CLAUDIA MYHERS

Jim has quietly supported many people over the years. When my partner died in 2001, his family owned the condo that we lived in and unfortunately I didn't get along with them, so I was going to be out on the street if I didn't buy it. MaryAnn [Rea, Jim's longtime assistant] called and said, "Jim assumes you'll want to buy the condo and said he'll do whatever you need to make it happen." My father had died two years earlier and I'd inherited money, so I was able to buy the condo myself. But Jim didn't know that, and the thought of his offer reduced me to tears.

—KEVIN RITTER

I met Jim when I was offered "The Kirkoff Case," the first episode of *The Rockford Files*. I read the script and thought it was great. This was the time of your career when getting the lead guest star on a series was a big deal. Plus I thought, *Ooh, James Garner, that's my guy!* I'd been a big fan of *Maverick* when I was a kid—it was my favorite TV show when I was ten.

He didn't disappoint me. We worked well together and I had fun playing a villain, a spoiled rich kid who plans a murder. Jim and I just hit it off and that was that.

Years later, I'd just done *Salvador* and my career was on fire—Oliver Stone offered me *Platoon* and there was talk about doing *Wall Street*. My agent called and said, "You've been offered the part of some retard in a TV movie. I'm gonna pass on it."

I was curious, so I said, "What do you mean, some 'retard'?"

"Oh, you know, it's a psycho part."

"Is it an offer? If it's an offer, I should be polite enough to read it."

"You're not gonna do a TV movie, okay?"

"I'm gonna read it anyway."

So he sent me the script.

Of course, it was *Promise,* written by Richard Friedenberg, one of our greatest writers.

I called my agent back and told him, "I'm doing this movie. No discussion. Just make the deal for whatever they offer and let's go. I wanna do it!" (This particular agent made another mistake, which finally caused me to fire him: he turned down *Reservoir Dogs* without consulting me.)

People ask me, "What's the favorite thing you've ever done in your life?" and I always say *Promise* because it was a perfect part for me and a perfect experience with Jim.

—JAMES WOODS

Jim has been better to me than anyone else in my life except my father.

—STUART MARGOLIN

Late in 1987, I published *The Portable Curmudgeon,* a small book of humorous quotes, anecdotes, and interviews with a modest first printing. A few months later, my telephone rang and it was James Garner. He'd gotten my number from the phone book.

"This is Jim Garner, I'm an actor," he said.

"I know!" I said. "How *are* you?"

"I'm fine. What kind of curmudgeon has a listed number?"

Jim told me that a fan, Donna Ismond, had sent him a copy of my book while he was recovering from heart surgery, and he was calling to thank me because, he said, the book had helped cheer him out of post-op depression. (Bob Newhart and Dick Martin had also sent a copy; Jim said he wasn't thrilled that they had to chip in.)

One Friday night a few weeks later Jim was a guest on *The Tonight Show*. He talked with Johnny Carson about his heart surgery, and then he brought out my book. He told the story of how he got it, then read from it until the first commercial, after which he handed it to Johnny, who read from it until the next commercial. The audience laughed and it put the book on the map: to date *The Portable Curmudgeon* is still in print and there are four sequels. I've been allowed to publish a couple of dozen other books, all, I'm convinced, on the strength of that *Tonight Show* appearance, without which I'd probably be selling real estate instead of collaborating with James Garner on his memoirs.

—JW

Films

Toward the Unknown ★★ (Warner Bros., 1956) C-115 min. D: Mervyn LeRoy. William Holden, Lloyd Nolan, Charles McGraw, Virginia Leith.

My big-screen debut, all about the pioneering days of supersonic flight. I had only seven lines and got killed early, but they talked about me afterward, which was nice.

The Girl He Left Behind ★★ (Warner Bros., 1956) 103 min. D: David Butler. Tab Hunter, Natalie Wood, Jim Backus, David Janssen.

The Girl with the Left Behind. A romantic comedy in an army setting. It was awful and I was awful, but it was the best I could do at the time.

Shoot-Out at Medicine Bend ★★ (Warner Bros., 1957) 87 min. D: Richard Bare. Randolph Scott, Angie Dickinson.

It was always fun working with Dick Bare, and Randy Scott was an old pro, but the movie isn't worth a damn. I was under contract, so I had to do what they put in front of me.

Sayonara ★★★½ (Warner Bros., 1957) C-147 min. D: Joshua Logan. Marlon Brando, Ricardo Montalban, Miiko Taka, Miyoshi Umeki, Red Buttons, Martha Scott.

A big-budget movie about an important issue, it was the first "serious" film I'd ever done. The highlight for me was working with Marlon. (See pages 46–48.)

Darby's Rangers ★★ (Warner Bros., 1958) C-121 min. D: William Wellman. Etchika Choureau, Jack Warden, Stuart Whitman, David Janssen.

I was originally cast as a young captain, but Chuck Heston dropped out and I was under contract, so the studio bumped me up to the role of Major William O. Darby, commander of the 1st Ranger Battalion in World War II.

"Wild Bill" Wellman (*Wings, The Public Enemy, The Ox-Bow Incident*) didn't take any guff. He had a short fuse and always gave better than he got. He'd been in the Lafayette Escadrille in World War I and ran his set like a military outfit. (Wellman, Raoul Walsh, and John Ford were considered the tough directors. If you could work with them, you could work with anyone.)

I don't think Wellman wanted to make the picture in the first place: he was doing it as a trade-off so he could do a personal film about his war experiences. I don't think he wanted me in the part, either, and I don't blame him: I was too young for it and he deserved a bigger star. But we got along fine because we respected each other.

Cash McCall ★★ (Warner Bros., 1959) C-102 min. D: Joseph Pevney. Natalie Wood, Nina Foch, Dean Jagger, E. G. Marshall.

Not much of a movie, but I liked Natalie. She was a sweet girl, and we had a good working relationship even though her husband, Robert Wagner, would come down to the set and watch us do love scenes and tell her how to act. I don't think she knew it herself then, but I thought Natalie was a lost soul.

Up Periscope ★ (Warner Bros., 1959) C-111 min. D: Gordon Douglas. Edmond O'Brien, Andra Martin, Alan Hale.

Up Your Periscope for the FBI or *Lieutenant Merriweather at Sea.* Another piece of crap that Warner Bros. stuck me in while I was under contract.

The Children's Hour ★★★ (United Artists, 1961) 107 min. D: William Wyler. Audrey Hepburn, Shirley MacLaine, Miriam Hopkins, Fay Bainter.

My first experience working with a great director. (See pages 69–71.)

Boys' Night Out ★★ (MGM, 1962) C-115 min. D: Michael Gordon. Kim Novak, Tony Randall, Howard Duff, Janet Blair, Patti Paige, Zsa Zsa Gabor, Howard Morris.

A little farce about midlife crisis. Kim was beautiful and she had a wonderful quality that audiences liked, but she didn't know how to act. I think she was insecure, because she was always running off the set to fix her face. She was more interested in her makeup than the script.

Move Over, Darling ★★★ (20th Century-Fox, 1963) C-103 min. D: Michael Gordon. Doris Day, Polly Bergen, Chuck Connors, Thelma Ritter, Don Knotts, John Astin.

The best part of this remake of the 1940 screwball comedy *My Favorite Wife* is Doris Day. I'd been slated to make it as *Something's Got to Give* with Marilyn Monroe, but I did *The Great Escape* instead, so Dean Martin took my part. Twentieth fired Marilyn for chronic tardiness and stopped production, retitled it *Move Over, Darling,* and made it with me and Doris.

Doris didn't *play* sexy, she didn't *act* sexy, she *was* sexy. And then she could take a sexy scene and make you laugh. Which is better in the bedroom than a lot of things. And Doris was a joy to work with.

Everything she did seemed effortless. She's so sweet and so professional—she made everyone around her look good.

The Wheeler Dealers ★★ (MGM, 1963) C-106 min. D: Arthur Hiller. Lee Remick, Jim Backus, Phil Harris, Chill Wills, Louis Nye.

A broad comedy in which my character is a lot like Bret Maverick: a Texas con man, only this time in New York City. I guess audiences liked it, because for years people came up to me and quoted lines from it.

The Great Escape ★★★★ (United Artists, 1963) C-168 min. D: John Sturges. Steve McQueen, Richard Attenborough, Charles Bronson, James Coburn, Donald Pleasence, James Donald.

A classic from a great action-adventure director. (See pages 71–83.)

The Thrill of It All ★★★ (Universal, 1963) C-108 min. D: Norman Jewison. Doris Day, Arlene Francis, Reginald Owen, ZaSu Pitts.

Better than it should have been, again because of Doris.

In one scene, I drive a convertible into a swimming pool and the car begins to sink. I started floating up and out of the seat, so I had to grip the steering wheel, hold myself under water, *and act at the same time*! Now you know why we make the big bucks.

The Americanization of Emily ★★★★★ (MGM, 1964) BW-117 min. D: Arthur Hiller. Julie Andrews, Melvyn Douglas, James Coburn, Joyce Grenfell, Edward Binns.

An antiwar film at a time when we were at war in Vietnam. Brilliant script by Paddy Chayefsky, marvelous direction by Arthur Hiller. And as for Julie, well, I just love her. *Emily* is my favorite film that I've ever seen or been involved in, and Charlie Madison is my favorite character, probably because I share his views. (See pages 83–92.)

36 Hours ★★½ (MGM, 1964) BW-115 min. D: George Seaton. Eva Marie Saint, Rod Taylor, Alan Napier.

I play an American intelligence officer who has knowledge of the impending Normandy invasion. The Germans drug me and fool me into believing the invasion has already taken place so they can find out what I know. The movie doesn't work because there's no suspense: everybody knew that in real life the D-Day invasion was a success, and that we'd won the war.

I loved working with Eva, a wonderful actress and a sweet lady, and with George Seaton. I remember driving on the freeway one morning to the set, rehearsing my dialogue to myself. By the time I got to the studio I had it all worked out in my mind. It was a tough scene that took all day to shoot. Driving home, I went through the dialogue again and realized I hadn't done a single line the way I'd intended. George had changed everything and I never knew it. *That's* a good director.

The Art of Love ★★ (Universal, 1965) C-99 min. D: Norman Jewison. Dick Van Dyke, Elke Sommer, Angie Dickinson, Carl Reiner, Ethel Merman.

I enjoyed working with Norman again, Dick Van Dyke is as nice as he seems, Carl Reiner is a good actor and a terrific writer, and there are some funny bits. (Mae West was originally cast in the Ethel Merman role, but she couldn't remember her lines.)

Grand Prix ★★★★ (MGM, 1966) C-175 min. D: John Frankenheimer. Eva Marie Saint, Yves Montand, Toshirô Mifune, Brian Bedford, Jessica Walter.

In my opinion, still the best picture ever made about auto racing. (See pages 101–11.)

A Man Could Get Killed ★★½ (Universal, 1966) C-99 min. D: Ronald Neame. Cliff Owen, Melina Mercouri, Sandra Dee, Anthony Franciosa.

Disappointing, though I did have fun playing backgammon

on the set with Melina and her husband, Jules Dassin. Didn't enjoy working with Tony Franciosa, who kept abusing the stunt men. He purposely wasn't pulling his punches in fight scenes, and he kept doing it despite my warnings to stop . . . so I had to pop him one.

Duel at Diablo ★★½ (MGM, 1966) C-103 min. D: Ralph Nelson. Sidney Poitier, Bibi Andersson, Dennis Weaver, William Redfield.

I loved working with Sidney and my old pal Dennis Weaver. Everybody did stunts in that picture, even leading lady Bibi Andersson. Sidney had to learn to ride—he didn't know anything about horses and I think he was a little afraid of them.

Mister Buddwing 0★ (MGM, 1966) 100 min. D: Delbert Mann. Jean Simmons, Suzanne Pleshette, Angela Lansbury, Katharine Ross.

I'd summarize the plot, but to this day, I have no clue what it is. Worst picture I ever made. What were they thinking? What was *I* thinking?

Hour of the Gun ★★★ (United Artists, 1967) C-100 min. D: John Sturges. Robert Ryan, Jason Robards, Albert Salmi, William Schallert, Michael Tolan, Monte Markham.

My agent called and said Sturges was doing a sequel to *Gunfight at the O.K. Corral* and I agreed to do it without seeing the script. I trusted John that much. It's a different kind of Western than I'd done; my character, Wyatt Earp, is the most steely-eyed of all my roles, and the movie is about Earp's obsession with revenge.

Great cast: Jason Robards as Doc Holliday, Robert Ryan as Ike Clanton, and a newcomer named Jon Voight as a baby-faced gunslinger.

We filmed on location in Torreón, Mexico, a little farming village that doubled for Tombstone, Arizona. Jason was a terrific actor and a good guy, but he was never on the set when you needed him. Fortunately, Sturges always knew where to find him, because Torreón had only one bar and one whorehouse. When Jason didn't show up for an 8:00 a.m. call until late that afternoon, Sturges dressed him down in front of the entire crew. Jason was contrite and his behavior improved after that.

How Sweet It Is! ½★ (Warner Bros., 1968) C-99 min. D: Jerry Paris. Debbie Reynolds, Paul Lynde, Terry-Thomas.

    Loved Debbie Reynolds. *Loved* Paul Lynde. *Loved* Terry-Thomas. *Hated* the movie.

The Pink Jungle ½★ (Universal, 1968) C-104 min. D: Delbert Mann. George Kennedy, Eva Renzi, Nigel Green.

    Hunting diamonds in South America, or something. I made this thing for the money and I'm lucky it didn't wreck my career.

Support Your Local Sheriff ★★★½ (United Artists, 1969) C-93 min. D: Burt Kennedy. Joan Hackett, Walter Brennan, Jack Elam, Bruce Dern.

    For a long time after it came out, when people came up to me in public, this is the movie they talked about, and when it's on TV, I'll sit and watch a little of it. (See pages 187–89.)

Marlowe ★★★ (MGM, 1969) C-95 min. D: Paul Bogart. Gayle Hunnicutt, Caroll O'Connor, Rita Moreno, William Daniels, Bruce Lee.

    Paul Bogart did a wonderful job with Stirling Siliphant's adaptation of Raymond Chandler's novel *The Little Sister*. Paul is a total pro, having directed scores of live programs during the Golden Age of television and countless episodes of series before moving on to feature films.

    In one scene, I'm in a restaurant with a date and someone sends over a bottle of wine. The waiter opens it and pours a little for me to taste. Gore Vidal had just referenced my butt in his novel, *Myra Breckinridge,* referring to it as "impertinent" and "baroque." (One of the two would have been sufficient.) I ad-libbed those two words, "impertinent" and "baroque," to describe a glass of wine in the scene and Paul kept it in.

I was in good company playing Raymond Chandler's legendary private eye, following in the footsteps of Humphrey Bogart, Dick Powell, and Robert Montgomery. Plus, I got to beat up Bruce Lee. (Only in the movies!) Bruce showed me some martial arts moves between takes.

A Man Called Sledge ½★ (Italian, 1970) C-93 min. D: Vic Morrow. Dennis Weaver, Claude Akins, John Marley.

Sludge. One of the few times I've played a heavy, and one of the last. I wish I could remember why I let Dino De Laurentiis talk me into this turkey. The poster says, "Not suitable for children." It should say, "Not suitable for human consumption."

Support Your Local Gunfighter ★★ (United Artists, 1971) C-92 min. D: Burt Kennedy. Suzanne Pleshette, Jack Elam, Harry Morgan, John Dehner, Joan Blondell.

Not as good as *Support Your Local Sheriff* and not really a sequel.

Skin Game ★★★½ (Warner Bros., 1971) C-102 min. D: Paul Bogart. Louis Gossett, Susan Clark, Edward Asner, Andrew Duggan.

A funny movie if you don't mind jokes about slavery. Paul Bogart did a masterly job with a story about a con man who travels the South selling his "slave" again and again, but they're really partners.

They Only Kill Their Masters ★★ (MGM, 1972) C-97 min. D: James Goldstone. Katharine Ross, Hal Holbrook, Peter Lawford, Harry Guardino, June Allyson, Tom Ewell.

I'd rather not talk about it.

One Little Indian ¼★ (Disney, 1973) C-90 min. D: Bernard McEveety. Vera Miles, Pat Hingle, Jay Silverheels, Jodie Foster.

I've done some things I'm not proud of. This is one of them. The only bright spot was a ten-year-old Jodie Foster.

The Castaway Cowboy ½★ (Disney, 1974) C-91 min. D: Bernard McEveety. Vera Miles, Robert Culp, Gregory Sierra.

M-I-C-K-E-Y M-O-U-S-E. The best thing in it is the Hawaiian scenery.

Health ★★ (Lionsgate, 1979) C-100 min. D: Robert Altman. Lauren Bacall, Carol Burnett, Dick Cavett, Glenda Jackson, Alfre Woodard.

We had a lot of fun making it, especially playing practical jokes on Dick Cavett, who took everything we could throw at him with grace and good humor. (Dick and I became instant pals.) It was a privilege and a pleasure to play opposite Carol and to work with Betty Bacall.

I loved Bob Altman. He gave actors tremendous freedom. Though we had completely different approaches—he hated scripts, I loved them—I enjoyed every minute of it. Bob was a true maverick and he had guts: he'd think nothing of starting a movie before he had all the financing, and he thumbed his nose at the studios. *My kind of guy!*

The Fan ½★ (Filmways, 1981) C-95 min. D: Edward Bianchi. Lauren Bacall, Maureen Stapleton, Hector Elizondo, Dana Delany.

Can there be more than one "worst-picture-I-ever-made"? The only saving grace was working with Betty Bacall again—we also did a *Rockford* together that wasn't all that bad. She's a wonderful actress and a beautiful woman. And so feisty. I just love her.

Victor/Victoria ★★★½ (MGM, 1982) C-132 min. D: Blake Edwards. Julie Andrews, Robert Preston, Leslie Ann Warren, Alex Karras.

My second chance to work with Julie, and it was a great experience because she's a great lady and a wonderful actress and singer. I wanted to ask Blake for the Robert Preston role, but my friend John Crawford talked me out of it. He said nobody would accept me as gay, but I wanted to try it.

Blake wrote most of the scripts he directed and he made *good* movies: *Breakfast at Tiffany's, Days of Wine and Roses, The Pink Panther, The Great Race, 10*. He was easy to work with, a total professional. He could get cranky if the set was too noisy and he had to shut everybody up, but he was open to suggestions and created a good atmosphere to work in. Blake was the first director I'd worked with who used video. He'd shoot a scene and then play it back for the actors. I never liked to see myself acting, but I would look at the video occasionally to see if a stunt looked right.

There's a scene in which I kiss Julie, who plays a woman posing as a man posing as a woman. In an early draft of the script, my character kisses her before he's sure she's a woman. Blake said he chickened out and wrote it so I know she's a woman. I'd love to have done it the first way.

Tank ★★ (United International Pictures, 1984) C-113 min. D: Marvin J. Chomsky. Shirley Jones, C. Thomas Howell, G. D. Spradlin, James Cromwell.

Just a workaday movie with nothing outstanding about it. I had fun making it, though, because I got to drive a Sherman tank and crash into things.

Murphy's Romance ★★★★ (Columbia, 1985) C-107 min. D: Martin Ritt. Sally Field, Brian Kerwin, Corey Haim.

A sweet, American story about a normal guy and a normal girl, except for the age difference. Wonderful script by the husband-and-wife team of Harriet Frank and Irving Ravetch from the novella by Max Schott.

Sally's character is always asking me my age, but I won't tell. In the last scene, we're outside her house and she asks me to stay for dinner. I say, "I won't have dinner unless I stay for breakfast." "How do like your eggs?" she says. On the way through the door, I tell her: "I'm sixty." I cheated: I was only fifty-eight at the time. (See pages 203–6.)

Sunset ★★ (TriStar, 1988) C-107 min. D: Blake Edwards. Bruce Willis, Mariel Hemingway, Malcolm McDowell, Kathleen Quinlan.

Wyatt Earp and Tom Mix team up to solve a Hollywood murder. Blake had wanted Robert Duvall but got Bruce Willis instead, who ad-libbed all through the picture. At one point, I took him aside and gave him some friendly advice: "No matter what you think, you're not a better writer than Blake Edwards." He didn't listen. He just wasn't serious about the work. I've heard he's changed since then, and if so, more power to him.

The Distinguished Gentleman ?★ (Hollywood Pictures, 1992) C-112 min. D: Jonathan Lynn. Eddie Murphy, Joe Don Baker, Charles S. Dutton, Kevin McCarthy.

I can't remember a thing about this picture. I can live with that.

Fire in the Sky ★★ (Paramount, 1993) C-106 min. D: Robert Lieberman. Robert Patrick, D. B. Sweeney, Henry Thomas.

Based on a supposedly true story of alien abduction in Arizona. Whether the incident actually happened, I don't presume we're the smartest thing in the universe. It's *big* out there. (Maybe we're somebody's golf ball.)

Maverick ★★★ (Warner Bros., 1994) C-129 min. D: Richard Donner. Mel Gibson, Jodie Foster, James Coburn, Alfred Molina, Graham Greene.

Mel bought the rights to *Maverick* from Warner Bros. because, he told me, it was one of his favorite shows when he was a kid and he'd always wanted to play the character. Dick Donner, whom Mel had worked with in the *Lethal Weapon* pictures, had wanted Paul Newman as Zane Cooper, but Paul wasn't interested, so they decided to hire the original Bret Maverick.

Mel and I got along fine. I didn't know that he hates Jews and everybody else. I didn't know he was drinking, either, because he held it pretty good. But when I came on the set, I thought, *What are these people doing?* Mel didn't know his dialogue and we had to improvise a lot. He wouldn't rehearse, either. He was just running off at the mouth on camera. I thought it was nuts, but Dick Donner assured me Mel knew what he was doing. Jodie and I looked at each other and figured we might as well join in. When we got through with it, I'm sure William Goldman didn't recognize his movie.

Of course, I loved working with Jodie—I had fallen in love with her when we did *One Little Indian* when she was a little girl.

My Fellow Americans ★★ (Warner Bros., 1996) C-101 min. D: Peter Segal. Jack Lemmon, Lauren Bacall, Dan Aykroyd, John Heard, Wilford Brimley.

Jack and I are ex-presidents trying to expose a kickback scandal. It was the first and only time I worked with him. Such a sweet man. He was a joy to work with: thoughtful, generous, always prepared.

Jack had a black standard French poodle named Chloe who went everywhere with him. She always rode shotgun in his Aston Martin, even when there were other people in the car, she flew with him in the first-class cabin—they were inseparable. Chloe was a bit of a princess who drank nothing but Evian water, but she was obedient to Jack. When they were on a soundstage, Chloe knew exactly how to behave.

One day we were about to do a scene in which Jack was seated at a desk. While we were rehearsing, Chloe roamed the set. When it was time to roll the camera, she plopped down under the desk. When the director yelled "Action!" she froze and didn't move a muscle or make a peep until she heard the word "Cut!" That dog took direction better than some actors I've worked with.

I wish the director were so professional. He was a self-appointed genius who didn't know his ass from second base, and Jack and I both knew it. He had no idea where to put the camera, he didn't know what he wanted, and he was a whiner. The movie could have been a lot better.

Twilight ★★★ (Cinehaus, 1998) C-94 min. D: Robert Benton. Paul Newman, Susan Sarandon, Gene Hackman, Reese Witherspoon, Stockard Channing.

I play a minor character in this mystery set in Los Angeles. I was attracted by Richard Russo's intelligent script. I don't mind doing a small part. I've always felt that any time you have a film where you've got one or two really good scenes, it's worth doing.

Space Cowboys ★★★½ (Warner Bros., 2000) C-129 min. D: Clint Eastwood. Tommy Lee Jones, Donald Sutherland, Clint Eastwood, Marcia Gay Harden, James Cromwell, William Devane.

Space Geezers. When we shot it Clint was seventy-two, Donald was sixty-six, Tommy Lee was fifty-three, and I was seventy-two.

I've known Clint for about a thousand years. He was in a *Maverick* episode in 1959. We were playing golf one day and I said, "We should work together more often than every forty years," and about a year later he hired me for *Space Cowboys*.

Clint makes it look easy and gives you a great environment to work in. But he lied to me: That scene where we all show our butts— Clint told me the other guys were going to do it, so I said I would, too. But he'd told Tommy and Donald that I agreed to do it. He conned us all into dropping our trousers.

Divine Secrets of the Ya-Ya Sisterhood ★★½ (Warner Bros., 2002) C-117 min. D: Callie Khouri. Sandra Bullock, Ellen Burstyn, Maggie

Smith, Shirley Knight, Ashley Judd, Fionnula Flanagan. Angus Mac-fadyen.

All those wonderful women! I got to play Sandra Bullock's father and Ellen Burstyn's husband. It's a strange marriage . . . but aren't they all?

The Notebook ★★★★★ (New Line, 2004) C-123 min. D: Nick Cassavetes. Gena Rowlands, Ryan Gosling, Rachel McAdams, Sam Shepard, Joan Allen.

A magnificent love story based on the Nicholas Sparks bestseller. (See pages 207–9.)

The Ultimate Gift ★★ (Fox Faith, 2007) C-117 min. D: Michael O. Sajbel. Drew Fuller, Ali Hillis, Bill Cobbs, Brian Dennehy, Lee Mer-riwether.

I play a dead man. Not typecasting, I hope.

Television

SERIES

Maverick (1957–61)
The training ground where I learned my craft. (See chapter 3.)

Nichols (1971–72)
Nichols is a drifter who returns to his Arizona hometown in 1914 and reluctantly becomes its sheriff. (See pages 189–92.)

The Rockford Files (1974–80)
Still in syndication and streaming on the Internet, whatever that is. (See chapter 7.)

Bret Maverick (1981–82)
Twenty years after the original *Maverick* series, Bret wants to settle down, so he rides into Sweetwater, where he wins $50,000 and the deed

to a saloon in a poker game. But somebody swipes the fifty grand and the saloon turns out to be a losing proposition. Unfortunately, so did *Bret Maverick*.

Man of the People (1991)

The series, in which I play a scam artist appointed to my late wife's city council seat, was short-lived and rightly so.

Chicago Hope (1994)

A David E. Kelley production with good scripts and good actors. I enjoyed the few episodes I did as a ruthless head of an HMO who comes in and cuts the budget.

God, the Devil and Bob (2000)

A controversial animated show in which I provide the voice of God. It's a shame we went out of business so soon, because I *loved* playing God.

First Monday (2002)

I played a *conservative* US Supreme Court justice (*act*-ing!). Loved working with Charles Durning.

8 Simple Rules (2003–05)

I joined the cast for a guest shot after John Ritter's untimely death and stayed until the series ended. Everyone made it very nice for me. The writing was good, and I enjoyed working with Katey Sagal, David Spade, and Suzanne Pleshette.

I never used to like working with children. For a long time I thought they were unpredictable and, well, unprofessional. But Amy Davidson, Kaley Cuoco, and Martin Spanjers were terrific. Who cares if they steal a scene? If any actor can steal a scene from me, they're welcome to it.

MINISERIES

Space (1985)

A big-bucks production based on James Michener's best-selling book. I'm not nuts about the miniseries format: you work one day, then you're off for three weeks. I like to work every day and immerse myself in a role. But James Michener was on the set a lot and that was a treat.

Larry McMurtry's Streets of Laredo (1995)

The sequel to *Lonesome Dove*. I play aging bounty hunter Woodrow Call chasing a bandit who's been robbing the railroad. I'd been slated to do the Robert Duvall part in the original, but I got sick. Bobby was so good, I didn't really mind losing the part.

Great cast: Sissy Spacek, Sam Shepard, Sonia Braga, Randy Quaid, Ned Beatty, George Carlin, Wes Studi, Charles Martin Smith.

Mark Twain's Roughing It (2001)

Mark Twain was one of our greatest writers, of course, and I admire him a lot, but it was a little scary to play him. I don't think I did a very good job, but I enjoyed the experience, especially working with Charles Martin Smith, who did a fine job of directing.

TELEVISION MOVIES

The Rockford Files (1974)

The first of a series of made-for-television *Rockford* movies, as they were called back then.

The New Maverick (1978)

Charles Frank in a *Maverick* revival attempt that didn't quite make it.

Bret Maverick (1981)

We had to stop production for two months after I got thrown off a mechanical horse and broke a bunch of ribs.

The Long Summer of George Adams (1982)

Stuart Margolin directed and composed the music for this delightful film about a railroad worker in the 1950s whose job has been made obsolete by technology. I treasured the experience of working with Stuart again, and I always loved Joan Hackett.

Heartsounds (1984)

Based on the autobiographical book by Martha Weinman Lear about her husband's struggle with heart disease. Norman Lear produced—Hal Lear was his cousin—and Glenn Jordan directed. Mary Tyler Moore and I had never met before, but it was a joy to work with her. She had instigated the project, and she really threw herself into the part of Martha Weinman Lear.

The cast members were all staying at the same hotel in Toronto and there was a fire in the middle of the night, so I banged on Mary's door and shouted to wake her up. We walked down eighteen flights together with her insisting all the way that I probably saved her life. I didn't think it was such a big deal. Turned out the fire wasn't serious—probably somebody cooking cucumbers with Sterno.

I think they may have begun to think about me differently after *Heartsounds*. At least that's what I hoped. I wanted them to see that I could do something other than a cocky detective.

The Glitter Dome (1984)

I play a senator who goes from age thirty-five to sixty-five. Shooting it, on any given day, I didn't know how old I was. I was forty-five in the morning, sixty in the afternoon.

Promise (1985)

Our first Cherokee production for Hallmark and my first collaboration with Jimmy Woods. (See pages 192–95.)

My Name Is Bill W. (1989)

The founding of Alcoholics Anonymous, through the eyes of Bill Wilson and Bob Smith. (See pages 195–201.)

Decoration Day (1990)

An African American World War II vet (Bill Cobbs) turns down the Medal of Honor to protest discrimination in the military. I play a retired judge who tries to get the medal for him decades later. My wife had died, I'd withdrawn from life, and I was content to sit in a boat with my dog. ("She knows the English language but can't speak a word of it.") Most of the characters I play are people who try to do the right thing. In this case, he was trying to get other people (the government) to do the right thing.

I supplied my own wardrobe. I got an Indiana Jones hat out of my closet—Stu Margolin had given it to me—and cut the brim down a little bit. The pants and the fishing vest are mine, too. I think it's always better if you can wear your own things.

Barbarians at the Gate (1993)

All about the takeover mania of the 1980s and '90s. The sheer gall of those guys, ripping companies apart, saddling them with all that debt, putting all those people out of jobs. I hadn't read the book, because high finance and rotten people don't interest me. But I loved Larry Gelbart's script. Larry was a great satiric writer. He was funny and, boy, he had a *knife*! But he was a pussycat of a man.

People said I made Ross Johnson into a nice guy, but I didn't deviate from the script. He was no hero, but he wasn't exactly a villain, either. I think he was just a salesman who got in over his head. I haven't done any out-and-out villains; they don't hire me for that because of the persona I've had for forty-five years. I think they hire me to make a bad guy a little more presentable, but I never play an out-and-out killer.

It was going to be a feature, but Columbia dropped it from the schedule as part of an austerity program. The producer, Ray Stark, went to cable and it was great fun. Later they put it on Fox and ruined it. They wanted me to loop dialogue for the broadcast version, but I refused. I hate the way that looks—your lips are doing one thing and your voice is doing another. I said, "Go get somebody else," and they did, some guy in town who sounded like me.

Breathing Lessons (1994)

Joanne Woodward and I play an old married couple who have nothing in common except their love for each other. (See pages 206–7.)

Rockford Files: I Still Love L.A. (1994)

The theme song was slower and so was I. Practically everybody from the original series came back to do the TV movies, though we'd lost "Pidge"—Noah Beery Jr.—in the interim. We did eight *Rockford* movies in all:

Rockford Files: A Blessing in Disguise (1995)
Rockford Files: If the Frame Fits (1996)
Rockford Files: Godfather Knows Best (1996)
Rockford Files: Friends and Foul Play (1996)
Rockford Files: Punishment and Crime (1996)
Rockford Files: Murder and Misdemeanors (1997)
Rockford Files: If It Bleeds . . . It Leads (1999)

Dead Silence (1997)

I'm an FBI negotiator trying to secure the release of a busload of deaf kids. Marlee Matlin and Lolita Davidovich starred.

Legalese (1998)

A bit convoluted, but I'm a slick defense lawyer defending Gina Gershon's character after she shoots her brother-in-law. I think. I loved working with Glenn Jordan again.

One Special Night (1999)

My third time out with Julie Andrews and it *was* a charm. We shot it in Montreal thirty-six years after our first collaboration, *The Americanization of Emily,* but who's counting?

We've both lost our spouses and take refuge in a cabin on a stormy winter's night and . . . guess what happens?

In one scene, I had to hold a cigar and Julie noticed that my hands were shaking. "What's the matter?" she said.

"I'm nervous!"

"After all these years, you're still nervous?"

"I'm always nervous when I work. It keeps me on my toes. When the camera starts to roll, I'm all right."

The Last Debate (2000)

John Badham directed Jon Maas's adaptation of Jim Lehrer's novel. I'm a newspaper columnist who conspires to sway an election in favor of a Democrat. How did they know?

INDEX

INDEX

About the Authors

James Garner has starred in numerous television shows and films, from *Maverick* and *The Rockford Files* to *The Great Escape,* with Steve McQueen, and *Victor/Victoria,* with Julie Andrews.

Jon Winokur is the author of various nonfiction books, including *The Portable Curmudgeon, Zen to Go,* and *Advice to Writers.*